AGAINST THE GRAIN

Studies in Austrian Literature, Culture, and Thought

Translation Series

Against the Grain

New Anthology of Contemporary Austrian Prose

Selected and with an Introduction by

Adolf Opel

ARIADNE PRESS
Riverside, California

Ariadne Press would like to express its appreciation to the Austrian Cultural Institute, New York and the Bundesministerium für Wissenschaft, Verkehr und Kunst, Vienna for their assistance in publishing this book.

Library of Congress Cataloging-in-Publication Data

Against the grain : new anthology of contemporary Austrian prose / selected and with an introduction by Adolf Opel.
      p.   cm. -- (Studies in Austrian literature, culture and thought. Translation series)
  Sequel to: Relationships. Anthology of contemporary Austrian prose: Riverside, Calif. : Ariadne Press, c1991.
  ISBN 1-57241-031-0
  1. Austrian prose literature--20th century--Translations into English. I. Opel, Adolf, 1935- . II. Series.
PT3826.P7A35   1997
838'.91408089436--dc200
                              96-95830
                              CIP

Cover
Art Director and Designer: George McGinnis
Illustration: Marino Valdez

Copyright ©1997
by Ariadne Press
270 Goins Court
Riverside, CA 92507

All rights reserved.
No part of this publication may be reproduced or transmitted in any form or by any means without formal permission.
Printed in the United States of America.
ISBN 1-57241-031-0

TO LEO AND CLARITA

Table of Contents

Adolf Opel 1
  Introduction
  Translated by Francis Michael Sharp

Acknowledgments 9

C.W. Aigner 10
  The Anti-Cupid
  Translated by Heidi L. Hutchinson

Hans-Jürgen August 16
  Europe in the Rain
  Translated by M. Veteto-Conrad

Christian Baier 29
  Joseph, A German Fate
  Translated by Donald G. Daviau

Ilse Brem 38
  The Boat
  Translated by Heidi L. Hutchinson

Heidrun Brunmair 41
  Feelings like Winter Burs
  Translated by Renate Latimer

Stephan Eibel 49
  The Particularly Engaged Poet
  Translated by Paul F. Dvorak

Janko Ferk 51
  Work Is Liberating
  Translated by Paul F. Dvorak

Marianne Gruber 58
  Freddy
  Translated by Alexandra Strelka

Norbert Gstrein 64
    One
    Translated by Lowell A. Bangerter

Erich Hackl 72
    Instead of an Honorary Salute
    Translated by Carvel de Bussy

Wolfgang Hermann 81
    The House
    Translated by Francis Michael Sharp

Margarethe Herzele 97
    Paralysis
    Translated by Beth Bjorklund

Graziella Hlawaty 106
    Easter Stroll
    Translated by Donald G. Daviau

Paulus Hochgatterer 112
    Mr. Little's Last Days on the Job
    Translated by Todd C. Hanlin

Konstantin Kaiser 119
    With Love from Inspector 19
    Translated by Donald G. Daviau

Marie-Thérèse Kerschbaumer 121
    Alma
    Translated by Lowell A. Bangerter

Ulrike Klepalski 127
    Midsummer Night
    Translated by Helga Schreckenberger and Jacqueline Vansant

Walter Klier 134
    King Sepp
    Translated by Lowell A. Bangerter

Ulrike Längle 145
  The Plunge
  Translated by Margaret T. Peischl

Robert Menasse 152
  Long Time No See
  Translated by Eva Dukes

Inge Merkel 160
  The Death of Odysseus
  Translated by Renate Latimer

Felix Mitterer 173
  To the Edge of the Village
  Translated by Jerry Glenn and Jennifer Kelley

Barbara Neuwirth 180
  Villa Dolorosa
  Translated by Michael T. O'Pecko

Martin Ohrt 192
  Vico
  Translated by Paul F. Dvorak

Elisabeth Reichart 202
  The Benefit Concert
  Translated by Richard H. Lawson

Kurt A. Schantl 208
  Noon Song
  Translated by Donald G. Daviau

Robert Schindel 211
  The Despairing
  Translated by Michael Roloff

Evelyn Schlag 220
  Touché
  Translated by G.G. Gardner

Wolfgang Schöner 229
A Life
Translated by M. Veteto-Conrad

Julian Schutting 238
Innocent Dream of an Innocent Man
Translated by Paul F. Dvorak

Wolfgang Siegmund 240
Arrival under Dramatic Clouds
Translated by Jerry Glenn and Jennifer Kelley

Erich Wolfgang Skwara 250
It's a Cliché, Isn't It?
Translated by Michael Roloff

Wilfried Steiner 256
Scarlet Flight
Translated by Heidi L. Hutchinson

Gerald Szyszkowitz 260
What? How Long Has It Been?
Translated by Heidi L. Hutchinson

Sylvia Treudl 266
Road War
Translated by Beth Bjorklund

Elisabeth Wäger 273
How a Doll's Skin Grows Tough
Translated by Richard H. Lawson

Wolfgang Wenger 281
A Vigilant Eye and a Vigilant Ear
Translated by Margaret T. Peischl

Authors about Themselves 290

INTRODUCTION

AUSTRIA'S LITERATURE AT THE MILLENNIUM
A QUESTION OF DIRECTION

ADOLF OPEL

> "Today's errors are often
> tomorrow's norms!"
> J.W. v. Goethe

THE authors whose works are represented in this anthology are above all those who began to publish in the eighties or whose main prose works began to leave an impression on public consciousness during this period. In the earlier volume, *Relationships: An Anthology of Contemporary Austrian Prose* (Ariadne Press, 1991), we attempted to give an overview of the most important Austrian literary figures in the post-World-War-II period. These included authors who began publishing after 1945 as well as those who continued a literary career already begun before the War. This new selection of texts reflects the increasingly noticeable change in style of the generation of writers that has since emerged, the generation which today constitutes "Contemporary Austrian Literature."

Observers of the literary scene—not only of Austria's—agree that from about the beginning of the eighties a "directional change" made itself felt. However, opinions on the precise direction toward which this change points vary quite widely. The source of the directional change, on the other hand, seems evident. The new literature is a reaction against the so-called "classical modern" literature that appeared at the end of the fifties, itself a counter-trend to what was then the dominant literary view. This immediate precursor to contemporary writing found such a strong reception that the label "classical modern" does not at all seem out of place. It was a progressive "avant-garde" that was radically unsettling to the reigning paradigms of narration, language, and power at the time. Since linear narration could no longer do justice to social discrepancies and indeed had an affirming effect, it was necessary "to develop a narrative form that deconstructed and exposed the old realism," as it was formulated, for example, in the critical theories of Horkheimer and Adorno. Tendencies that had eked out a miserable existence in the literary underground up to that point began their confrontational march—at least in Austria—against all of the establishment's hurdles, only to become in turn the establishment themselves. Experiments with word constellations and word fragments were intended to expose the manipulative character of the bourgeois understanding of language. In "practical actions" and later in "happenings," new "realities" were supposedly created, realities that eluded every canon of authority. The creation of an autonomous feminist vocabulary was to lead to a democratization of language itself. These actionists developed finally into Austrian "state artists" some of whom even today set the tone and not just in literary matters.

In our search for a label for the recent trend (and counter-trend to "classical modern"—as a kind of antithesis to it), we unfortunately cannot avoid that often strained concept of the "postmodern." As ambiguous as it is arbitrary, this concept covers the most diverse areas, always according to the viewpoint of the observer. Umberto Eco, one of the most prominent representatives of the "postmodern" in world literature, has referred to it as the "skeleton-key concept"—which might be said of other such terms as well.

The period in which the change in direction of the eighties began to be felt coincides with a phase of the rapid growth of the most divergent alternative and counter cultures. We would not go wrong to interpret the one as a response to the other. Everything that declared itself to be "innovative" was gradually seen as "art" and "culture"; the claims for recognition, for a public and for subventions were heard and met. Although pressed between the covers of a book, there are phenomena in contemporary literature comparable to that "creative" spirit in the fine arts whose own canned metabolic products were found worthy of a museum exhibit. Those who wanted to belong to the "progressive," tone-setting circles were well advised—and still are today—to give both their admiring applause.

Apparently it is in the nature of things that progress finally turns against "progressives" themselves since ultimately, when in increasing measure *everything* counts as art and culture and can be fabricated by the do-it-yourself method with no attention to any binding standards, then *nothing* is any longer art and culture. When the social order has become so permissive that it tolerates and sanctions *everything*, the possibility of "originality"—let alone "scandal"—becomes more and more constricted. And according to progressive thinking, it is scandal that has become the criterion for the novelty of an artistic production. It is the most visible form of every "novum," which in turn must always be topped in an ongoing progression by the next "novum" to make it possible even to talk about progress.

That stylistic change, however, which gradually began to unfold at the beginning of the eighties, places the idea of progress and its linear model of time into question. The actual political development also reflected the loss of a "progressive" perspective. The surprising collapse of communism carried along with it the "leftists" of the world, those whose ideals were pinned to the concept of "progress."

What form have the new trends in Austrian literature assumed at the threshold of the coming millennium?

The protagonist in the narrative "The Anti-Cupid," the first published prose work (1994) by the renowned poet C. W. Aigner, is a physicist who retreats to the isolation of a mountainous region in Italy in order to devote himself entirely to the scientific elaboration of his quantum theory. In the process he reflects on the concept of time:

> Psychologically, time could be described as a sensation within the bounds of the habitual. We experience the world in which the sun rises and sets as something habitual.
> Physically, time is a fixed but relative dimension registered by clocks. Even if an experience seems short to us or painfully long, the physics of the clock tells us how long it lasted.
> Expressed philosophically, time is a hypothesis of expectation. Or it is an interpretation of duration in a world of becoming and passing away. . . . I tend to doubt that my reasoning powers are adequate to comprehend the phenomenon that we indicate with the term *time*. We cherish the illusion that we are forced to understand time in a linear fashion, in the direction from yesterday via today toward tomorrow.
> Whatever belongs to yesterday, however, is only real through our conscious memory and I can only remember in the

moment. Memory then cannot be a factor of a linearly flowing time, but a momentary experience.

About one hundred years after Ernst Mach—the philosopher whose epistemology provided the literary scene of fin-de-siècle Vienna with an intellectual foundation—the narrator's ego in "The Anti-Cupid," awash in the waters of modern science, also turns out to be a quite fragile structure. It is a proposition of dubious worth. The reader is reminded of Mach's "empirio-criticism" that interprets the world as the unique mental conception of every individual and dissolves our world of experience into purely sensory impressions. The current vocabulary is of course completely different. Yet the dialogues and monologues in the prose of the contemporary writer recall narrative techniques that seem to belong to the past. The partner in dialogue with Aigner's physicist, a charismatic beekeeper who steadfastly diagnoses so-called "love" as self-deception, could be a direct descendant of the sectarian "traveler" from the Galician novelle of the same name by Leopold von Sacher-Masoch (1869). Both protagonists are part and parcel of a specific landscape from which they seem to have sprung and whose topography is an integral component of the narrative. Both are characterized by a skeptical world-view reliant on scientifically ascertainable knowledge, a world-view with roots in two of the most influential thinkers of the nineteenth century, Schopenhauer and Darwin.

Above all, however, it is Nietzsche and his thoughts on "eternal recurrence" who provides the theoreticians of the "postmodern" with a philosophical springboard. Scarcely any other Austrian writer has found wider acclaim with a single book than Christoph Ransmayr with his novel *The Last World* (1988). It has been instrumental in illuminating the significance of Nietzschean thought in a contemporary context. When the historical Ovid in this book—in defiance of history—steps up to a battery of modern microphones to give his famous speech in front of the emperor and senators, we have one of the most obviously postmodern passages in recent literature—which, unfortunately, we were unable to include in this anthology due to copyright restrictions.

Instead of following the further sequence of threads that theoreticians of the "postmodern" have woven, citing Mircea Eliade and making reference to that "exemplary recurrent event of archetypal dimensions" that Ransmayr possibly intended to depict, we will rest content in recalling an anecdote that attained a certain literary pedigree when

Alexander Lernet-Holenia mentioned it in his book *The Secrets of the House of Austria* (1971). The story concerns Ludwig van Beethoven who is interviewed by an American reporter and greeted: "Hello, Van!" etc. Finally, when the maestro does not answer, the reporter concludes: "And you wouldn't believe it, the guy was deaf!" A parody of the "postmodern" and its method of depicting time and history is anticipated here long before there even was such a thing as postmodernism.

Its polar reversal of the concepts of "time" and "history" as well as its definition of the past as a "prefiguration of the future"—as found in Eliade—have also had an effect on the aforementioned stylistic change in recent Austrian literature. Striking as well has been the return to traditional narrative techniques.

Wolfgang Hermann who published his first book in 1988 said in an interview:

> Basically I long for tradition. I read Gottfried Keller and Goethe with great enthusiasm. I know that it is no longer possible to write like that, but I struggle against something that might be called the pure materiality of language. For a time the avant-garde was essential here but today it is mere mimicry. I have long been looking for the essence of language, something that comes from an existential gesture. The one gesture is life, the other is writing and they both come from the same force. . . . I don't intend to make anyone believe anything. While I'm working with language I don't want to act like I'm not working with language. It is not only a transparent medium, but simultaneously participates in the image and the word form. I'm not after my own tone like Thomas Mann's nasal writing— his njämnjämnjäm sound—or the eternal repetition in the writing of Thomas Bernhard. I want mine to be light and unhindered. The reader shouldn't hear the author's tone, but the voice of the world.

Walter Klier, whose first novel appeared in 1983, also complains that this world was rapidly lost to the Austrian writers of the "classical modern" and that they "took flight into language." He attributes to the "recent Austrian national literature"—as he derisively calls it—an anemic, feeble quality which "takes refuge from subject matter in an intellectual marginalization and from reality into the unreality of the subjunctive." And he too supports the reaffirmation of traditional narrative techniques: "Let's not be deceived: the modernist strategy of the anti-narrative works with the same model only in its negative form. This negative form—characterized by the absence of the traditional—can be read as the basic pattern. The essential lies somewhere else entirely. It is between the lines."

One of the most respected Austrian authors of the younger generation, Robert Menasse—his first novel appeared in 1988—refers to himself as a literary descendant of Heimito von Doderer, the last representative of the "big" novel that presents a total world view, and comes to the following conclusions in the essay: "There is life after Doderer": "I am completely convinced that novels cannot be written today, for example, without looking around to see what novels have previously been written, how they were written, and how they reflect the location where they were written. What other source of training could be better and how can one otherwise avoid falling behind the standards already set?" He places himself in opposition to that least strenuous type of literature, the so-called "prose of self-experience." Producers of such prose write in more or less conscious ignorance of literary tradition, tradition already "established," and take themselves and their surroundings as the measure of all things.

The change in direction will also mean that another widespread species of "official" Austrian literature will have a great deal to endure. It includes poets of "resolutions" and authors of "appeals" from the left whose timely public embrace of political programs was often the surest way to be taken into the privileged ranks of the "New Austrian National Literature." The economic crisis that hit Austria brought with it the necessary surrender of ideological positions and the elimination of works that are ideologically too radical for a larger readership and can only be sustained by public subsidies.

What the art historian Sir Ernst H. Gombrich had to say in an interview in 1994 about the issues raised here—mainly concerning the fine arts—is undoubtedly also relevant with regard to literature: "The concept of mastery has been lost and something like self-realization has taken its place. Artists seem to me at times like swindled swindlers. They have the mistaken idea that art is simply communication. Admiration of mastery, what art used to be about, has gotten lost. But it will return."

Many writers of the younger generation also reject a regionalism which is nothing more than a cover-up for encrusted positions of social criticism, a kind of inverted regional novel. The Austrian protagonist in Gabriel Loidolt's novel *Le Cafard or the Master Torturer* is in the foreign legion, yet his story takes place in France. Wolfgang Pollanz or Wolfgang Siegmund describe cities, landscapes, and continents in significant, minimalist prose which—far removed from the stale air of Austria—echoes the "voice of the world."

Yet these examples in no way mean a flight from Austrian themes and problems. Wolfgang Siegmund reports the following about his new and still unfinished novel *Concerning the Good Fortune of Being a Simple Man*: "The novel is set in Austria and tells about the crisis of European intellectuals since the fall of the left. My hero takes flight from his 'city of thoughtless speech' into the icy cold of a posh spa in midwinter. At one point he calls his short journey there 'his trip to America.'" This journey ends abruptly, however, at the Pörtschach train station. Hofmannsthal's "Andreas" (1932) immediately comes to mind. Its hero gets stuck in Carinthia and is unable to reach Tuscany, his goal, although at least in the text fragments he gets as far as Venice. In Siegmund's new Austrian work, on the other hand—part *Bildungsroman* and part travel novel—the hero "who has always only read and pondered is now forced to set out for the masculine world, the world of action and deed. And of course he also encounters the question of what masculinity really is in the post-feminist age. On the shore of Lake Wörther, a site for showing off and superficiality, he meets other outsiders who spend the winter here. In short, I want to tell about homelessness in this novel and how one can perhaps somehow gain a foothold in this age without roots . . ."

In spite of individual originality and distinctiveness, a few common characteristics that can be interpreted as trends do emerge on closer inspection of the self portrayals and "position papers" of the authors in this anthology:

- the writer as an outsider situated on the fringes of society;
- the writer's lack of relevance (in a new decadent, fin-de-siècle mood);
- the multilingual nature of literature which no longer remains a marginal phenomenon in an age of uprootedness, disintegration and migration in Europe and the entire world;
- the necessity of pursuing real events instead of writing "invented stories";
- the demand for "traditional" narration;

- the demand for "intense precision";
- the presence of an expanded perception;
- the turn to fantastic literature and science fiction—an almost virgin terrain in German-language literature—which are now considered equivalent and integral to traditional belles-lettres;
- positive on neo-existentialism;
- negative on neo-romanticism;
- revolt against the "terror of the media industry."

As different as the viewpoints and starting positions of the individual writers may be and as divergent as the currents and countercurrents, which carry and retard them may be, today's writers do battle above all against an epidemic-like media and "event" culture. Perhaps anti-culture is a better expression for a phenomenon that leaves no room for books and no time for reading.

There is a call to take up the pen against tendencies that the poet Joachim Gunter Hammer so aptly reduced to a common denominator in a letter to me: "the rise of indifference and cynicism and with them the rise of fascism, the disgustingly clever profiteering and the parallelism between the grand buffet and the morbid joviality. . . ." In other words, a summons for action against the spirit of the times and a life style whose virulence is not restricted to Austrian borders.

Translated by Francis Michael Sharp

ACKNOWLEDGMENTS

We wish to express our appreciation to the authors, all of whom granted permission to publish the selections included here, and to the translators. Particular thanks go to the authors who wrote position papers and self portrayals especially for this anthology.

In addition we would like to thank the following publishers for allowing us to use the texts noted:

Deutsche Verlags-Anstalt, Stuttgart for C.W. Aigner (from *Anti Amor*); Suhrkamp Verlag, Frankfurt am Main for Norbert Gstrein (from *Einer*) and Barbara Neuwirth (for "Villa Dolorosa" from *Phantastische Begegnungen*); Residenz Verlag, Salzburg for Inge Merkl (from *Eine ganz gewöhnliche Ehe*); Otto Müller Verlag, Salzburg for Elisabeth Reichart (for "Das Benefizkonzert" from *La Valse*); Verlagsbuchhandlung Pichler, Vienna for Felix Mitterer (from *An den Rand des Dorfes*); Deuticke Verlag, Vienna for Paulus Hochgatterer (for "Die letzten Arbeitstage des Herrn Klein" from *Die Nystensche Regel*); Ariadne Press, Riverside, California for Marie-Thérèse Kerschbaumer (from *Woman's Face of Resistance*) and Robert Schindel (from *Born-Where*); S. Fischer Verlag, Frankfurt am Main for Evelyn Schlag (from *Touché*); hpt Verlag, Vienna for Gerald Szyszkowitz (from *Der Vulkan*); Wiener Frauenverlag for Sylvia Treudl (for "Strassenkampf" from *Sporenstiefel halbgar*); Residenz Verlag, Salzburg for Wolfgang Wenger (for "wachsames auge, wachsames ohr" from *die gleichgültigkeit der wüstenbewohner*).

THE ANTI-CUPID

C.W. AIGNER

I was feeling devastated, for my lover had been unfaithful to me. I had trusted her one hundred percent—and then this cliché! Like a bad joke. You come home early and find your woman in bed with another man. The shock isn't so much in the sight of familiar skin rubbing against unfamiliar skin but in the realization of having been so wrong.

So: you need to get a grip on yourself. I went to Italy, to stay in a house belonging to some friends which is empty in winter and whose only source of heat is an open fireplace. But it is ideally situated for solitude. At an altitude of six hundred meters, no neighbors far and wide. Late November and there was spring weather on the mountain, a layer of clouds covered the broad valley below, and when I sat at the window of the old stone house, I could imagine myself sitting in an airplane stopped in mid-air. I took long walks, adopted a primitive form of nourishment consisting of noodles mixed with something or other, sometimes just butter, sometimes a couple of tomatoes. Tea, coffee, and a little wine were also available, and I relished not having to shave or shower any more. I became a skunk on two legs, and if I had ever slipped and fallen on one of my panicky, breakneck walks or climbs, on which I regularly lost my way, no one would have been able to identify me. This thought gave me pleasure, for in spite of my relative youth, I am a famous man of science. I have worked with the best minds of this century and trained some very good minds myself. My discovery of the individual behavior of elementary particles has been nominated for a Nobel Prize, at any rate. Still, all that doesn't do a thing for a wounded ego, and so I continued to run away from myself on my hikes. Nobel Prize or not, I still couldn't figure out where I had gone wrong. And so I came to a rocky plateau not far below the pass, where I sat down, sweating, to contemplate the choppy sea below, as if a Neptune of the soul could emerge from it and open my eyes. The harmony of birds singing reminded me of the springs of my school days, somewhere a brook was rushing by, I hovered between self-pity, tearfulness, and pride, the very ingredients that make anyone look ridiculous. To the left below me was a small stand of oak trees, out of which a hiker emerged and climbed up my way. He had thick, black hair, a full black beard, a short, stocky build, and a hearing aid behind his right ear. With a brief word of greeting, he sat down beside me. Then he began to speak in the following manner: after every second word, he would close his mouth and draw in several short breaths through his nose, somewhere in this forest of beard. He said that the problem which was agitating me so much that I could barely keep my balance was a very trivial matter. I didn't know what he was talking about. He couldn't possibly know anything about me, for aside from "hello" I hadn't said a thing.

He said: We would like life to be predictable. That is the purpose of scientific research, of logic and philosophy. You see, what do we really want? We want to understand the soul, or whatever you want to call it, that driving force of life and of the world. And how do we seek to discover? By destroying. Never leave anything whole in order to understand it as a whole. Just as a child cuts open his teddy bear to look inside, to find out what it is that makes the animal so alive. For after all, the child lived with it, played with it, talked with it, shared its thoughts and loved it. All research is the search for our own illusions. We ourselves are the driving force. There is no point in asking *why* something is the way it is. The consequences of this *why* lead to the destruction of our own thoughts. Just as love cannot exist. We project our own illusions and ideas upon another person. It is like a mirror. We are admiring ourselves when we believe we love something or someone else. That's all. If we humans could just see ourselves as the piece of flesh, water, blood, cartilage, bones, and intestines that we are, we wouldn't find ourselves very attractive. We need the imagery of our own illusions to make ourselves bearable. Love is absurd—that is demonstrated by our use of language: I love my wife, I love my job, I love my hobby, I love pork roast, I love potatoes with my pork roast, I love the English, I love my country, I love being free, I love motorcycles, I love a certain pop singer, I love guinea pigs, I love peace and quiet, I love love.

Then he sniffed a couple of times and said I didn't have to believe a word of what he was about to say. In fact, I should assume the opposite for the time being, and decide later.

He said: All humans probably fall in love the same way, regardless of the reasons they think they have for needing to be in love. In this there is no difference between servants and masters. Yet each one believes himself to be unique in his feelings. That is the curious thing about such conditions. Just as the most intelligent man turns into an embarrassment in a drunken condition, that's how strange the sum total of these drunken conditions is.

We can see that a child at play perceives a rag doll as a living being. She transfers her ideas, wishes and fears to the doll, furnishes it with her own illusions, talks to it, receives answers. If a lifeless object can receive a character courtesy of our imagination, why not then a person furnished by our affections. These projections can be so strong that the person can even be the opposite of what we have always wished for. Then even the coward appears to be a hero, the rag doll a princess, and the pug a noble, elegant animal. There is apparently nothing stronger in our belief system than self-deception.

The expression *love* is not a concept because there is nothing to conceive of. It represents a word for an idea, a synonym like the non-concepts *honor* or *justice* which give names to things which don't actually exist. The expression *love* is a wrapper for something vague that intends to be all-encompassing. Shouldn't we be able to ask what this thing is made of that is bought so dearly and treated so cheaply?

We must be aware that a person we grow fond of is, in principle, randomly interchangeable. It is absurd to believe that among billions of people, there should be just this one who is our destiny. The point is not to find the *right* person, the point is to come to an agreement with someone who has struck our fancy at one time or other, to keep our loneliness within bounds. Searching for the *right* person would mean fluttering about like a butterfly until you have forgotten why you are fluttering. So you sniff around a bit more and end up taking the first person who halfway meets your expectations. And together you then think you are unmistakable and uninterchangeable. In the end it doesn't matter whom you live your life side by side with.

We have to recognize the other person as a symbol. We can either glorify or condemn a symbol, but not a piece of flesh. The idealization of the other person is a self-defense against our own weaknesses. We are only admiring ourselves in the other, at least our image of ourselves. That is why the other person needs to be idealized. When we are disappointed in him it only means we are disappointed in ourselves.

Certainly the strong and immediate attraction to a being heretofore unknown to us is always an affection for the illusions that we attach to that being. A spot on the nose, a certain movement, a shimmer, and in an instant images emerge from our subconscious: some germ has been stimulated by a strange force, and it in turn infects this and that, and before we know it, our imagination has woven a creature out of the being standing before us that would sicken it to realize what we had fashioned it from.

And so we take parts of the mosaic from the other being to craft our own mosaic, which then consists mainly of our own pieces and of very few of the borrowed ones. We believe we know the other person, since, after all, we have constructed him ourselves. But even the most carefully selected stones of the other person are not as we would wish them to be, and do not have the characteristics we selected them for. We will attempt to convince the other person to act in this small particle as we imagine they should. For the fulfillment, for the adjustment of just one particle, we tolerate an overwhelming majority of parts to create a picture that doesn't appeal to us at all. But we are thankful and are therefore more likely to give up a small stone from our own crown, fashioned by our imagination from an old hat.

Even mating is *per se* neither an erotic nor an aesthetic matter. It is merely a biological-physical process which would be repulsive if we were to think about what takes place, how our blood shifts, how our innards work. It is therefore only the image of something that mates. Two illusions rub against one another. It must be illusions and repressions; how else would, say, a gynecologist be capable of arousal? Our capacity for carnal pleasure is nature's anaesthesia. That the senses of two people who are attracted to one another are generally deadened to all external truths may be nothing more than the necessary narcosis without which both would have to recognize from which antipathies they have come together, just to keep them from doing battle with one another.

Love is such a generally accepted concept that no one doubts its existence. You can find thousands of pseudo-definitions. There is reason to suspect, though, that this thing that people believe in so unshakably simply does not exist. A graven image.

Hardly any of the original human instincts that were necessary for survival are still necessary. What of these did we retain? Nothing but the illusion of being able to displace nature. And so the instincts and reflexes that once had a particular significance for the harmony of man with his environment have grown useless. In a life where buying is the only necessity, these instincts are undesirable. An internal ice age is approaching. With the atrophying of our former abilities and instincts, one human's interests in another also shrink. Our main interest consists in making ourselves useful to others. Behavior patterns replace behavior. In keeping with a simple cost-benefit analysis we want to quickly get rich before everything falls into ruin. Even in the area of emotions. But anyone who only remembers how to pull out his wallet will receive packaged emotions. Anyone who never learned how to live with a certain amount of feelings will sooner or later panic. Then, like in a supermarket, he will reach for anything that shines or sparkles. All that remains for us, then, is the flashing neon sign *Love: free admission*. But only the admission. This Las Vegas of feelings, the great, sparkling illusion awakens our passion for gambling. Again and again we are drawn along in the hope of getting a maximum of affection for a minimum of investment. Dreamily, we emerge, like out of a movie theater. Like in the comic books, when someone runs into mid-air and hovers there, as long as he is dreaming. Not until he awakes and becomes aware of the abyss beneath him, does he fall, hair flying.

An instinct only forms where conditions make it necessary for survival. It will disappear if it is no longer needed. Our survival is apparently no longer threatened by any other species, at least not by any species in the mammal family. The lions are in cages. We no longer need a keen sense of hearing, no highly developed sense of smell. Our survival, our senses can be entrusted to machines, the only things the human spirit still trusts; after all, we created them ourselves. Only the sexual drive remains, which is in the process of being neutered just like all the other senses. One of the wildest errors is that the spirit rises above the body. This vain levitation theory discredits the body as a living thing, which means that the body as machine is at our disposal. To be at our disposal means to be for sale cheap. The cheapest thing there is on earth is money. Humans as goods are available by the billions. They are no longer the *summum bonum*. A *summum bonum*, we know, is not easy to come by. That stupid fallacy of the free spirit. Just go to a prison, then it's easy to see how the exalted free spirit twitters about behind bars.

Our spirit sees our body as a prison. But the body has paced off the world step by step; hands were the first to grasp the world. Without arms and legs, no brain, and vice versa. We need to see that the brain, the spirit, is present even in our little toe, and that it is not imprisoned behind the eyes up there in the thing we call a head.

He stood up and said no more, but kept on sniffling. We stared at the sea of clouds. Above it, a plane was plowing a furrow, its belly in the wet cotton. He turned to me and said—

Isn't it a fact that we understand the foundation on which affection for us grows least of all? He who really likes someone does it most inconspicuously. He makes no demands, for he knows instinctively that great affection and possession are mutually exclusive. Good-bye.

Translated by Heidi L. Hutchinson

Europe in the Rain

Hans-Jürgen August

THE sound of bending and finally splintering plastic stabbed ever more clearly through the monotonous whistling of the wind that had flooded the valley for days. The man located the source of the popping high up behind his shoulder, though—as he deduced from the hollow, desolate remnants of the noise—at a safe distance. In the glass of the abandoned gas station, the reflection of the plastic sign attached to the edge of a steel mast being progressively destroyed with each passing moment careened from one side to the other before it tilted into the darkness within. When the man had closed the door and turned to the row of metallically gleaming pumps set against the pale green background of the hills like a relic of a lost culture, one more fragment of green plastic fell off and revealed another segment of the flat gray sky.

His gait almost dancelike, the man sought to avoid the remnants of plastic strewn over the damp asphalt. Due to the varying pressure of the wind, his movements seemed like those of someone suffering from poor balance. Nonetheless, it crackled beneath his boots, so that the man stumbled a little as if a nail had pierced the soles of his shoes and painfully entered the ball of his foot.

The woman, who had got into his car while the man had opened up the electronic lock of the pumps, formed a dark silhouette behind the tinted glass of the windows. He had already noticed her on the side of the road but hadn't paid any further attention to her, because she had given no sign of wanting a lift.

As he stuck the nozzle into the tank, his gaze slid over the side windows, in which the distorted image of the gas station was reflected, onto the side mirrors. The implacable face of the woman caught his eye, he felt the sudden static tension that built up between them, this feeling that took him captive in moments now quite rare, rather like déjà-sentí, and allowed memories presumed lost to return. Not until the nozzle clicked did the moment dissolve; only now did he notice the woman's sunglasses.

A glowing orange spot of color that faded slowly traced his path, plumbed the borders of the interior as the man pulled the door shut against the pressure of the wind. The woman put the cigarette lighter back into the holder, took a deep pull on the smoldering cigarette.

"Where to?" asked the man, halfway swallowing the final syllable, unsettled at the implausible matter-of-factness of his own voice. The woman rolled down the window and blew the smoke outside before she leaned back in her seat, and with an imperceptibly tired look, indicated the dark gray ribbon of asphalt that stretched out before them.

T: Was it unpleasant?
F: Of course it was. It always is, every contact is unpleasant, isn't it? Especially with strangers. With everyone.
T: Why is every . . .
F: Well, because the people are all . . . are all sick somehow. They have odd ideas. They always want something . . .
T: From you?
F: Yes, from me, from fate, from life, what do I know.
T: And this man, was he sick, too?
F: Yes, no, sick . . . he was perverse somehow, not like you think, harmless, harmless-appearing, but it made him special . . . dangerous, confusing.
T: Fine, go on.

The man had shifted into neutral, the car rolled slowly out onto the rather sloping road. At a distance of a few hundred meters, just under the line where the mountains hemming in the valley met the cloud cover, the man had made out a point of light that now came ever closer, grew clearer until the car halted. The man observed the point a while, registered the scarcely noticeable modulations of its light's intensity. The woman had taken off her sunglasses and was following the gaze of the other. When he picked the camera up off the back seat and opened his door a crack, she turned to him . . .

"What's that?"

Her voice was barely audible over the continuous whistling of the wind that penetrated the interior of the car in softly changing modulations, she whispered as if they were witnesses of a holy event or a base murder.

"A station."

He opened the door wider, the wind grabbed the material of his pants leg which beat about his lower leg like a flag.

"A station? What . . ."

The woman interrupted herself, vexed by her much too openly exhibited uncertainty.

Her eyes stayed fixed on the point of light.

"A light station that . . . well, I don't know, they must not have a name. They don't give themselves any in order to be invulnerable, like nameless gods that you can't defile."

His voice was as calm as that of a knowledgeable guide in an apocalyptic art exhibit. He looked at her profile, observed the slight trembling of her black lashes.

When the woman realized that the man had opened the door wider and had stepped out, she turned around, leaned onto the driver's seat, and shouted something after him.

He no longer heard her.

F: The points of light increased, there were more and more of them, and now and then I had the feeling that . . . that they were a part of a big whole, as if they made up a cryptic sign.
T: A sign?
F: Yes, as if a circle were closing, an encirclement.
T: What did the man do?
F: He kept stopping and standing still, the same ritual over and over again: he stared at the points of light, at the ones in front of us, then again at the ones behind us as if he wanted to organize them or . . . read some sort of information from them. Then he picked up the camera off the back seat, got out and took pictures.
T: And you didn't say anything else, you didn't ask any questions?
F: No, not at first.
T: And the man explained nothing about these . . .
F: Stations?
T: Yes.
F: Yes, stations he called them, he couldn't say anything more about them, or he didn't want to.

T: Whose stations they were he didn't say?
F: No, he didn't know, he didn't know their names.
T: Then he really didn't know?
F: No, or at least he pretended not to. Do you know? Maybe everyone knows already, do you know?
T: Calm down. Probably he really didn't know. And other than that he didn't say anything about them?

"At night there are hundreds. At night the forest glows."

The man turned off the camera and laid it carefully onto the back seat. He waited a few seconds for her next question, but when he became aware of the absurdity of his game, he broke the silence.

"They are only symbols, they are symbols. Signs of their presence."

"They? Who are they?"

"Some of the symbols are in the forest, the others," he indicated a group of giant spaces lit up yellow that rose up from the horizon before them, "the others are there."

"And we . . . "

"We are right in the middle."

The man smiled at the woman, whose eyes he could only imagine behind the dark lenses of her sunglasses. His features reflected this mixture of uncertainty and fascination that captured some strangers catapulted into this landscape and slowly but all the more surely abducted them into the inescapable labyrinths of their own morbid logic.

The road led directly to the areas glowing pale yellow. Due to the incline of the road, the vertical plateaus sank beneath the approaching horizon, the visible sections became simultaneously lower and wider.

"And why are you photographing that?"

The man was silent a few seconds, stared at the areas before him coming closer and closer, that—flat and wide as an immaculate movie screen—had already taken up an considerable part of the horizon.

"Probably to keep me from losing my hold on the world, to keep it from becoming too strange to me. In holding on to it, I can at least become accustomed to it."

The woman now looked at the driver for the first time. She took off her glasses, folded them absent-mindedly and put them into the pocket of her jacket. She looked the man over, his hands holding the steering wheel, the wind-tousled hair. Her gaze was caught within his eyes that now followed the way the yellow street markings were swallowed up by the vehicle.

The car neared the crest of the street. At a few hundred meters' distance the cooling towers, lit up by dozens of spotlights, stretched into the narrow sky. The escaping steam formed a single unit with the low-lying clouds whose uniform gray had brightened slightly in the light of the midday sun.

The shadowless mushroom steam-cloud covered the valley like a tight-fitting lid, even the wind, corralled in this hoselike space, had lost its power. Tiny drops, more condensation from the moist air saturated with the steam of the plant than actual rain, began to cover the windshield.

At the fork in the road, which lay between the car and the plant, a tank was partially obscuring the traffic signs painted over with black enamel.

The man took his foot off the gas pedal, let the now decelerating car roll down the slightly sloped lane. He observed the three people who broke away from the tank and positioned themselves to block the street that led to the plant. Their machine guns hanging horizontally at belly level turned them into three dark crosses in front of the yellow cement backdrop.

With a rapid motion, the man reached behind his seat and threw a woolen blanket on top of the camera before he rolled down the car window.

A woman broke away from the group of three and walked toward an imaginary meeting point. Clutching the machine gun with her right hand in the vicinity of the trigger, she moved her outstretched left arm slowly and clearly up and down. The driver continued to slow the car down; shortly before it came to a halt, the uniformed person appeared in the frame of the open car window. The driver glanced briefly at the glowing colorful symbols on the gray-green background of the clothing, which he interpreted as insignia—incomprehensible to him—of a hierarchical system, then at the hand whose fingers were crooked around the trigger of the weapon, finally at the angular face of an approximately thirty-year-old woman.

Her quick, precise, and conspicuously mechanical-appearing glances caused by the accompanying abrupt head movements were not directed initially at those within but at the empty space of the interior. Not until the soldier had acknowledged the emptiness of the car as such did her glance rest on the passenger, lingered on her face a few seconds, clearly as long as her practiced powers of assessment required to store the characteristics of a face with all its details, and to register betraying reactions, a change of the pupils perhaps.

As the uniformed woman took stock of the driver, she slowly raised the weapon with her right hand and suddenly straightened up. She took a step backward, pointed at the car with the gun, gripped the barrel with her left hand. A quick movement with the weapon, shimmering metallically in the diffuse light, beckoned the driver to drive on.

"They're leading us to the mountains," the woman stated, after the driver had closed his window again. Her eyes jumped from the yellow areas that were growing even smaller in the make-up mirror of the visor, to the white-lit markings in the forest before her.

> F: I assume that we were searched and detoured because the plant people were afraid of attacks, because of the radiation that would then be released. But he . . .
> T: What was his name, actually?
> F: What his name was? No idea . . .
> T: Okay, go on.
> F: Well, he said the plant hadn't been in operation for years, none of these plants were operating anymore.
> T: And did he reveal why?
> F: Yes, it was too expensive and too dangerous. I was surprised at the effort being put into protecting the plants, but . . .
> T: Go on.
> F: He said it all had to do with just the symbol. Even the steam from the cooling towers was fake, useless, except to maintain the illusion of a functioning plant. He . . .
> T: Yes?
> F: He kept blathering about symbols, a war of symbols. It was rather unclear to me, somehow not tangible, until we, this . . .
> T: Slow down. We'll get to that later. He acted very knowing, then, like he was superior.
> F: Yes, . . . and no. He talked about everything with a matter-of-factness that wasn't . . . how should I put it . . .
> T: Wasn't condescending . . .
> F: Yes, exactly. I think he only wanted to . . .
> T: Yes?
> F: To talk.

T: Talk?
F: Yes, talk; talk to me.
T: And what did you want?
F: I? I wanted to go south.

The street, about halfway up the mountain, now ran parallel to the bottom of the valley. Now and then it disappeared into tendrils of the low-lying cloud cover. The moist, black ribbon of asphalt was bordered by fallow vineyards, houses, and the stumps of sawn-off utility poles hidden behind old, huge billboards for nougat cookies and insurance, shredded by wind and rain.

The row of white lights winding its way through the forest had moved nearer now. After certain bends in the road it gave the appearance that one was entering the foreign territory, but the direction of the street always asserted itself as a line of demarcation.

The driver observed the ribbon made up of the spots of light, only partially shimmering through the clouds and then enlarged in patches, tried to make a sensible connection between them and the plant that had already disappeared from view.

Completely immersed in the fog, five points of light stacked up on a mast now appeared to the right of them like warning fires. The man brought the car to a halt, began driving again slowly so that he could devote his attention more to the lights than to the curving road. He observed how the changing perspective caused the position of the lights to each other to change, vertical became elliptical, then as the road led on, more and more approximated a circle. When the right side of the car stood opposite the glowing symbols like the broadside of an old warship, the driver came to a stop.

The man took the camera off the back seat with an automated motion that testified to long practice. His gaze never wavered from the pentagon of light, he gazed at it, as if it threatened to otherwise vanish irrevocably from reality.

Miss, um, could you open the . . .

When he heard his whispering, voiceless words, he smiled at this senseless precautionary measure, the admission of his fear. He watched in the viewer of his camera as the tinted window slowly moved downward and let in the diffuse light of the outer world, accompanied by a cold draft of air.

On the right edge of his right field of vision he discerned the indistinct contours of the woman's head, bordered to the left by her profile, turned almost completely away from him. The blurred lines exposed her high forehead, the wide arc of her cheekbones, the dully shining dark hair. Succumbing to a need to hold close, for intimacy, the man centered this image in the viewer and briefly tapped the shutter button. The motor of the autofocus whirred, for fractions of a second the sharply bordered image of the woman appeared in the viewer before the man, startled by the cold noise of the apparatus, pointed the camera once again at the outside world. When the woman reacted to the whir by turning around, the lens was already aiming at the chain of lights enthroned on the pole. Again the noise of the little motor sounded before recurrent clicking confirmed that a further portion of reality was archived.

The road now led into the cover of clouds, the radius of the circle of light enlarged, and slowly the dim silhouette of a town defined itself in the fog. When they had passed the rusted city limits sign, also painted over with black enamel, the driver realized that one of the spotlights was mounted on a tower in the town. The road wound through the assortment of whitewashed houses. Not a soul was to be seen on the streets, even the dogs, normally so typical of these regions, were missing. Behind the closed windows no light shone, not a single even secondary sign of life was discernible.

The museumlike inertia was disrupted by a violent pounding on the car's chassis. At short intervals a droning rat-a-tat-tat was to be heard, beginning under the motor block and making its way through the car in a matter of seconds. The right foot of the driver leapt from one pedal to the other, and as the car moved slower and slower, accompanied by the scraping sound of tires sliding on the oily damp lane, the man saw the bent tin sheets appearing out of the fog in quick succession which, stirred up from beneath the car, sounded their brief *tremendo*.

When the car came to a stop, the silhouette of a small transport van appeared, barely discernible in the contourless light of the car's headlights.

    F: Afraid? Yes, I believe in this situation I really was. A happy kind of afraid, somehow.
    T: Happy fear?
    F: Yes. A feeling of . . . a sign of life, a sign of . . .
    T: A being there emotionally.

F: My God, yes, if you want to call it that, yes. Whatever it was, at least a feeling . . . Not a good one, but one nonetheless, an intense one even.
T: And how did you . . .
F: After a long time.
T: And how did that feel to you? Only happy?
F: No, of course not. It was . . . strange.
T: Did you express your fear, your anxieties?
F: What?
T: Well, did you express your feelings to the man, did you . . .
F: No.
T: . . . share?
F: No.
T: . . . tell them to him?
F: No.

Both doors were yanked open almost simultaneously.

The sooty openings were adjoined by barrels of a gun off center in perspective, then a mechanism gripped by hands scraped bloody. It was not discernible whether the masked person who now slowly withdrew the barrel of the gun from the interior of the car was male or female, just as with the half dozen compadres, the reflective visors of the motorcycle helmets, the heavy jackets and pants had buried any gender beneath them. Only their lanky frames, the studied hurriedness of their movements, the firm skin of their hands, of these few uncovered body parts revealed that youths were who had circularly surrounded the car.

No order to leave the car was necessary; the man was led hurriedly—as was the woman—to a wall of a house. While some pointed their rifles—whose archaism lent a penetrating aura of immediate dangerousness—at the intruders, others searched first the car, then the clothing that the man and woman wore. With rapid movements a pair of hands felt along the contours of the bodies distorted by fabric of clothing, yet without haste, without unnecessary exertion which would have betrayed a trace of emotionality, dedicated itself to all body parts with the same indifference that degraded the body to a shapeless technical object. When the man carefully broke away from the wall after this examination and turned around, he saw the male or female leader directing the procedure with hand motions that were more an indication than a gesture and which made and unmade dozens of ciphers in seconds. Already, the first masked ones were leaving, and before the man had reached his car door, the van backed into a tiny street that swallowed up the gray-enameled metal in its shadows. The man peered into the interior of the car, his gaze scanned every square centimeter as if to assess damages, circled anxiously around the woolen bulge on the back seat and rested a few seconds on its crest. When the man noted that he could detect no difference in the condition of the interior, that no trace testified to the reality of the past ten minutes, he jerked back, tore his gaze from the inside of the car as if blinded by a demonic vision and looked searchingly in the direction in which he thought he had seen the youths vanish. On the way to the light enthroned on the tip of the church steeple that pained the eyes and made the pupils contract into tiny black points, his gaze skimmed over the figure of the woman, who had already got into the car.

F: No, actually not. Not for me.
T: But for the man.
F: Yes, certainly. But for me . . .
T: Was it different with him?
F: With him? He was quieter, said less. Oh yes, and he didn't take a single picture after that.
T: Why?
F: My God, how I do know; I've already said he was odd. At any rate, he never touched the camera again; he even left it in the car, under this wool blanket, when we got to the farm.
T: You said someone had given you the address of this farm as a place to stay overnight.
F: Yes, right.
T: Where did you get the address?
F: I don't know. From some guy probably, it was a while back.
T: It only seems that way.

The halogen spotlight was trained on a dead chicken that was nailed by its spread wings to the whitewashed wall of the farmyard, the light penetrated its plumage, made the animal appear an obscene offering. In the sand of the courtyard a dozen persons knelt with lowered head and hummed monotonously a melody whose changes in pitch were lost in time and that were vaguely reminiscent of Gregorian chorales.

The man turned his gaze from the scene, closed the window and pulled down the blinds, while he, as furtive as a sinner, threw a glance at the murdered god. He turned around slowly; the cold that coursed through his naked feet anew at every step on the tile floor caused him to limit his movements to only the most essential.

He looked for the origin of the water, the source that fed the shower. His eyes followed the noise of the vibrating pipes hidden behind white plaster, along the ceiling, down the wall of the bedroom into the fittings, whose shine had become dull.

He observed the forking of the stream of water as it struck the head of the woman and now, conforming to the shapes of her body, coated her skin with an ever-changing film shimmering in the artificial light. The coat of water covering the woman collected like the remains of a snake's molting on the floor of the shower stall only to shortly vanish in the black hole of the drain.

When the eyes of the man constricted, irritated by the chaotic variety of the light's deflections, he turned around and withdrew into the darkness of the room. The woman turned off the water, grasped a towel and dried the last traces of water off her body. When she stepped onto the cold flagstones of the floor, around the spot where she'd stepped a moistly dull sheen of condensed steam formed that enclosed her feet like a fleeting aura. Scarcely had the woman moved into the room before these traces of her presence were extinguished.

The woman remained at the entrance to the small bedroom, the one side of her body was dimly lit by the diffuse light that penetrated the bathroom through the plastic strips of the blinds, while the side of her body turned to the door melted seamlessly into the dark spacelessness of the background. The woman kept her eyes firmly shut a moment in order to become accustomed to the darkness, and then peered into the barely distinguishable shades of gray the room offered.

With apparent constancy of interest, her gaze skimmed the windowless walls, the mattress lying on the floor, the body of the man lying on his back, the doorless old wooden wardrobe.

It seemed as if the woman was using these moments to absorb topological data which could be of decisive importance to one in a strategic game of unknown rules. When the light in the courtyard was gone and the darkness was almost unbroken, the woman, as if she had waited for this sign, approached with assured steps the man lying at her feet.

Europe in the Rain 27

F: My God, what it was like?
T: Well, did you sense anything special? Something . . . ?
F: A feeling of nearness, of intimacy.
T: Of nearness?
F: Yes.
T: Good. And what did you do then?
F: I stood up and went outside.
T: When? That is very important.
F: Immediately afterward.
T: You mean, you hadn't gone to sleep yet?
F: No.
T: You didn't sleep during the whole night in question, then?
F: No, I . . .
T: Why? Were you tense?
F: No, I just don't sleep next to . . . strangers, mainly because he, as I said already . . .
T: was strange.
F: Exactly.
T: And how did you get the weapon?
F: It was lying . . . I found it in the kitchen, yes, that was where it was lying. On top of the refrigerator.
T: It was just lying there on top of the refrigerator?
F: Yes.
T: Good. Go on, do you remember what happened then? So you took the pistol . . .
F: Yes. And I went outside with it right away. It was already getting light.
T: Good, very good. And then?
F: That's all, I mean, I don't know.
T: Try to remember. Did you see anyone?
F: No, I . . .
T: Did the man follow you outside?
F: I think . . . no, I don't know.
T: Did you fire? Try to . . .
F: No, I don't know. I don't know!
T: Good. Good. Did you ever see the man again?
F: No.
T: Do you suffer from this uncertainty?

F: No.
T: Good, then it's okay.
  And now, what do you want to do now?
F: I want to go on.
T: Go on? Go on to where?
F: South. Further south.

Translated by M. Veteto-Conrad

JOSEPH, A GERMAN FATE

CHRISTIAN BAIER

AS a child he was afraid to be the center of attention. The presence of many people irritated him.

He is timid, says his mother in her harsh Rhineland dialect. She is a descendant of Dutch immigrants.

Go ahead and baby him, your mother's boy, thunders his father, the worker's son who has risen from messenger boy to purchasing agent in the wick factory of W. H. Lennartz in Rheydt. He has his own ideas about his son's future but harbors great expectations for Hans and Konrad, perhaps because they take after their mother. Joseph, on the other hand, resembles him.

You have to give him time, he's still young after all, the boy, he'll soon learn.

It is Sunday. Joseph is sitting on the sofa in the parlor, the "good room." The previous day the family had taken a trip to Geisterbeck. He was probably thinking about that.

The others find him, whimpering, with cramps. Fetch the doctor, Konrad, quickly.

He doesn't know what else happened to him. At some point the pains let up, moderated to a dull, laming feeling. Except for his mother and the doctor he sees nobody. Then he seems to be surrounded by whiteness. Snow, he thinks, winter. The women who bend over him wear strange, bobbing caps. Angels, he thinks. His mother had told him about angels. The angels show great interest in his right leg, stick long needles into it, but it doesn't hurt. Can you pray alone? asks an angel. He doesn't understand and nods. When his mother comes it is Sunday, and when she leaves again, he begins to cry and won't be consoled. On one occasion his father comes, puts his heavy hand on his forehead, says nothing. When his father departs, the boy doesn't cry.

On his right leg hangs a clump of bony mass and numb tissue. He has difficulty walking. His leg gives way constantly. That's normal, reassures the doctor, the muscles have to regain their strength first.

Hans and Konrad take turns assisting him through the room. Movement, the doctor advised. But the brothers have no patience with Joseph, they want to go out, to be with the others.

His mother shows him pictures in the catechism. Jesus curing a leper, Jesus curing a blind man, a crippled person, angels hover about, looking altogether different than the women in the strange, bobbing caps. You must be brave now, the good Lord tests us all.

The perspective of his childhood is the growing distance between himself and the others. He experiences everything from a distance. Rarely is he in the middle of things, and he never feels any compulsion to assert himself among others.

His development is restricted to his head, which stands in an oddly disproportionate relationship to the rest of his body.

Everything will be all right, Joseph, you only have to believe it. He goes to church holding his mother's hand; kneeling side by side, they pray for strength for Joseph to bear the burden of his impairment. Joseph, he thinks, I am he.

His father sits over his blue account books. A bookkeeper of his life. The operation gobbled up a fortune, the specially fitted shoes, out of which the boy has soon grown again. Sometimes he summons Joseph to him, says nothing, just looks at him. A cripple. What is to become of him in the future? He had wished for sons, straight and strong, who make their way, get ahead in life.

He breaks a plate, stands amid the pieces, waits for what will happen, waits for punishment which doesn't come. After all, he didn't do it intentionally.

Joseph soon knows how to function with what he is, he doesn't learn to live with it. He has a beautiful, powerful voice. At Christmas he sings a song, his mother taught it to him. Aunt Stine is there and Aunt Lieschen, his father's sisters, uncle Heinrich (he deals in cloth) sits next to them wheezing. All praise Joseph. He is very excited. It took great self-control to step up in front of so many people and sing. He has achieved a victory. Even his father appears moved. At mass his mother squeezes Joseph's hand quite firmly and, while putting him to bed, she says: you see, it has helped, the praying.

Still, the distance to the others decreased only slowly. They had nothing in common. He prefers to sit with his mother in the kitchen, browses in the catechism. He turns the pages carefully. Books are something valuable. He soon knows the pictures by heart, but always discovers new details, refinements in the beautiful facial expressions of the saints and martyrs. What torments they had to endure, and all the while looking toward heaven which was full of angels who made no effort to hurry to help the suffering with the swords they swung threateningly above their heads. He made up the names of the saints according to the manner of their torment. He has an amazing memory.

His father comes in, takes him aside. Now show what you can do. Then he sits in a room with others, children of the same age, who know each other, have long childhood days in common. Benches in rows, sit quietly. That is not difficult for him. Anyone who doesn't pay attention is singled out, punished. To a question there is only one answer. Anyone who doesn't know it has to stand up and go to the lectern. Teacher Hilges has a small blond beard. His strictness unites, punishments create a sense of community. In the very first weeks groups are formed, leaders develop. Paul is one of them, takes charge. His father owns a Konditorei in town. Joseph sits next to him. They walk the same way to school. Paul is strong, can lift Joseph with one hand during recess, and everyone laughs. Since then they have become friends. At any rate Joseph thinks so and makes sure that nobody interferes with Paul's friendship. He tries to keep up with Paul, but he doesn't succeed. He is too slow, and Paul isn't willing to wait for him. He takes a fall, lands flat on the schoolground. Don't run if you can't do it, says Paul. Then he turns away from Joseph and goes over to the others.

He disappointed me. I don't belong to anyone. He sticks out his lower lip. I am alone. During class work he covers his notebook demonstratively with his hand, so that Paul can't copy, although with teacher Hilges this is impossible anyway. But Paul should notice. His father has a Konditorei in town. So? The son, who can throw a ball so high that it bounces as high as a man when it lands, doesn't even know how much twelve times seven is.

There is a sister, Elisabeth. She is weak and pale and looks off into the distance. If one holds out a finger, she often grabs next to it. Something is not right with her. Joseph doesn't know what to do with her. One has to poke her in the side or tickle her under her chin before she emits a forced laugh. She doesn't want to eat. With children one has problems, complains his mother, holding the child in her arms.

He is pushed away more and more when he wants to hug his mother. You are a big boy now, Joseph, says his mother. She rarely calls him Juppche any more. Sometimes he begins to cry without reason, the vein in his forehead swells—something that he has in common with his father. Don't be stubborn, Joseph. Oh, be quiet, Konrad gives him a poke in the back.

A severe winter. In the morning the frost crackles. The windows have grown together in a bizarre way. From some distance he watches his other schoolmates—and how clearly at this moment he perceives them as the others—throw snowballs at each other. Their breath shoots out of their noses and mouths in thick gray columns. Suddenly Paul claps his hands before his face, screams with an overpowering voice: an ice ball! Next to his right eye there is a gash. Paul sinks to his knees. That is his punishment.

When he comes home, there is a strange coat hanging in the hallway. His mother intercepts Joseph right at the door, pushes him into the parlor. He would like to ask what has happened, she simply presses a finger against his mouth. He sits on the sofa, lets his legs dangle. When he lets them swing freely, the right one stops sooner. Sit still, Hans hisses. The frost etches the windowpanes.

There is little hope. His father came home from the factory with a high fever and pains in his chest. It is nothing, he said, but still he lay down. The fever won't go down. Pneumonia. His mother stands in the doorway: your father is dying. That is a cue for everyone to get up and follow her into the bedroom. The children have always been forbidden to enter the parental bedroom. Now no one dares to look around. His father is lying on the bed, the center of the room. His breathing is raspy. The mechanical rising and falling of his chest. His father has opened his eyes half way, but he recognizes only shapes, outlines against the light, the fever blurs his gaze. There is the smell of vinegar and mustard plaster.

They stand there and don't dare to move from the spot. None of them has ever seen a dying person before. That's how it is, they may be thinking, that's how somebody dies. Reality closes itself off to them, they are not conscious of it. The man who painstakingly keeps track in blue account books of every penny he loses at cards, of every penny that he gives to a door-to-door salesman, of every coin that he throws into the charity box, the department head before whom the workers remove their hats when he walks with his family on Sundays after church, their father cannot die so simply. To whom will he delegate the right to praise, to criticize, to punish? Over the bed hangs a crucifix.

Joseph will still remember this later, even now at the moment when they are kneeling and praying, it is an almost unreal memory: the hairy back of father's hand, worker's hands, his fingers clutch at the cloth of the bed covering. Out of these fragments is created a memory that lasts.

A small miracle happens. His father reemerges from the bedroom into life a changed man, more reflective, more serious even than before. He owes his life to us, thinks Joseph.

In this winter it still snows often, and, fascinated by the speed of her spinning top, Elisabeth claps her hands. Paul—it appears that he will not be promoted at the end of the school year—wears a bandage on his head, loosens it, shows those standing around the stitched wound on his temple. Did it hurt? Na! He who can stand pain is strong.

Joseph would also like to stand pain, be strong, but no ice ball hit him, he only knows the correct answers to the questions of his new teacher—Hennes is his name—and that doesn't count. A class photo shows Joseph in the third row at the end on the right.

Teacher Hennes urges Joseph's father to send the boy to the *Gymnasium*. He is ambitious and industrious, he can become a doctor, says his mother. His father has reservations. The *Gymnasium* is expensive. It has already been decided that Konrad and Hans will leave school after their obligatory military year and learn a trade. His father looks at Joseph with concern. What is to become of him with his foot, if he is not a doctor? He has a good head on his shoulders. The decision is made. We'll just have to cut down on things.

The long, echoing halls of the *Gymnasium*. The covered windows of the main hall. We are not learning for school but for life. It is a great gift, Joseph feels, he must prove himself worthy. Separate the wheat from the chaff, thunder the professors and the school inspectors. Voss teaches German, Professor Bartels history; he knows how to inspire the class. Professor Foerster (in their notebooks they call him Kaes because he abbreviates Caesar as "Caes") gives Latin instruction, a dry-as-dust, humorless schoolmaster. Geography with no-nonsense Rentrop—"Hm. Hm. Hompesch dismissed!"—French with Klass, Mathematics with Schmidt-Hartlieb. Chaplain Mollen leads the class in prayer. I belong to the wheat, Joseph tells himself.

His father gave him permission to set up a study in the attic. Studying requires quiet. Meyer's *Lexicon* and Mommsen's Roman history move upstairs. He paces back and forth between the slanted walls. Voss mentioned in class that Goethe also paced back and forth while he dictated to Eckermann. Joseph stops in the middle of the room, puts his hands behind his back, poses.

He reads a great deal. Connections come of their own accord. He sprinkles his conversations with what he has put together from books, emroidered with a knowledge of details. His vocabulary grows. He knows how to express himself in elegant language, even if he finds it difficult to debate. Whenever he finds himself confronted with opposing views, he immediately withdraws, pulls in his reins. If there is no other way out, he pretends not to understand.

Events arrange themselves into a biography. Sometimes he looks around the attic, thinks: *he* studied here. Or: *his* study.

If the class is blamed for something, his name is usually mentioned as a praiseworthy exception. Then he looks back. Sometimes the reprimand also includes him. That shames him. He doesn't belong to the group, doesn't want to either, lets the others know this more and more clearly. During the recesses he stands to one side and waits for someone to join him or for a group to call him to join it. But that happens rarely.

When he answers a question, he raises his right eyebrow and looks at his questioner from the corners of his eyes. In class he generously lets his work be copied. Privately, however, he selects who may share his knowledge. Max Flacke, Eugen Camphausen, Ernst Heyn—for all I care. Peter Backes should do his own work. And there is Richard, Richard Flieges, farmer's son, tall, silent for long periods and reflects before he speaks, sometimes gives the impression that he had just strayed into the classroom. Nothing can disconcert him. In the indifference with which he accepts criticism and bad grades the professors smell the seeds of rebellion. Listen to the important comments that colleague Flieges reported on the problem of the Classical elements in Schiller . . . When Richard says "I," he means himself, he never generalizes.

The solidarity in a class photo is deceiving, Joseph never stands in the center as in this photograph. His place would be at the very back, in the last row next to Flieges, who is the only one who doesn't look into the lens of the camera. Even friend Fritz sometimes finds it difficult to stand by Joseph. Nevertheless, for the brief seconds of the picture he places his hand on Joseph's shoulder, as if to draw him into the class.

Long conversations with Fritz. Joseph doesn't want to know anything about women but listens attentively when the names of girls are mentioned, occsionally makes deprecating remarks, purses his lips, waves them away, as if he were standing above this strange, unknown, mysterious world.

    He also knows a girl. Her name is Maria. Whenever he meets her, he acts stiff and reserved. She must not notice anything. He fears rejection. But inwardly he is glowing. She senses that and makes fun of him. Then he burns in full blaze.

    He would like to write letters to her, creeps around her house, sees her illuminated window. How does he know it is hers? He feels infinitely alone. His fantasies run away with him. Women on warm spring days, the women from the factory in their blouses, Mrs. Morkheimer from the neighborhood, Maria, he thinks, Maria, and could attack everyone who crosses his path. During the evening hours his yearning grows strong, changes into melancholy. Why are you so restless today, Joseph? It's nothing, Mother.

    I despise life, he says with clenched lips. He instinctively prepares such staged outbursts, limps next to Fritz on the promenade, his head lowered, his hands behind his back, his upper body bent slightly forward, this posture, he finds, gives him an intellectual look. For a long time he says nothing, stops, looks into the distance, growls with furrowed brow: filth, everything filth. He gets a jolt out of it himself when he hears himself talk this way. Life isn't worth anything, Fritz. I sometimes feel a great emptiness in me, looks at his friend, searches his face for signs of alarm. Sometimes I'm afraid of myself.

    Dahlen Street is still the center of his world, the study with its slanted walls, from the window the view of a stone mason's workshop. Behind the board fence crosses are intended for graves. Death, he thinks, to die, there is so much yearning for peace within me.

    Maria. How she would react, if she were suddenly told: Joseph has . . . here—his farewell letter. It is addressed to you. He imagines the scene. Each time, after she has read the letter, Maria covers her face with her hands.

    He has to think of Richard Lennartz, the son of the wick manufacturer. They had become friends. Joseph was twelve. Herbert and he sometimes did their homework together in the afternoon. Afterwards they played together. Herbert was sick. Something wasn't right with his nose. He had to be operated on, but it didn't help.

    One afternoon Joseph was about to go visit Herbert. When he rang the doorbell, he had such a peculiar feeling, and when Mrs. Lennartz opened the door with a puffy face, then he knew right away. Then he wrote a poem.

Who will write a poem for him? Maria. Maria! He bites his knuckles.

Chaplain Mollen evaluates his pale top student thus: he has the qualities to be a priest, even if there is still so much confusion within the second-year student. Chaplain Mollen sees it as his mission to find a servant of God in every class. Many things in Joseph already have clear outlines, others, by contrast, are still not settled, show no organized form, don't find a direction. He must feel his calling, the Chaplain says to the boy's father. I will keep an eye on him, show him the way. Thank you, thank you, Your Reverence.

Assistant Master Voss removes his pince-nez, blows on his glasses, begins to clean them with great care, rocks his head back and forth. He doesn't like Chaplain Mollen. He doesn't know what to think about Joseph. Must one have an opinion about a person, who, scarcely has one called on him, jumps up and answers as if shot out of a pistol? His manner of expression is exaggerated, ocasionally also inflated, mannered, precocious, his handwriting pointed and cramped, his views for the most part are not his own, everything about him tries to create the impression of individuality. Assistant Master Voss sets the pince-nez on his nose again, adjusts it, and says: I prefer a person without overwhelming insights but with character to a clever person without character. Another of Mollen's victims, he thinks. Freemason, thinks Mollen.

An unusual summer begins. Everything swims in heat and haze. Streaks shimmer in the air. People walking cast long shadows on the clover of the paths in Kaiser Park. Geraniums flame. Swarms of mosquitos in the air, small galaxies. A cloud stands immovable in the sky. The longer one observes it, the more it changes its shape. From the window of the attic it has the form of a Pavian head. Old light nests in the trees. It becomes twilight. Don't read much longer, Joseph, you will hurt your eyes. The nights are full of distant voices and demands. In the morning beer wagons will jolt over the stone pavement. At noon there will be dumplings. In the early evening shots will be heard.

They will read about it the next day in the newspaper. There will be war, his father prophesies. His mother crosses herself. They talk about the ultimatum. Joseph gets the atlas from his study. Maria is forgotten. For the time being. War, the word has resonance, greatness. The spirit of Sedan is in every German, his father says, the peace has already lasted too long. Joseph feels within him an excitement he has never known.

The newspapers proclaim the declaration of His Majesty before the Parliament: The desire for conquest does not drive us, but rather the unbendable will to preserve the place where God has put us. Yes, our Wilhelm stands by his pact with Austria. When forced to defend ourselves, with clear conscience and clean hands, my father stands up, for a moment his voice fails him before he can continue reading: We will take up the sword, strong and true, in knightly humility before God and resolute before the enemy. A great hour, like echoing thunder, like the clashing of swords and the crashing of waves: the German army and the Imperial navy are battle-ready, according to the mobilization plan. For the Fatherland! His father's eyes are shiny with moisture. From the pulpit the message resounds that God showed his love by sacrificing his son's life for us, so we must also sacrifice our lives for our brothers. Bells ring throughout the land. Firm and faithful stands the watch, the watch on the Rhine.

Translated by Donald G. Daviau

THE BOAT

ILSE BREM

"Love is being together in order to find shelter in one another." (Jules Feiffer)

FROM the very start, they couldn't abide one another. Perhaps that was the reason that they decided, in defiance of the normal conventions of an insurmountable affection, to form a partnership for life.

Neither of them had needed to use more than average persuasive power, since they were driven by one and the same motive and pursued one and the same goal, a goal which was uncertain, about which they knew nothing, about which they hadn't and couldn't have had even the vaguest notion.

They were both of the same dark, gloomy and cunning sort and both convinced that they had outsmarted the other and would continue to do so. In this sense they were, so to speak, treading the same path. That was the appeal of the matter, which was theirs alone and would have remained thus forever and always, and would never have been of any interest to a third, let alone a fourth or more persons, had they not both simultaneously been willing to pool their savings and buy a boat.

This desire for a boat originated in the bottommost layer of their being, where they had long since, even before they had met, become aware of their abysmal loneliness.

It was a loneliness that had started before them and would continue to exist after them.

This loneliness pursued them like a specter.

With the boat they wanted to flee this loneliness, their own as well as that of the other.

That is why only a motorboat would do, and not a sailboat, with which escape was dependent upon the wind.

They wished in their travels to be dependent upon nothing and noone, least of all upon the whim of the weather, upon a wind that would not submit to their will and want. They wanted to, had to, progress quickly.

That was their common goal.

At last, with the boat and through the boat they had a tangible image of their goal.

With this motorboat, they imagined, they could escape loneliness as swiftly as possible.

With the motorboat, they believed they could shake off the burden of this unsolvable problem.

When they saw one of those picturesque, romantic sailboats crossing the pyramids of light on the lake at a snail's pace, they would smile in disdain and in mutual agreement, until one day they found themselves bored with the navigable rivers and lakes of their small country.

Like the snail his shell, they put their motorboat on the roof of their car and made their way to the sea.

It was at this point at the latest that a dangerous, endangering suspicion arose within them.

The boat, for which they had sacrificed the last dime of their savings, was incapable of freeing them from their loneliness.

It was a fraud.

Since however nothing was as unbearable for both of them as the realization of the insurmountability of their problem, they began to take out their wrath over the unreliable boat on each other. Like two millstones grinding together, they rubbed themselves sore on one another. Everything and nothing became a point of friction in the closeness of coexistence into which the boat forced them.

Since the possiblity of avoiding one another on the boat was almost nonexistent, they spent more and more time in the water, for the purpose of soothing their sores and cooling their heated contact surfaces, until each of them, quietly and secretly, made the decision to end his misery by removing the other from his life.

During this brief period with a foreseeable end to their suffering, they even managed a certain mutual forebearance, respect and regard.

And when suddenly, quite unexpectedly, from one minute to the next, the great gale came up and drove the boat toward a steep cliff as if it had neither rudder nor helm, she huddled against him seeking shelter, while he put his sheltering arms around her.

But the sea had no sympathy for their fickleness.

It was persistent, straightforward and bent on thorough work, and it fulfilled their months-old secret desire to be rid of one another.

Their death was an unsolvable mystery to the shore police, just as the two unfortunate ones had found the torment of their loneliness to be an unsolvable problem.

On the day of the accident, the weather stations had not registered any unusual occurrences, aside from a light breeze.

Translated by Heidi L. Hutchinson

FEELINGS LIKE WINTER BURS

HEIDRUN BRUNMAIR

SHE had wanted to hold on to him, hold him back with a word that wasn't even on the tip of her tongue. it was stuck in her throat, this word.
it caused her pain, a wild, unconscious pain.
stay!
since she did not say it, he did not stay.
who knows whether he would have stayed, had she said it.
when he drove away, she tried not to gaze after him.
she fumbled for her keys and while she was fumbling for them, not finding them at once, she walked toward her house.
her field of vision was wide, much too wide, and so she saw nonetheless how he turned right at the next intersection and once again vanished from her life for a long time.
only a year ago she would have cried after such a good-bye. she would have unlocked her apartment door with suppressed sobbing. she would not have turned on the light in the hallway. she would have thrown her purse into a corner, the door would have slammed shut behind her, while she would not have been able to restrain her tears. she would have lain down on the bed and wept into the pillow. the next morning she would have left the house with eyes red from crying. a year ago she would have done . . . would have gone . . .
now no longer.
now she was quite calm. although the word "stay!" was still stuck in her throat. she could not get rid of it, could not swallow it, it was too big, it was still growing.
nonetheless she was calm and did not cry.
she unlocked the apartment door, entered, turned on the light, softly closed the door behind her, put down her purse.

no uncontrolled motion. very calm.
she thought about him and how he always withdrew from her in the same way. she loved him.
yes, i love him, she was thinking. and just to see what it sounded like and to test it, she said aloud:
i love you.
she said it to her mirror image. not to him, for whom it was meant.
the next time she would say it, even if she would fall over dead afterwards: stay! i love you!
she undressed slowly, without haste.
i love him, she was still thinking, as she turned off the light.
falling asleep was impossible.

it'll be dark in a minute, the child says as the train approaches the tunnel.
it'll be dark, and it will stay dark, because no one thinks of turning the light on in the compartment. the tunnel is not very long.
the train has three eyes.
it whistles before it enters the tunnel.
when the train has sped past, you see red.
and when you sit inside, you see nothing at all as long as it speeds through the tunnel.
the child was not afraid. it was told the train exited again at the other end of the tunnel and then it would be light again.
it was told it would always be light again after the darkness, and each night would be followed by a new day.
because the earth is turning, the child says, and the train is moving.

he withdrew from her each time in the same manner with a charm that sometimes provoked cold fury in her.
he sauntered off, brushed his hair from his forehead, protected on all sides, with catlike movements. protected himself.
she thought, if she approached him just one step, he would spit at her, show his claws, arch his back. his third eye—in the middle of his forehead.
and when he was gone, she saw red.
the weekend in the city was . . .
summer, empty streets, noise from opened windows.
turkish music, a whiff of orient above the street dust.
black martins in an unnatural blue sky. the cry of a falcon.

now and then a car, driving by below.
burned smell.
and in the background the asthmatic breath of the big city.
the eyes red from crying were the past. now everything took place within.
thoughts spread out in her, sank from her head into her larynx, caused her difficulties in swallowing, branched off into her coronary arteries and constricted them. they stopped at her heart. strangled it until it was beating twice as fast in its mortal fear.
these thoughts.
his third eye did not irritate her as much as his catlike gait.
i love him, she said again and again to her mirror image, as if to assure herself.
something had gone wrong with her attempt to tame the panther.
something that she had overlooked, missed.

the train whistles before it enters the tunnel.
the child is not frightened. it associates the whistle with the immediately following darkness.
the whistle is a warning signal, which does not make the child fearful because: it'll be light in a moment.
then, after the tunnel, the track extends across a narrow deep valley. the child stands at the window and enjoys the ensuing eerie sensation as it looks down into the valley. the bridge sways while the train traverses it. far down below the child sees a river among the rocks. the water foams because the rocks are in its way. the water plunges over the rocks, seldom yields.
the child is amazed. light goose bumps spread over its neck and arms.
the train whistles and enters the next tunnel.

she managed to cope less and less with her vulnerability.
and she was no longer able to reject feelings she encountered.
when she was at her wit's end, she went into the shower. she let the hot water envelop her body. when she closed her eyes and was on the verge of losing her balance, her hands seemed to cling to the stream of water.
she tried to rinse from her body her feelings that were sticking to her like winter burs. she opened her mouth and held it under the stream of water. the water ran out again, on the right side differently because here in the corner of her mouth was a scar, which gave her occasionally when she was particularly tired a suffering expression.

as one gave—an order or a title.
the water ran out of her mouth: the word, the words remained stuck in her throat.
then, while drying off, she was overcome with an old sensation which she could not integrate, and she did not know whether others knew it too because she never discussed it with anyone. a sensation—not a winter bur this time, but rather a transitory yet recurring one.
every time while drying off: this feeling of homesickness. at least that's what she called it.
a certain serene sadness, a sad smile of her body.
the mirror was still clouded long after she had opened the door.

the child is dreaming.
it often dreams during the day, to the annoyance of grownups.
and from time to time it dreams a certain dream, which winds like a red thread also through the other dreams.
there is always something subterranean, earthy, animalistic.
the dream recurs in various forms.
the forms make no difference to the child. it sees the connections because it knows nothing of their meaning.
the child trusts its dreams.
this unconditional trusting . . . in dreams . . .

no more eyes red from crying.
she thought she had herself completely under control. although she abhorred every kind of control.
when her feelings threatened to suffocate her, she gently plucked them off and failed to notice how treacherously they adhered to her again. winter burs.
at night she dreamed the dreams that she had chased away with effort during the day.
and then the old dream returned, descended upon her with elemental force and imbued her with fear, and she was helplessly at its mercy.

the child is standing by a steep, left-winding cellar staircase. irregular steps, as if someone had scraped them with bare hands out of a rock.
the walls are wet, shimmering snail tracks in the light of a flashlight.
the child descends the stairs. it holds on to a narrow black railing that leads down along the right wall at the child's eye level.

Feelings like Winter Burs 45

it is dark down below, the flashlight casts only a faint beam, focused on the ground.
high heaps of soot beneath chimney gates, screws, dead rats on the well-trodden clay floor.
sometimes tree stumps are lying about. the child climbs over them.
forced open cellar compartments, the dripping of water, rats are scurrying.
the hallway never leads straight ahead, runs into corners, branches off.
the child knows precisely where it has to go.
it comes to a grating made of wrought-iron.
the grating is leaning on a black opening in the wall.
the child takes a chunk of wall that has fallen off and hurls it into the black hole.
the chunk hits a water surface with a splash: a lake in the middle of the cellar.
the child walks on.
in the rear of the hallway, an overflow pump, where there is no more water. beside it a washroom with stove, sink, table.
the child searches for the panther,
it can smell it, hear it breathing.
he must be behind the next corner.
but there is no more corner. the hallway ends here.
somewhere glass is splintering. no other sounds aside from the dripping water.
the child looks up: water pipes everywhere.
the pipes are leaky, the water drips into pails that are filled to the top.
the child empties the water from the pails into the lake.

she had tried to tame the panther.
as a punishment he withdrew from her, not without first having bitten her.
and then: nothing but dreams for a long time.
while she confined herself, inexorably cut off every escape route, drove herself into a corner, she observed herself as if she were a stranger.
very interesting what that stranger was doing.
she would never do that . . . no, not she.
her reptilian brain drowned out everything else at that time: saber-toothed, panther-skinned, blind with rage.
covered with scars, unabashedly obstinate.

already narrow halls closed completely behind her. for the first time in her life she had succumbed to a fallacy.
that was immensely painful.
she had offered him her throat, had relied on his bite-restraint and was as if paralyzed when she felt his predatory breath on her neck, his sharp teeth.
afterwards he had briefly shaken himself, had stretched and extended himself, and then had settled down at a safe distance from her;
from there he observed her with amazement, with tilted head. looked on as she was threatening to bleed to death from his bite.
did he want to know if it hurt?
it was her fault alone. she had caressed a wild animal against her better knowledge. a nervous cat. a panther.

the child cannot fall asleep. an entire day's demons and spirits keep it excitable.
the child is not afraid. still not afraid.
through the window the light of a street lamp enters the room.
when the child raises its left hand it can cover the window's square of light. the hand is very big, clenched into a fist it sits like a huge black panther in front of the window.
the child knows nothing of pleonasms: a black panther.
the wild animal does not move. it waits.
the child is tired.
suddenly the panther attacks, claws at the rectangle of the bright window. and the child is frightened. it turns on the light in the room.
hesitantly it approaches the window.
the light of the street lamp is weak, the night is blacker than before.
and the window becomes the mirror in which the child can see all that is behind it.
the panther is no longer there.

the first time she entered the cellar, of which she had dreamed her whole life, her legs gave way.
she had to sit down on the steps of the cellar staircase, she lit a cigarette. then she rose slowly and with hesitation walked step by step along the dream path, turned the corner. she knew precisely where she had to go.
the dripping of the water.
the lake was here behind the wrought-iron railing.

she threw the chunk of wall into the black hole and shone the flashlight upon it.
the lake was deep.
a good place to let yourself disappear too, she thought.
she also heard the panther breathing. she could feel, smell him.
around the next corner . . .
he had attacked and bitten. the wound on her neck had healed, even though her blood would always pulsate more strongly at this spot than anywhere else.
she should not have come so close to him, he had warned her.
when she had approached him, he was still lying on his back, purring and playful. he had licked her face and hands, had permitted her to stroke his stomach, ruffle his chin. then he had softly begun to rumble like distant thunder. he had risen and had left. she had followed him, enchanted by his beauty and the elegance of his movements.
and now she sat in the web of her memories and entangled herself more and more.
dandelion seeds were whirling about and clinging to her hair, taking root, burying themselves, clearing a path for themselves.
dandelion seeds. they also don't reflect.
they drift.
they also arrive. somewhere.

the child draws up a plan for life.
it sketches, speaks about it. with everyone.
when it is asked what it wants to become, it answers:
i want to tame a panther. when i grow up.

now she was grown up. and felt very small.
she did not move.
although she longed to touch him gently, she did not do it.
she spoke softly with him, talked to him, accustomed him to her voice.
at least to her voice. words.
and looked deep into his dark eyes.
i love you.
she said it with her eyes, her mouth spoke of other things.
he sat beside her and hypnotized her with the third eye on his forehead.
the wound on her neck was hurting.
he slanted his head.

then he rose and left. and withdrew from her, with a friendly smile.
and returned. and sat down beside her. and listened to her.
now and then she approached him at arm's length.
not closer.

Translated by Renate Latimer

THE PARTICULARLY ENGAGED POET

STEPHAN EIBEL

THE engaged poet lives in the big city or in the country. He calls himself a writer or a scholar.
He is in a constant struggle with his writing. To write or not to write? He consistently decides in favor of writing. Writing for the oppressed. Against the powerful.

The engaged poet quickly found his way to humanitarianism and constantly ponders whether he really shouldn't kill the leader. The regional political leader, the federal leader, or the industrial leader. The engaged poet drinks or doesn't drink. He has or doesn't have a car.

In any case, the one who drinks and has a car, or who doesn't have a car but drinks, or the one who doesn't drink but has a car, or doesn't drink and doesn't have a car, or the reverse, quite frequently drives as if back and forth by taxi.

He appears with politicians and is constantly plagued by doubt. The doubt shows in his engaged writer's stomach and in his careworn, engaged writer's face.

To give his hand or not to give his hand—and he has already given his hand to the politician. What would it have accomplished if he had killed him? Well, maybe, but what good is it going to do. He sympathizes with every revolutionary group, above all with armed groups, but doesn't join any of them, because he knows everything better than they. His deep sense of humanity is hidden behind his know-it-all attitude, but the engaged writer only realizes that when he is older and wants to be called a poet again.

Moreover, if engaged poets embrace a communist party, it becomes possible for their feeling of oppression to gain great support. But the engaged poet or poetess must additionally become an especially engaged or oppressed poet. The engaged scholar uses all his powers of creativity to become an especially engaged scholar. The one who is especially engaged seeks out allies in a large party and is the greatest of all antifascists, when all is said and done. He or she lashes out without restraint against the dead fascists or the ones whose days are numbered, writes a play for a seven-by-ten meter stage, is praised by the fascists who are still living and those who have currently become party members in one of the major antifascist parties, and despairs of the success.

By then this particularly engaged person is seeking out more allies and broader themes, and no longer considers going into politics. He becomes more generous. Even this one confounded conservative party is to a large extent pitiful. The other, previously despised right-extremist party is fundamentally even more pitiable.

The particularly engaged poet is now criticized by the left. This again serves a considerable purpose for him. He now no longer wants to be called a writer or a scholar, but a poet. Why shouldn't he insist on what he now actually is?

The engaged poet internalizes that in an engaged way, because there is nothing greater than being a poet. In addition to that, he will become a painter or a consultant. Actually he succeeds in becoming a poet laureate, without a body of work. But who has what he has?

Translated by Paul F. Dvorak

WORK IS LIBERATING

JANKO FERK

HIS story actually started at the point where his wife no longer let him. Since her refusal he thought up the most ghastly things at those times when he would otherwise be lying on top of her.

No more talk about total marital commitment, or especially about cohabitation, or about fidelity, or proper conjugal behavior and support, as it states in the law, but only about the terrible things in his head.

Franz K. was frequently busy in his cave—that's how he labeled the house in which he worked—where the best writings were confiscated from all those who could write well and then presented some time later in a more or less attractive form and design to a public that even read now and then. In a manner befitting the diligence of his occupation, he thought mostly about those who write and about what they write. Other, unknown women with long hair and beautiful eyes were out of the question for him, for he was actually a good man and would only consider such things or other later on when permitted by the law or death, which for him were always one and the same thing. Death, that master, he said to himself, is law, which is why he decided one day to just wait for death, because it was surely more reliable than any sort of law that a human being could twist and interpret according to his own ideas, however and whenever it suited him. That means that he, Franz K., never relied on the daily disposition of a man in black, but rather only on the incontrovertible, the true, the eternal, as he himself called it.

The cave, in which a room was set up for his body and also for his mind, was a tall, dark, warped building behind whose every corner lurked the ill-fated hand of that master who had built it. A dreadful building that in addition had been excavated for a cellar and thereby offered extra space. Here in the cellar, where he once conceived of it in this way, he wanted to erect several small caves—in this instance he meant it literally—with everything necessary for survival so that he then might be able to detain writers there as he deemed necessary.

To maintain the caves, for which nature had already made certain provisions in the cellar and for which only a brick was needed here and there, he summoned a friend. This friend had once sat next to him in school and subsequently had failed and had dropped out before him; meanwhile, amid the greatest duress, he had learned to work with sand, water, and lime as well as with tools.

Not having shared his company for a long time and telling him nothing at all about his life, and also quietly hinting at nothing, Franz K. dispatched his friend without delay into the cellar so that he could look around and then slowly begin to set to work with the tools and with nature.

The friend, who made the descent into the cellar in accordance with K.'s most exacting directions, wanted to carry out what the latter had ordered; after all, he was being paid to do that and nothing else, but he didn't know how to initiate the plans. As a result, he also didn't give the matter any further thought.

Working nonstop both day and night for days, he brought water into the caves, installed a drainage system, arranged the discarded items that K. gave him and shamelessly called them table, chair, and bed; he enclosed the caves with bricks right down to the hole which a grown person could squeeze himself through, took a serious look around again, and tried to focus on and take note of what he saw there, which in part had come about by his hand and thus by executing his orders from above. He would have preferred to forget everything right there on the spot, for he certainly was not stupid. Then he packed his things, hurried out towards the daylight and the fresh air, and went off, because, all of a sudden, his friend Franz K. began to make him feel uneasy.

The next day, when K. set about checking what had been accomplished, he seemed satisfied. There was a series of holes, in which a writer had space and in which there was enough water for washing and for drinking whenever he got thirsty. The makeshift furniture was there and the necessary incidentals. K. had thought of every amenity, assessing the needs of others in terms of his own standards.

After examining the caves, so to speak, Franz K. did not want to delay any longer before barricading a writer in each, where the latter would have to work strenuously, honestly, and assiduously and would be obliged daily to hand over everything he had written.

Franz K. initiated his search. He sneaked out onto the street and over to the inn across from the cave, where he intended to confront the first writer and then abduct him.

In the inn with its stench and suffocating air, he immediately found a man who had just published a book about his country and another about its people and had put them on display himself, a person nonetheless whose impertinence would vanish under K.'s careful watch. Once and for all. Since K. knew exactly how much this scribbler reacted to money and young girls more than to anything else, he enticed him to the cave across the way with the promise of showing him an attractive girl and offering him some money. Under the pretense that the pretty little girl and everything else was there, he led him right into the hole in which he would write until his crooked fingers were sore and his eyes dimmed. When the wheezing and gasping avaricious lover of girls had crawled into the hole—he was no longer the youngest of men—K. barred it up immediately and instructed him to go ahead and adjust to the situation and to arrange things as best he could for himself, since he could certainly count on being there for some time.

K. found the second writer, a person for whom fame meant everything, strolling along the busiest street of the city in a crowd; he was certainly not difficult to find, for the clothes he wore attracted everyone's attention. K. made him believe that the newspaper—one which he just happened to edit—had dedicated an entire page to him, the second page at that, and, if he wanted, he could take a look at it right away and take it along home with him. The man, for whom fame was an addiction, urged K. to hurry off with him to see this second page right away, whereupon K. allowed himself to move along only at a moderate pace. When they arrived in the cave, both were already breathing heavily; but the writer would not let himself be deterred from squeezing into the hole—accompanied by the biggest grunt he was capable of—where the newspaper with the second page supposedly was. Repeating the same words with which he had already informed the first man about his circumstances and given him instructions, K. locked him up and slowly went home, where—lying in bed—he pondered over how and where he would be able to acquire two more writers.

The next morning on the street he met a writer whom he enticed into the cave by promising that he would eat with him. Thereupon, the man, whose stomach was growling noticeably, did not give the matter a second thought but rather latched onto K. immediately and would have followed him in like manner to the ends of the earth, if he had periodically been given the hope of being able again soon to sink his teeth into something.

The hungry man was quickly taken prisoner, and K. immediately seized the last one by force.

Franz K., who now knew he had everyone he wanted in his hands and in his cave and sensed the feeling of power in his innermost being, checked again before he set about giving orders to make sure the writers had at their disposal everything they really needed, both for survival and for writing: candles, pencils, sufficient paper, food, and naturally the necessary utensils and other incidentals.

Franz K. took away his writers' clothing by force, so that even if they might somehow or other manage to escape—a virtual impossibility—they would be able to flee from the cave only at the expense of offending public morality and decency. From the holes in the cave the most terrible obscenities were shouted at him: that he was nothing but a filthy wretch, who kept them prisoners in a subdivided vault of corpses. And they would scratch all sorts of rotten things on the walls with their fingernails so that later on people would know about his reprehensible treatment of the writers. He was a criminal and nothing more, with the greatest indebtedness to the writers and, therefore, in reality, to humanity at large. Moreover, he is going to get his comeuppance some day, for at some point the tables will turn, since he was certainly too cowardly to wring their necks, even if he thought that it was time to do so.

Franz played deaf and dumb, walked away, and intended to return only when they had calmed down a little.

They really did not know what was in store for them, nor were they very curious about the details, since only the fear that seized them and filled the whole cave, this little room, remained with them. One tearing out his hair, another whimpering, and all of them thinking about mother at home. They were now like little children again.

When Franz K. believed that they were now compliant enough, he returned and played the role of the loving father. By then they were almost broken individuals—which was moreover not a bad thing for a writer, as Franz K. thought he knew; they were perfectly quiet and acted submissively. They just wanted to get out of there as quickly as they could. He swore to them with raised hand that he would immediately set each one free as soon as he had fulfilled his assignment; but he knew that he would let everyone out simultaneously and only under duress, because they would run off to court on the spot, in unison and full of vindictiveness, in order to report him and accuse him, who—he thought and was convinced—had provided a great service to the art of scribbling.

Perhaps they would also pounce upon him, as on a dog, if he did not act nimbly and if they still possessed the necessary strength. At the least he would come away with one less tooth and a black eye.

They lack nothing, K. maintained; in his opinion, they had everything and he himself wanted only to treat them well. He wanted to assist them in aspiring to what they were always striving for, to produce a good text he could distribute in public after they had written it, and then they would be back in the world again. Back in the world again, he emphasized, for he could never take their freedom from them, those who had their home in the realm of thought, and imagination, and dreams.

After he had made clear to them what he expected and they seemed somewhat consoled—their gnashing of teeth and cursing had subsided somewhat, he explained to them exactly what he had in mind.

He had the one who had always shown a predilection for young girls and money write stories. Stories and nothing else because they were his specialty; a novel, a work with some value, he had not yet produced despite his considerably advanced age, and at poetry he had proven himself to be completely hapless. With a whimper he crawled away from the cave entrance to behind the table, lit a second candle alongside the first, and began to write: "He did not know where he was, in a state of ignorance that caused him serious doubts about his survival." At least for once that was a start.

The one whom Franz K. called the stroller was commissioned to write a volume of poetry. That was his forte, K. said, and prompted him to begin right away. "one night / is won / he said / but what about the day" were the first lines of the poem in which he intended to describe what freedom meant to him, if he could add enough other lines to these out of his head onto paper.

The hungry one, whom he had enticed into the cave from the street, was to translate a novel. From a foreign language into his own.

The one he had brought into the cave by force made his own suggestion. He wanted to write a play. Franz K. immediately agreed and was apparently satisfied, for with a "Yes, please!" he shooed him over to the desk and called out loudly and clearly to everyone that they should begin and not waste any time, for time is writing, he said, and work is liberating. Besides, he was contemplating a collected volume that he might perhaps put together from these cave stories. He already had a title in mind: "Damage to One's Health." Franz K. was convinced that this was the only suitable name for the volume.

Franz K. visited his so-called masters twice every day. He appeared regularly in the morning and in the evening and collected what they had written. If one of them did not have enough to turn in, that is, if he had not worked hard enough, K. threatened to turn loose one, two or, worst of all, three rats in his hole, hungry ones to boot, with terribly long tails, who would definitely attack a man if the senses and instincts that they were born with told them that biting someone's foot or leg could fill their stomachs and set their digestive tracts in motion. He also could not guarantee that some of the rats would not be rabid, for that kind was easier to catch because they were more trusting and even tame. In certain cases he checked in a moment later. The mere tremors that K.'s threats caused to run down their spines steered their thoughts to that writer who had been bitten by a dog and who in his despair had taken his own life, because he was convinced the dog had fallen ill to this malady which, either unfortunately or fortunately as the case may be, was not so, as was determined after the writer had withdrawn forever from his work.

After K.'s talks it was at least certain that the masters were working. But it was not certain whether what they wrote under a certain compulsion and not solely out of feelings of pleasure—their surroundings and conditions spoke rather in favor of feelings of displeasure—was also good. This question did not concern Franz K. very much, although it seemed justified. In the past he had frequently published volumes for the reading public, which seemed important almost exclusively because of the particular rumors before publication and not because they contained the history of the century between their covers. K. was a businessman and not a loafer. He had probably lost his wife for that reason too, a long time ago, long before he had finally but too belatedly noticed it.

The last freedom, suicide, death through one's own hand, was pondered by one or the other of the writers in his despair, but the means to carry out this unnatural death were lacking. Franz K. had also thought of it, for he was familiar enough with the people with whom he had to deal in his profession. He had not let anything be brought into the caves that would make suicide possible. It would have worked against his advantage and profit: he had gathered his four scribblers to work and not to die.

In the beginning it was as if the kidnapped ones, who had been abducted from their habitats to a change of venue, were in a daze. One of them needed his accustomed surroundings in order to write, a rundown flat with a filthy bed and a plump little girl on it, and the other, for example, merely a red flower. Nevertheless, they slowly began to adapt to their surroundings, they wrote out of fear for their lives and actual physical dread of the rats.

This was torture, one of them said as he sobbed noticeably.

The reams of paper that Franz K. gathered up and kept securely on his desk grew considerably every morning and evening. The writers were obviously exerting themselves. Certainly more than in the so-called state of freedom, K. said to himself. He almost did not understand why they—their completely filled pages best expressed their wishes and hopes—wanted to break and force their way out of their caves at any cost, when the conditions there for men like them were excellent and really appropriate. Moreover, K. could not comprehend it, since twice a day he gave the one writer a lot of money and showed him drawings of young girls and generously gave the other plenty of good food to eat. Neither were the other two lacking anything, as he now even tried to appease the glory seeker as well. Once he dedicated the whole second page of his newspaper to him—someone had written something about him—and another time he reprinted one of his stories. And all that in a short span of time.

Three times, perhaps four, Franz K. took along his son, whom he loved more than anything else, to visit the writers. Once the little boy even tickled the lover of money and girls with a long pole through the fence—as he called the bars—and asked him his name.

I like you, you arrogant little ape, said the boy with a roguish look on his face. He was glad that his father had such delightful friends.

Only when K.'s small, black-haired son realized that they were locked up, did he ask him: "Father, Father, does it have to be this way?" Then K. released the writers and embarked with them and his son at his hand on a peace march through the country, from which none of them ever returned.

Translated by Paul F. Dvorak

Freddy

Marianne Gruber

He was incapable of performing for himself the simplest tasks of everyday life; one had to feed him, help him drink, wash him, take care of him almost like a baby. When he wanted to go to the bathroom, he made strange noises which only his father understood. Even there the boy needed help: with undressing, cleaning up, and dressing again. One time he and his father were stopped by a policeman. Here was a man who was using a public restroom with a half-grown boy. "May I see some identification?" Then a look at the light-skinned, moon-faced Freddy, a look into the face with the too small, narrow eyes, a face in which one could read no life history, and the policeman looked up, irritated. "He's your son?"

Yes, he was his son. The man leaned over and searched the face of the boy until their eyes met. "I'm going now," he said, "but I'll be right back. You stay here. You wait. I'll be right back."

"Here," repeated the boy and stretched his mouth into a wide grin which made his tongue stick out.

The man, desperate, stroked Freddy's hair. "Soon, Freddy, okay?" He fixed his son's posture. Back straight, hands on the table. Then he stood up with careful movements, his eyes fixed on the boy, as if he had to hold him down with his eyes like an animal. "You'll stay here?"

It was a pleading, insane question, which the boy answered with "here, here," without moving from the posture his father had placed him in.

They had arrived a week before, on Friday, and it had been the same as always. Initial confusion, then disgust were hidden behind statements framed with good will, like, "I admire you, how you handle that with the boy." Spoken by civilized middle-Europeans who would never admit their prejudices or reservations. One doesn't do things like that. They pretended tolerance, but the unasked question lurked behind everything they said: what did they want here, he and the boy, they who were interrupting their peaceful summer vacations, into which nothing strange or sickly was permitted to enter. And the father's answer, the attempt to calm them, the usual, that to which he had grown accustomed, and which was so often demanded, would it never end: he isn't dangerous, he's just different, and he's a good boy, who needs sun, light, fresh air, and contact with other people, so that his little, almost silent soul can live a little. He isn't bothering you, is he? Of course the boy was bothering them.—I admire you, ha! And always the helpless shrug which answered this question.

The man, now out of the boy's sight, walked quickly to a telephone. The benches under the chestnut trees were full, and from the pool behind the house came the whoops of Tim and a couple of other boys. They had pushed Astrid into the pool and now she was crying.

Freddy was still staring, motionless, in the direction in which his father had disappeared from view. A fly wandered over his plump, formless face, but he didn't dare to brush it away, as he sometimes tried to do. His expression didn't give away what he was thinking, if he was actually thinking anything at all. Perhaps he was imagining pictures, things which other people can't see. A different world, a small one, constantly filled when his father was there, was now flooded with his absence. The longer his father stayed away, the more insecure this world became.

The boy became restless. He awoke, whimpering, from his blunt posture, kicked his legs against the bench, as if he was bothered by terrible dream visions, hid his head between his arms, huddled into himself, and cried softly like a captured animal. Every person in his midst, even the touch of daylight, seemed to frighten him without his father present.

The man came back just in time to avoid a rather large scene. "Come on, it's okay," he said, "It's okay. I'm back." They touched each other's hands, and the boy began to smile again tentatively. His tongue was out of his mouth, his eyes looked up, and he kept his round face close to his father's cheek.

The man could feel the stares in his back, stares of wondering people. Don't give in, he thought. One can't notice that. Perhaps one day he would be able to see past the people, to live among them, and to not feel hurt in the boy's place because of their stares and their ununderstanding, crude talk. That such a creature was even able to live! No, he would never be able to make them grasp what this child had taught him—him, the successful, hard-working man, the man who had been, before, completely untouchable.

As he glanced up from the table, he looked straight into Astrid's curious face. She was five and wise with age—and a touch lonesome, like all people who think, or dream, or ask questions beyond their familiar boundaries.

"Why doesn't he ever say anything?" she asked.

What could he reply to that? That Freddy was sick? That there was no cure for his sickness? Perhaps she would feel sorry for the boy, and carry into the rest of her life the idea that one should give people like that over to doctors or stick them in hospitals; better yet, she would think later: shut them in closed institutions. Lock them up, lock them up, those who remind us that we're never thankful enough for living, for the sunlight and the cheerful days, for being able to run over summer meadows, to name the flowers, and to point at the clouds.

"He only speaks the language of the angels," answered the man, "if you understand what I mean."

She tilted her head and looked searchingly into Freddy's face. "And why does he look different?"

"Does he? Different how?"

That was one question too many. She didn't know the answer, so she turned away and went to the sand box, where she was building a castle.

The boy was completely calm again now, and he started the finger games that he and his father played so often. He went through the routine of sticking out his hand, making a fist, and so forth. Then his father brought blocks out of his pocket, and Freddy began, with difficulty, to stack them on top of one another. He panted with exertion and chewed on his lower lip. After a while he had enough, and began to watch Astrid. He obviously wanted to play with her. When she finally realized this, she came over and held her sand shovel out to him, but Freddy drew back from her hand.

"Here, take it!" she said. "Or doesn't he like to play in the sand? Aren't angels allowed to get dirty?"

"Well, they are," answered the man. "He just doesn't know what to do with the shovel. You know, he might not build a castle, or maybe he'd ruin yours, or he might try to eat the sand."

Astrid laughed and stuffed some sand between her lips. "I eat sand

too, sometimes, when we make sand pies."
"Would you want to play with him?" For a moment, a thought of hope flared up, a thought that he didn't want to complete. No, a healthy child would never play with his son, never.

But Astrid nodded.

"You have to be very careful. He gets frightened very easily."

"I don't believe that," said Astrid, "angels never get frightened." She laughed again and stuck the shovel in Freddy's hand. "Open your fist," she commanded, "and now close it!" Then she grabbed him by his shirt and pulled him to the sand box. He seemed to like digging around in it. He threw the sand in the air, squashed it between his fingers, and started to howl loudly when he felt it on his cheek. Astrid imitated this immediately, and the man began to fear that people would put blame on Freddy if the girl acted completely crazy. Not much later, Astrid's mother came and took her away.

"Forgive me," said the man, "I should have watched them more carefully." He expected bitter reproaches, but the woman didn't say anything. The silence could sometimes be even worse than the talk. The man pulled Freddy to the table. For a while, they couldn't decide on what to do. While they were staring ahead, Tim came over, and the man knew right away that he was up to nothing good. He had already surprised him once when he and the other boys had decided to entertain themselves by harassing Freddy. He fixed his eyes on Tim until he turned around without saying anything and went back to the pool. Then the waiter came and asked the man to come to the telephone, as he had an urgent call.

The call was urgent, he knew it. It came in response to his almost cowardly effort. From newspaper articles he had learned about a special training program for patients with brain damage. One could glean from these articles that with the required knowledge and infinite patience one could teach such children to complete certain tasks, for example, to make paper flowers or to roll paper cones. They could even learn to communicate better. One could improve their language skills. The boy was a fairly bad case, but not an impossible one. Now, during his vacation, the man might have enough time to work with Freddy, if he obtained the basics of the teaching program in time. He didn't want to institutionalize the boy. This lovable creature was his son, and he clung to him, he loved him, even if no one understood. He wanted to keep him as long as he lived, as long as they could stand it, he and the boy's mother.

Again the parting ritual. They looked at each other face to face. And: "I'm leaving now, but I'll be right back." And the fixing of body posture and the pleading looks, the slow distancing, keeping eye contact as long as it was possible, and having to see, once more, Freddy's falling countenance when his father was no longer in his field of vision. He has known this for many years now, but the boy's expression of lonesomeness still always brought his father the same helpless pain.

"I'll never leave you," said the man suddenly, more loudly than he had intended. "Never. As long as I live, do you understand?"

The telephone conversation lasted longer than he had expected, and it didn't bring the information he had wished and expected to receive. If he really wanted to further the boy's development in the best possible fashion, he would have to give him away, at least for a few weeks or months. In the summer heat he could feel his impatience rising while he talked on the telephone. They were all friendly, helpful people who were counseling him, but what it meant to live with this boy, with this charge who gave himself completely to his father's care, and the unintentional tenderness, this they could not understand. They knew a lot, but they knew nothing of the deciding factors. Freddy only knew a stunted, dwarfed world, but he was the only real, honest human being in that world. He existed without lies, without pretending, without traps. He was true in everything. And if he stayed alone too long again now, it would take him days or even longer to get the fear out of his soul. They have hardly any memory, the doctor had explained to him, these children have no memory, but the memory of fear was present. The boy must have had memories of how he was harassed, beaten, and tied to his chair in a moment when he was left alone.

The man hung up hastily, and only when he left the telephone booth did he realize that he hadn't said good-bye. He almost ran to the field behind the house, where the benches stood under the chestnut trees and where Freddy was waiting, where he possibly found himself in the midst of some sort of horror again.

As he came around the corner of the house, he saw Astrid sitting next to Freddy on the bench, and the boy seemed calm, despite all expectations. Astrid was talking to him, and he listened, to whatever he could understand of what she was saying. As he came closer, Freddy's father saw what they were doing. Astrid was playing the finger game with Freddy, which she had obviously observed. She said, even imitating the man's tone of voice: "Stick out your hand, make a fist, stick out your hand, make a fist. And now stick out your thumb."

Slowly, the man came nearer. It was the first time that the boy had sat next to a strange person without immediately crawling under the table. He was even laughing. Astrid said: "Pull your tongue in and close your mouth." Then: "Good, Freddy, good. I'll buy you some ice cream, too."

When she discovered the man, she lifted her heated face. "I think I already know it a little bit."

"Certainly. Your hands are very quick."

"Oh, that thing with the fingers"—she made a demeaning hand gesture—"that's easy. I mean the language of the angels. I think I already know it."

Translated by Alexandra Strelka

One

Norbert Gstrein

HE was the right age, fifteen, when he returned from the city, having firmly decided not to leave the village again. And she? And we? But nobody had ever talked about that, neither in school nor at home, and they knew after the first reprimand, often even before it, that there was nothing to say and nothing to ask, least of all when the sentences burned on their tongues and followed hot on the heels of each other, filled with unbelievable suspicions. The limits were quickly reached, in the evasive words, in the sudden silence that they noticed with the same curiosity they felt with respect to the gradually discernible mystery behind it. What was wrong with Father? At times he liked to turn off the television set so decisively that they knew he was watching them for a long time afterward, and they did not dare look at or away from him. Or he stopped in front of it as if by accident and began to search the drawers for the tablets he took three times a day.

We had to be inventive, and we pretended to be more ignorant than we really were. We perceived the slightest whispering with overly alert senses and stared into the narrowest fissure, in the continuing game of hide-and-seek that one generation imposed upon the next. And Jakob? He listened for hours to the adult conversations until a little piece fell off somewhere, which he could fit into his mosaic or at least save in the most dependable part of his memory and later put in the right place. And by the foxes' burrows? Something wonderful had to happen, something that had never happened before, or something very horrible for punishment, he thought. And later, when they walked back through the woods, from time to time he sniffed at his fingers and didn't dare touch Hanna's hair, the chestnut-brown ponytail that bobbed up and down in front of him. One piece was added to another, and once, Mother, your dressing gown was askew, a little bit, just a very little bit, and he didn't want to believe it. He looked away, looked at her again, and even days later stared at her like something foreign and saw her as a woman for the first time. And she? And we? In the cook's room, did we also . . . ? When the opportunity presented itself, he crept into the unlocked room and leafed through the magazines with trembling fingers, sat on the unmade bed with a mountain of dirty clothes in front of him, and turned the pages and saw, saw everything, had the complete picture, long before his return and long before the time he spent in the city, at an age when many still had no idea at all or only a vague one.

In the nightclub he watched the others, and beneath the magnificent gestures, behind the ponderous statements he recognized the oppressive speechlessness that they learn from childhood on. Alcohol inspired them to speak sentences that were not their own, foreign words, artificial High German, broken English. It dissolved the stiffness that had been passed from father to son and on down the line again and again; and held them tightly in its loose grasp and did with them what they thought *they* were doing. And over and over again they found a girl who still broke out in loud laughter about the most foolish things and obliged them, submitted to their kisses, or let them uncouthly talk her into submitting to their kisses and much more. Jakob watched the others, and sometimes he could not stand it. Then he closed his eyes and imagined the most fantastic things, or ran disgustedly through the nocturnal village. Or he drank, and the alcohol gave him no inspiration, just a painfully clear awareness of himself, in double numbness and a silence that seemed final. Then he thought he would do things differently, did not know how, knew only: differently, more tenderly. That is what he thought, and how short-sighted women were, all of them—and stupid.

And then.
And once.
"What's your name?"
He was sixteen.
And she?
"And you?"
How old is she?

He had stared at her for a long time. "You looked at me," she said later, as if he were going to break out crying or laugh insanely at any moment. "I didn't know it." And they went for a walk in the middle of the night, to the church and then back to the other edge of the village where the steeply climbing slopes made penetration of the snow-bound darkness impossible. And then? They leaned against the garage door in front of the restaurant and listened to the soft music from the dance hall. Should I? Should he kiss her? Jakob didn't know, and suddenly her hands were there, suddenly he was breathless, with every limb taut. He stood there stretched to the breaking point, stiff. *Stop!* he thought, *Stop!* and said nothing. And then he felt something warm and wet between his legs. He did not dare look down at himself. It hurt. He didn't dare look at her, didn't dare look anywhere nor close his eyes, and only the voices of an approaching couple tore him from his immobility, and he pressed himself tightly against the strange body whose fragrance seemed to come from so far away. He wanted to creep deep inside it. In his shame he wanted to disappear within it, and he wished that he were somewhere else—or nowhere. Later he lay awake and watched the slowly falling snow gradually cover the skylight.

For a long time, female tourists remained the only women for him. He became acquainted with them, at least by name, but never more closely or closely enough to feel safe during the two or three weeks. And then they departed into another world as if they had never been there. They demanded their portion and left nothing behind but the emptiness that grew from one time to the next, even when it had long since begun to seem infinite. In his memory the differences blurred into a constant repetition. Or they seemed unreal, only invented. And sometimes, when he actively thought about it, at the same, last moment everything shrank together into a single scene: He followed a departing car with his eyes in the cold of a winter morning, and in his pocket his fingers closed around a photograph, the desired trophy, or they pressed his soft penis. Otherwise there was little to say, nothing worth remembering, and especially no particular woman at all. He had never slept with one and had talked about death with all of them, in sentences that always stayed the same. He said that the fact that everyone had died until now was no proof that he would also die. And then he had laughed, had often not been able to stop laughing because he felt like crying about himself and his megalomania and about death. The walks always led to the church, and in the cemetery he showed them his father's grave or told about the girl who carried a child to full term and gave birth to it alone with her lover, hidden from her parents, her sisters, and the whole village. And after its birth they had slain it and buried it there, on that very spot. An old story that he had possibly heard years ago or had later invented in his misguided thoughts, at least parts of it, as an exciting episode. In the church he usually lit the candles, talked about himself or silently held the stranger's hand. And once, on a sudden whim, he had stepped behind the altar, but the place was empty, with a thick layer of dust on the little box, where we, as acolytes, had discovered the skull, our great secret. We had stared at it again and again and could never get enough.

On one birthday he received a red sweater, we remember, and was as happy as a little child. He wore it every day until people began to tease him, and then on the weekends—and never again, long after it ceased mattering to anyone. He, the youngest boy, had carefully guarded the memory of that summer, had sometimes climbed up to the foxes' burrows with his accordion, and had never followed them into the age where you forget or only remember inappreciatively. He said nothing in response to the gossip about Hanna and stared at the speaker when he heard the comments that had been brought along from somewhere. Did he feel good? Why the question now? On Sundays he went skiing with her or met her in a café, remember, and sometimes he still stared at her as he had done back then. Yes, they remember. Hanna was a beautiful woman when, with glistening eyes, she said she wanted to go to France. "Jakob, you won't believe it. I'm saving my money." She was going to Paris.

He often waited, sitting at the counter until she finished her work late at night. And he looked at her in the almost total silence after the bar was closed. He liked the thought that the people were all asleep, so far away in their houses; and he could have stayed for hours, just looking and listening, where there was nothing to hear, or only the soft clinking of the glasses when they bumped against each other. Sometimes Hanna opened a bottle of champagne and they silently drank it in the semidark room. Or once she wanted to dance, and he followed her with soft movements across the plastic floor, breathless and almost blind because of her closeness. Then suddenly he stopped and simply watched the way she turned as the sonorous music played. There seemed to be nobody in the world during those nights, when they stepped outside, invisible in the dark village.

Sometimes she let him fix breakfast for her, and she watched from the kitchen table as he danced around the stove, set up the large pans, and cooked "Hanna, whatever you want!" She only had to tell him—and excitedly poured the wine into the glasses. He was a different person during those hours, perhaps himself at last. He liked to remain silent for a long time and then be unexpectedly boisterous, laugh, or tell silly little stories as he had done back then when they had played in the woods and groped their way back in the dark. On the way home she took his hand, or he walked ahead, suddenly lay in the middle of the street, and shouted loudly into the night that he was fine—"I'm fine!" But once she bent over him and saw the tears flowing silently across his cheeks. He waited in front of the building until she had climbed the stairs and the light went on in her room, and then stepped beneath the balcony whenever she looked out the window. He took his time on the way back and strolled to the church. Through the clouded windows he watched the baker at his work, and often he couldn't help but play his old tricks during a sudden attack of bravado. In front of some door he built an enormous pile of snow that would be frozen hard by morning, or he gathered skis together from everywhere and carefully laid them out in a long line from one side of the village almost to the other. Everything seemed possible in those nights, and once he actually climbed up on the bridge railing and balanced his way across it with his arms stretched out wide.

Yes, he felt good, but Hanna always warded him off when he wanted to talk about it or about the future. She laughed at him and dissipated his misgivings—or increased them by her actions. He accepted it and saved his words, stood on the balcony and did not shout them into the darkness, just into himself over and over again. Or later, while lying in bed, he whispered almost inaudibly to the wall. He accepted it? On a warm night—it was already spring—when they had strolled far out along the road, out beyond the tunnel, he had begun talking about it again and, prepared for the usual response, had not been able to believe her answer. He looked at her—"Say it!"—and then at the sky, the ring around the full moon that filled the entire expanse of the valley from the left edge to the right.

Only once during all that time did she invite him to her room, where they sat on her narrow bed and enthusiastically told the old stories and drank red wine from the bottle, hand in hand. Or they were silent, with their eyes closed or directed at the wall across from them, and the only sound was the ticking of the alarm clock, doubly loud in the silence, when they thought about it. He watched her undress and slip under the blanket, and touched her face, her breast, and between her legs, so that she moved her pelvis with his hands and screamed, and muffled her screams in the pillow. She had fallen asleep when he left. Dawn was breaking over the village. The street was covered with a heavy layer of new snow, and he walked slowly toward the bridge, backwards, so that nobody could follow his tracks or only in the wrong direction. And with happy excitement he thought of the bottle of wine that he would open and perhaps finish off when he got home.

———————

Once he thought that the women in the village were not women, and only later . . . . But what then? And suddenly he found enjoyment in impossible sophistries. Were the women men? Ridiculous, when he thought about it carefully. So they were neither, and therefore not human beings. It really meant something when he often didn't see some of them for months; and he repeatedly thought that it had to be the first time since his school days, when autumn came and they sat in the midday sun or got ready to go to church or to walk for a few minutes from one end of the village to the other in the early darkness. During the other seasons there was never time, and they would hardly leave their houses, let alone go skiing or do something they didn't have to do. And they would only have entered a strange restaurant if a husband had gone on a drinking binge and hadn't been seen for three days. Instead they would stand in their own restaurants for half the night, reproaching the customers whose wives drank as they made sarcastic remarks, laughed, and talked about Greek islands where they had been or intended to go during the summer.

Jakob remembered: as children we had gone in and out everywhere, and he knew how they sat on the buffet or behind the kitchen table after serving the food, how they stared at the plastic cover and would have preferred never to lift a finger again. There was always work: cooking, washing dishes, cleaning the rooms. They had to be everywhere at once because they couldn't trust the personnel. And in the winter they had carried the washed laundry to the attic in large baskets and pinned it on lines that were stretched between the beams beneath the gable. And? Once he stopped in front of a closed door and heard a loud argument—and nothing more. Then he retreated along the corridor, confused by the noise that suddenly ended. And not long afterward, he entered the unlocked cellar, remember, and watched Mrs. Fender drink large gulps from a bottle, standing in front of the shelves with her legs apart. She paused while bending over, and then began again. They remember. Saliva was dripping from her mouth when he saw her face.

On Christmas he stood behind them in the church and looked across their scarves and the tops of their heads toward the altar, where the priest was asking heaven for fresh snow or whatever else was needed. And he dreamed he was sitting on a meadow with Hanna in the summer. She would wear shorts again, stretch her bare legs out in front of her, pull the cork out of the half-filled wine bottle with her teeth, and unpack—and laugh as only a woman can.

What did he blame the guests for? As long as he was a child, they had treated him as a child and had followed him clear into the attic with their questions and the sweets they offered him so that he would come out from under the kitchen table and talk or listen to what they knew about the wide world and how you are supposed to behave in it. He never understood exactly what they wanted from him, and he himself wanted nothing from them, except his peace when they told him not to act that way. Basically, he did not have much against them, as a child, in any case, no more than he had against people in general. And at the time, during his first years, it was only his shyness, his shyness with people. That was the expression they already used to describe him even before he could walk.

Later it became visibly more difficult to find appropriate terms for the questionable relationship. And a term that was hesitantly written down for lack of a better one, selected in the end only because it was at least applicable to itself, would also be questionable. What did they want? One season after another he watched how they presented to him the illusion of a life, the comedy and tragedy of their ostensible everyday existence, and he stood there, a spectator, who was supposed to regard everything as reality and shout "Beautiful!" or "Terrific!" and clap his hands excitedly. When they needed him, he was brought out and permitted to go on stage with them, as a ski instructor, yodeler, dishwasher, or whatever occurred to them, a rhododendron, perhaps a chamois hunter, and that was all. Once he talked about his time in the city. He had attended the secondary school for a few months. And they said it could not have been important to him—"Or did you fail?" And even if he had finished, a diploma would never be the same as the German equivalent. It would always be only something Austrian.

He still didn't want anything, just his peace, and would have liked to scream loudly when he didn't get it. He could stand their constant know-it-all attitude, but not the uninvited nearness with which they pestered him and did not let go, every winter, every summer, and at last completely, if he was not careful.

And all the flirtations? "The daughters of Germans are not Germans," he said, as long as he hounded them and tried to fool them. In the semidarkness of a cafe, he held their hands and tenderly called them *Piefke*.[1] And later, or if they let him touch them between their legs, he sometimes could not suppress a feeling of triumph. He had gotten even with them, all of them, and whispering with excitement he confessed his love or some other nonsense. When they departed, he sat there lost in thought, and the relationship remained forever unclear, until he forgot it. Or sometimes one of them came back years later and didn't know where to look or what to say, or looked past him and talked about the old days and what naughty children they had been.

He didn't want anything.

Translated by Lowell A. Bangerter

---

[1] Austrian derogatory term for a German.

INSTEAD OF AN HONORARY SALUTE

ERICH HACKL

1. How Victor Learned German.

ON the first day in the quarry, the boss said to him: "You blockhead! Give me the shovel." Victor did not know the word blockhead and also did not know the meaning of "shovel." He looked around and saw a tin can and brought it to him. "You blockhead!" the other said again and hit him in the back with his fist. "That is a tin can. I told you to bring me the shovel." Victor looked around again and picked up a U-bolt which he handed to the boss. The latter hit him over the head with his stick. "You blockhead! That is a U-bolt. You are to bring me the shovel."

In this way Victor learned the basic vocabulary of the German language.

2. How Pedro Denied on a Wednesday that It Was Sunday.

When Pedro returned from a leave of absence, he was told to wait a bit. A pure formality.

Later Pedro learned that during his absence a Hungarian refugee had come to see Mr. Gidney. He said he had heard that Pedro Gómez would return. "Yes," said Mr. Gidney. "Pedro is coming back." "But this Gómez is a Communist!" "Pedro has been working for us for seven years," Mr. Gidney replied cautiously, "since 1947. Pedro is a good mechanic." "Gómez is a Communist," the other man insisted.

Then Mr. Gidney started to worry and made a report. When Pedro returned from Spain, the CIC (Counterintelligence Corps) called him in and hooked him up to a lie detector. "Don't worry," they told him. "It doesn't hurt, only relax, don't sit there so rigid. Calm down. It is only a formality."

Instead of an Honorary Salute 73

Then the officer said: "Today is Sunday." And Pedro answered: "No. Today is Wednesday." And then the officer said: "You are wearing shoes." And Pedro replied: "Yes. I am wearing shoes." "Your pants are blue." "Yes. My pants are blue." "You are a Russian spy." "No. I am not a Russian spy." "Today the sun is shining." "Yes, it is really shining." "You are spying for Franco." "No. I am not spying for Franco."

And so it went on and they gave Pedro a cigarette. An hour later he was allowed to go home. They said they would let him know. A week later men dressed in gray appeared at the home of his parents-in-law at Bindermichl and asked questions about Pedro's way of life, his favorite foods and political preferences. Pedro waited till May for the Americans to allow him to go back to the shop. Then he had had enough of waiting and went to the employment office. "I need work as a pipe-fitter," he said, and the official sent him to a company for which he worked for seventeen years, earned a good salary and lived well.

3. How Victor Learned His First Word of German.

Victor Cueto had been a lieutenant in the Spanish Republican Army. After its defeat, he fled to France, where he was interned. Then he reported to a French engineer company. He and his comrades dug trenches for the infantry and built casemates. They carried no arms. When the German Army stormed the front, Victor became a prisoner of the Germans. After being held for a few days by the military police, the Spaniards were loaded onto a ship and taken to a small town on the Belgian-German border. The Gestapo took over the transport and took them to an internment camp outside of Hanover. They were told they would be returned to Spain. A two-day trip and then the train stopped. That was August 6, 1940.

The sign at the railway station read: Mauthausen.

And the first words Victor learned were "Let's go."

4. How Pedro Became an Austrian.

When Pedro returned from Spain, the police wanted to get him out of Austria. "Look," Pedro said, "my wife is Austrian. My son was born here and I have worked here for eight years. I spent five years in a concentration camp. So don't expect to get rid of me."

They made things hard for him.

He was given a residence permit for one week.
Then he went to the employment office.
He applied for Austrian citizenship. The police headquarters at Gusen made a determination. Although Pedro Gómez did not have a record, his request could not be approved. And so up and down. Pedro went to get his papers at the Security Headquarters, which sent him to the Provincial Government. There he was told that it was a matter for the Security Headquarters.

"I am married," Pedro said. "I have a child to support. I have had enough of your playing cat and mouse with me. I want to know just where I stand."

"Do you belong to a party?"

"I am a foreigner. Under Austrian law I am not permitted to join a party."

"Then find someone who has connections. He should inquire from the head of the Security Headquarters where your dossier is."

Pedro turned to an official of the Socialist Party. Two days later he was informed that his application for Austrian citizenship had been approved, and he was to pay the outstanding costs at the Finance Office.

5. How Victor Was Forced to Give His Signature.

From the railway station they were driven up to the camp, beaten from right and left. Up there the Spaniards were interrogated in German. It was a dialogue of the deaf. "How old are you?" was the question, and the answer: "Victor Cueto." "What is your name?" "Twenty-two." Then they put a sheet of paper in front of him. "Sign it!" Victor said. "I will not sign. First I want to know what it says. I'll not sign without a translator."

Then they beat him.

"Now. Sign!"

"I am not signing."

They dragged him out, tied his hands behind his back, and hung him up on the wailing wall with his feet twelve inches from the ground. He hung with his whole weight on the joints bent behind.

He became unconscious. When he came to, they again asked him to sign.

Now he did so, but for the rest of his life he never found out what he had actually signed.

6. How Pedro Went to Spain and What Happened to Him There.

The Americans employed him two years after the liberation. Pedro advanced quickly and became a foreman, repairing tanks. The Americans liked him. Pedro this and Pedro that. Pedro here and Pedro there. He married in 1952 after having spent two years in getting all the papers together, and the next year he decided to go to Spain.

"I want to go to Spain," he said. "I want to see my parents again. I have not seen them for eighteen years."

"Stay here, Pedro."

"No, I am going. I am a free person. I want to see them again."

And Pedro went, with his wife and the child. But at the frontier they confiscated his passport and only gave him in return a pass which he was to present to the Guardia Civil in Málaga. There he stated what he had already told the official at the border, namely, part of the truth. That he had been a *carabinero* during the war; that he had fought at Madrid; that he had fled to France, and had fallen into the hands of the Germans. He did not tell that he had been an officer of the Republican Army or that he had served in a special unit dealing in counterespionage.

His passport was not returned. Also he found no employment. He held on and then wrote to an American Army captain who had been a diplomat before the war and who had said to Pedro before his departure for Spain: "You are going to Spain. It is rash, but I understand why. Let me know if the Spanish authorities cause you any difficulties." And the fellow did help. The US Army asked for Pedro, saying that it required his services. And his sister-in-law was able to obtain a stamp on her permit identity card allowing her to leave the country.

7. How Victor Found Something to Eat.

This is what we had to eat: in the morning a ladle of coffee substitute without sugar. At noon a quart of watery soup with traces of potatoes or beets in it. At night a kilogram of bread with a small piece of margarine for every ten prisoners. The staff in our block had already cut off part of the margarine.

Victor owed his life to SS Sergeant Spatzenegger, who transferred him in 1943 to the quarry garden, and also to a Bible student and a work foreman. There, Victor could eat vegetables.

Spatzenegger was a bloodhound, a monster, a death machine, but he was like a father to Victor.

8. How Pedro Became a Tour Guide.

And it came about that an ambulance rushed up and stopped beside Pedro.
"You speak English?"
"No."
"Parlez-vous français?"
"Oui, je parle français."
"Et qui êtes-vous?"
"I am a Spaniard."
Then the door opened and a Puerto Rican stepped out, happy to be able to speak to someone in his mother tongue. Man, a Spaniard! "Why are you wearing that striped stuff?" Pedro explained: it was a prisoner's suit. "We are Spaniards from the concentration camp. We were locked up there."
"Just what we are looking for. A concentration camp. Get in."
Pedro got in and showed them the road to Gusen. And he led them through the camp. The Puerto Rican vomited. Another fainted. For the camp was full of dead bodies, everywhere, on the ground, in every corner. He showed them the crematorium where, since the end of 1944, eight to nine hundred corpses had been burned every night, not only from the camp, but also from Linz. Victims of air attacks, and new arrivals from the transports bringing Jews from Hungary, children, their mothers, every night, a frightful smell. The washrooms, the storerooms, dead everywhere and everywhere that stench. There was no more ammonium chloride to get rid of the body smell.
Pedro said: "And now let us go to Barracks 29. The TB patients are there."
"No. That does not interest us," the Americans said. "We have already seen enough. No tuberculosis."

9. How Victor Took Up Boxing.

In 1942 Victor was so despondent that he decided to go out into the wire. It would have been a release. But he was too weak to do it.
That was also the time he started boxing.
Every Sunday they had to put up a boxing ring on the parade ground

and egg on two prisoners to fight against each other for the pleasure of the guards. A weak one against a strong one. As a prize, the winner had his bowl filled up twice. Victor boxed against a Pole who had only been in the camp for two months. Victor lost on points.

10. How Pedro Was Once Lucky.

At the end of 1943, Pedro was assigned to the plumbers' workshop. From that time on he risked his life every day. Because as a plumber, he could leave the camp and return to it. He tied the legs of his pants together over his calves and pulled his workman's suit over them. Outside, everything was already organized. They gave him food that he stuffed into his pants. For anyone who appeared in proper garb was respected. Anyone who came along in improper dress was beaten. He bribed the bosses in the hospital with part of what he smuggled: "Leave that one here until he is well."

So Pedro's job was to bring food from the kitchen into the camp. He reported at the camp entrance: Unit commander. Plumber. Spaniard.

"What do you do?"
"Work. Kitchen."
"Go on!"

At most, the commander took a look at the tool chest.

Often somebody was caught. He was hung up by the hands, his arms behind him, and questioned. "I stole something." "Impossible. Who gave it to you?" "I stole something." No one dared to tell the truth: he would not have lived long after that. If he held to his story, it was possible that he might survive the interrogation. Then he was put into the hospital and nursed until he was well again.

Once Pedro carried in his pants a can of lard, a glass of marmelade, two sausages, a piece of bread, two pipes and razor blades. Then from a distance he saw a group of officers standing beside the camp entrance. And the cook came out of the door. The Commander said: "Spaniak! Come here!"

The officers looked up.
"What are you doing here?"
"I repaired the lock on the door."
A long, long look and then the saving word: "Get going!"
Pedro arrived at the hospital bathed in perspiration.

11. How Victor Almost Ate Himself to Death.

When the liberation came, he was in the camp at Ebensee. Atop the second tank that rolled into the camp sat a lieutenant from Texas who spoke Spanish and gave Victor a box of canned food from Army supplies. He placed a loaf of farmer's bread on top of it.

Victor ate it all: two kilos of meat, blood sausage, the bread. Then he could not stand up. They had to take him as fast as possible to the hospital in Gmunden to have his stomach pumped out. He had scarcely recovered when he got onto a bicycle and set off in the direction of Spain. American soldiers took him off the bicycle in Lambach.

12. How It Looked Bad for Pedro.

Shut up for three days in a railway car. And one day, in January 1941, the car door was opened and an SS man stood there and shouted: "Pronto! Pronto!" and beat them with his rifle butt. It was about four o'clock, four o'clock in the morning, and the Spaniards were formed into five ranks. SS on the left and SS on the right. That is how they went up the street to the camp. When it was light, a truck appeared, filled with emaciated men, with shaven heads, in striped jackets. Then Pedro whispered to his neighbor: "We are going in, but will we come out again?"

13. How Victor Repaid Wrong with Right.

He lived in Lenzing, on the same street. He had been with the SS and had tortured Victor at Mauthausen. Now he came to look up the Spaniard. He stood before the house door and speaking in a whining, muted voice, asked for mercy.

"Please do not turn me in."
"I shall not turn you in."
"Hit me."
"Not going to hit you."
"Why not? Go ahead and hit me."
"If I hit you, I would be the same kind of beast as you."

Then, benevolently, Victor suggested to him.

"You don't know me and I don't know you either. You don't even need to say hello to me."

But this was of no avail. The good Lord was to punish him in the shape of a drunken driver.

14. How Pedro Was Put into Prison.

When the war began on September 9th, the Spaniards were assigned to work on the fortifications of the Maginot Line. They laid barbed wire, built concrete bunkers, dug trenches. For this they were paid fifty centimes and were given free meals. They were constantly retreating, always on foot. Until one day they were told: "It's all over. Everyone out. The Germans are here. Get out as fast as you can."

When they trotted back to the camp, they were surrounded by German soldiers.

"French?"
"No. Spaniards."
"Ah! Franco!"
"Nix Franco. Republic!"
A major asked: "If not for Franco, for whom were you fighting?"
"For right and freedom. To have work. So that we can live."
Then the German looked long and reflectively at Pedro.
"We are fighting for that too," he said. "The world is crazy."

15. How Victor Went to Spain.

Because he had fought for democracy, his brother was sentenced to death under Franco and then his sentence was commuted to seventeen years' imprisonment. A similar fate would have been in store for Victor. But by 1957 he had not seen his mother for twenty-one years and he took the risk. By then he had been an Austrian citizen for six years, but in Spain he was reported as missing. So he went to the Embassy in Vienna and applied for a visa. His request was rejected. He could only enter the country with a Spanish passport. Victor went to the Ministry of the Interior. Helmer intervened and Victor was again called to the Embassy.

"Were you in an execution unit?"
"I was not."
"Have you ever killed anyone?"
"I was a soldier at the front. There is shooting there, of course."
"Sign here that you never took part in an execution."

Victor signed, received a visa and went to Spain with his wife. At the frontier in Irún, they had to wait for the train to Madrid. Three men approached them. Secret police. Your papers please. "A Red Spaniard. So. Coming home now." One of the three policemen sat in the same railway compartment. At three o'clock in the morning, Victor and his wife changed trains for one to Gijón. "We have gotten rid of him," Victor said. Three days later they went to a bullfight. Once Victor turned around and saw the man sitting in the row behind.

16. How Pedro Could Not Bear to Hear a Certain Word.

He could not stand it any more. The word followed him everywhere. It was a constant attack. A war without end.

"Yes," Pedro said. "Foreigner. I am a foreigner. But I am not ashamed of that. I am working. And I was a political prisoner. I did not need to work. I have repaired your drain-pipes. Hundreds, thousands of Austrian drain-pipes. Isn't that enough?

"Now," Pedro said, "I feel comfortable here. I have a wife and children and grandchildren. But after the war, I should have preferred to live among Spanish people. For a foreigner is very isolated in Austria. I could not listen to it any more: "You are a foreigner." Something inferior.

17. How Victor Got Along in Austria.

Victor could not imagine living in Spain again. "You are more Austrian than the Austrians," his relatives said to him. "And," Victor answered, "people know how to live better in Asturias than here. But I am an Austrian. One hundred percent. I am loved and I am content. Even though people once spat on me. But everything was different after the liberation."

Afterword.

Pedro Gómez Carriolo died at Linz on March 31, 1990. He was seventy-three years old. Three weeks later, on April 22, Victor Cueto Espina died in the hospital at Wels. He to was seventy-three years old. I just learned of his death today.

Translated by Carvel de Bussy

The House

Wolfgang Hermann

The Garden

MY brother is running in the garden. He's running to sweat the poison out of his body. He bought the poison in a city in the north. Give me your understanding, give me your understanding, my brother said to me at the spring on the mountain and I didn't understand. That was before the spirits caught up with him. He sat there and told us what he had seen.

The sky is split by a huge, continuous bolt of lightning, he says. The earth is lit up from inside. Trees, streets, houses are illuminated through and through. A gigantic hand reaches out over the land and a cemetery glows with a green light. My hands are transparent; I see the bones. It smells like burnt flesh. I want to cry out but I have no voice. I'm running, running as fast as I can but not moving from the spot, and spirits are rising up all around me.

My brother is pale, his cheeks are hollow. His eyes are glowing with a black fire. He comes through the door with a glassy look and says like a prophet: I know that father was a general in the war. He fought and defeated them all. No one wants to believe it. But maybe he was even Napoleon. His cabinet where he keeps his treasures is locked up. Maybe there are chests full of gold from Russia in there or jewelry from Egypt. Like a commander father rode in front of the tanks. No one shot at him since his breast was made of steel. He was Hitler's greatest general and, if he had wanted to, he would have conquered the world. Maybe he was even Hitler himself. And he had an operation so that nobody knows that Hitler is still living. As proof that I'm right I'm going to hypnotize the city. I'm going to put them all to sleep. The whole city is going to dream about a red land, above which eagles circle on blue wings. They dream until I give the sign. Even up on the hills outside the city they're dreaming. They look out their window into the dream. But they have to be careful; they can't let themselves be seen, or the eagles will come and get them.

My brother stands there with raised arms, gathers up all of his power and trembles. He utters a high, jarring scream, a scream like you sometimes hear from the slaughterhouse. His arms fall and he leaves the room with a triumphant look.

The grass is as fresh as the dew. My brother running in his bare feet. He writes a big figure eight with his feet in the garden grass. He keeps running. He runs past the old apple tree, under the laundry pole, and past the hiding place for playing doctor. At the corner of the wall with the big spider he turns. It's the spider to which he sometimes brings flies. He tears off one of the fly's wings and throws it into the web. Sometimes it's a long time before the spider comes; the fly tries to get free, but its effort is in vain. The web trembles and the spider comes to get the fly. I'm learning from my brother. I catch flies and mimic him. I tear a wing off and throw them into the web. Sometimes I torture them too with needles. I pierce them with five needles and let them run on the table. I don't understand why the fly doesn't die. I go to play. The fly is still wriggling in the evening.

Sweat drips from my brother's brow. His T-shirt is soaked through with sweat. He lifts laundry drums filled with stones. He blows out his cheeks and counts. One two five fifteen thirty . . . My brother is strong. I've seen him fight. He beat up everybody.

One time, Karl, who lives two houses away, had him on the ground. He pounded my brother's head on the asphalt again and again. I ran away and screamed. My brother got a bandage around his head.

My brother takes me along bird-hunting. He has a big bow and a lot of arrows. We sneak through the big meadow. My brother puts an arrow on the bowstring. He shoots at a bird in a tree. The arrow gets stuck in the trunk. The bird flies off in a circle; he's all mixed up. My brother is the best shot on our street. One time he almost put out the eye of a neighbor boy. In juvenile court he said the arrow slipped. He told me that the arrow didn't slip. People talk about my brother in the neighborhood. I'm carving myself a bow and cutting arrows. I'm going to be a hunter like my brother. The other boys are now afraid of me. My arrows sail a long way. I often hit the mark. I also have a real knife.

Father is going to take a picture of me.

In the winter the garden is beautiful, just like in a fairy tale. The snow lies way up in the pines and the bushes. Lots of times there's a blackbird on the laundry pole. It turns around, pushes off with its tail feather, jumps and flies away. Behind it snow falls off the pole. My brother stomps through the deep snow and shakes the pines with a broom handle so the snow falls off. The pines stand up straight. There are footprints everywhere. You don't know where a rabbit has been hopping or a cat creeping along. The pines are standing bare. Father arranged it that way.

I hear my brother breathing. His step is heavy. He runs slowly along the figure eight. The grass is yellow where he's running. The trees are quiet without any wind in the branches, only the stride of my brother getting slower and slower.

The Living Room

Father is sitting still in his large blue chair. He's reading the newspaper. A heater is whirring next to his chair. His feet are snug in his slippers. It's very quiet; now and then my father leans forward and puffs air out of his mouth. That's a funny sound, like it's coming from a well shaft.

I open the sliding door a crack and stick my nose into the living room. The living room smells of father. Nobody besides father lives in the living room. Father has cookies in the cabinet and a box with cheese and rancid margarine. He has his own bread that's white and he eats it when it's hard. When father was small he had wanted his own loaf of bread for his birthday—his family was really poor. The box with the cheese gives off its smell even when it's closed up. Nobody else lives here.

Father discovered me. He motions with his finger for me to come to him. I'm standing right in front of father. He says, I play too much. I run with my buddies all day through the meadows. You have to learn something too, father says. You're old enough. School comes first. You have to learn to make sacrifices. Later in life you'll be happy if you know something. You'll think about me. Father turns the pages of his newspaper. He reads without moving. There's a plate on the table with apple peel and an apple core. Beside it a knife. On the wall there's a bar counter and on it there's a television set. We have the first television set on the street, even in the whole area. The neighborhood children come on Wednesdays and we watch *Kasperle*. The whole living room is full of children. When Kasperle asks "Are you all there?" we all shout Yesss! Thank goodness that Kasperle always wins and defeats the crocodile. I'm afraid of the crocodile. One time I stuck a knitting needle into the wall socket and was thrown back by the shock. I shouted, "The crocodile's here!" and mother came to comfort me. I dreamed about the crocodile too. It wanted to grab me and I ran and ran. But I kept running on the same spot and couldn't get away. I woke up covered with sweat and was happy that it was only a dream. The crocodile is in the toilet too. It comes up through the drain and wants to bite something off. I hurry when I'm peeing.

After *Kasperle* we run out into the garden. We play tag or cops and robbers. We have to stop soon since father is standing on the terrace in his work clothes. We're making too much noise. We go to the meadows where the grass is tall and you can find good hiding places. We stomp down the grass. The farmer will be mad.

When father and mother are gone we sit in the living room and watch television. On Sunday afternoon there's an American movie. My ears get warm. I don't like it when there's so much kissing in the movies. And then the violin music and I get red. I go into the kitchen and make myself some oatmeal with cocoa, milk and sugar. *Bonanza* comes on then and we laugh at the fat Hoss. Once we see a movie where a man has Hoss's voice. How is that possible? The sound of a door opening surprises us, my brother turns off the television set and father and mother are standing in the room. Making excuses we creep out of the room, my brother to the garden, my sister into the toilet and I go to my room.

Father calls us into the living room. We sit there stiffly. Father says, "I'd like to know what I've done to you." My brother, sister and I look at the floor. Our chairs are electric.

The Dining Room

Mother sitting at the table in her housecoat. A heater is whirring at her feet. She's writing the tax returns. She's writing figures in a big notebook and drawing lines with a ruler. She's entering this year's expenses into the notebook and the figure that comes out at the end has to be right. Mother's housecoat is yellow. The wallpaper is yellowish green. A yellow lamp is hanging from the ceiling. Mother has a lot of wrinkles. For every wrinkle a handful of worries. Mother works until late at night. Father comes, looks around, pulls the plug from the socket. It's much too warm here; we have to save, he says. My mother is just about to say something but father has already shut the door. In the living room tires are squealing and there's a crash. Shots. Father is sitting in front of the television set. Working the whole day, she says, making plans, sketches and calculations and I'm supposed to freeze at night. Mother tells a story from her childhood. We lived near the train line by a lumber yard. There were mountains of wood. We hid behind those mountains of wood. One of us closed our eyes and counted. I can still remember just how freshly sawed wood smelled. One time we went along the train line to the tunnel. We lined up along the sides and waited for the train. Suddenly the train came steaming out of the tunnel and a black cloud with it. We were black as ravens. On the way home we thought about how we should explain it to mother. There was a black cloud over the house, much larger than the one from the train. People were running everywhere and the fire department was spraying water on the house. The mountains of wood were in flames along with the house. Father was running around with the workers while mother cried. We all were crying. I've never seen so many people. My little brother died from a rotten tooth the same year.

    Mother likes to be cozy. She likes it when the heater is whirring. Sometimes she sings a little to herself. My mother sings operettas. She sings on stage. I think the operetta is called *The Gypsy Baron*. Mother has make-up on and is wearing a colorful dress. She sings very loudly and the people applaud. I fall asleep and my brother wakes me up since my mother is singing again. My eyes hurt and it's late when we drive home.

    Father doesn't like mother singing operettas. He says he's proud of her but her place is at home with him and the children. That was the agreement, he says. Otherwise I wouldn't have married you. My mother goes into the kitchen and cries. Father has a cane. The cane lies on the rail behind father's back. It has four edges and you can see by the paint residue that it was once white. We're not supposed to speak while eating, father says. Eating is for eating. You get sick from talking too much. The radio is talking. It's talking harshly and in a clipped way about things in the outside world far away, about an earthquake, about a murder, about money, about a war on the other side of the world. Father eats quickly and nervously. His eyes are downcast. I don't think that father knows happiness. My brother is talking. Father tells him to shut up. My brother doesn't listen and keeps talking. Father takes down the cane. The cane goes back and forth across my brother's head. My brother quiets down. The radio talks. Father turns it up. Do we always have to listen to the radio while we're eating, mother says. Don't interfere, father shouts. You always are cooking so late. I have to listen to the news. I have to know what's going on in the world.

I hate the world. I hate the earthquakes and the presidents who visit each other. I hate the famines and the war at the end of the earth. Why can't we live in the forests like the Indians? Why don't we have any horses and live in the wind and on the steppe? I want to be like Winnetou or Old Shatterhand or Long Rifle or like Unkas or I want to be Robinson Crusoe. I hate school and I hate Mr. Friedrich, the teacher. I hate the stiff collar on the minister's greasy neck who plays "moon landing" with me. I saw the moon landing on television. What the minister does is completely different but he calls it moon landing. He calls me up front to the desk, takes me by the ears and pulls me up with them until I'm standing on my toes. The minister does that with everyone while he talks about Israel and the Promised Land and the desert war.

The dining room is mother's room. It's small like the room in a tree house. I like to scoot back and forth on the dining room bench. You can do anything with mother. It's a long time before she forbids it and sometimes she shouts. Sometimes at mealtime I secretly throw a piece of meat under the bench. Mother says that I'm fussy. I eat only a few things. When I'm eating alone my brother comes and says you're eating a cow patty, just look. He says it until I'm sick. Then my brother takes my plate and eats my meal.

Underneath the dining room table I discovered a sentence. Written there is: "Love me touch me." That's English and I don't understand it. My brother must have written it or one of his friends, those guys he has orgies with in the summer. Father says that my brother has orgies while they're at the mountain house. I don't know what orgies are. But since my brother's been having orgies, I'm afraid of him. He has a strange look when he stares at me. He laughs out loud and says: the little boy, look at the little boy and he shakes his head.

My mother has a cane too. It lies untouched on the rail behind her back. It has four edges and is white.

The Kitchen

Mother standing at the stove. She's cooking something wonderful. There are three kinds of lettuce. You have to give yourself a treat when the weather is so bad, she says. The tilt window is open. Mother is singing arias, ones from *Tosca* and the "Ave Maria." The neighbors go past the kitchen window and look in. Mother says "Hello!" and keeps on singing.

Mother's kitchen is old. The paint is peeling off the ceiling. The floor is wavy. The drawers are worn and without paint. I take a carrot and dip it in sugar. It snaps in my mouth as if I were a big rabbit. I set the table in the dining room. I tell mother that the pastor played "moon landing" with me again. And my teacher is making the whole class copy page three of our reader again.

Mother is cutting up onions. But she hasn't stopped singing. During carnival mother wants to take us to see the parade. We're standing already dressed in the kitchen. Father comes and says: you're not going to carnival. Mother has to do something for me. Today is a holiday, mother says. Nobody has to work today. You'll stay here, father orders. I'm going with the children, mother says. Father slams the door shut and goes upstairs. I'm going, mother screams up at him. Not a chance, father shouts back down. Mother goes upstairs. We hear her screaming and crying. We run upstairs. We hears screams coming from the bedroom. My brother pounds on the door and yells "Open up!" It gets quiet in the bedroom. Only mother's crying. Father opens up: "What do you want?" Mother's coming with us, my brother says. Mother is sitting on the bed and crying. She's staying here, is that understood, my father shouts. My brother pushes father into the bedroom. Mother is coming with us, he shouts. He pushes father to the edge of the bed. He throws him down on the bed. Father's face is gray. Father is an old man. My brother is young and strong as a bear. He takes mother by the arm and leads her away. Father sits alone and lost on the bed's edge. We go to the carnival parade.

My brother is sitting outside near the closed-down train line. My brother is naked. He is scratching himself on the face, on the chest, on the hips, on the legs. His head is bobbing up and down and he leans to one side and then back. Slowly, very slowly, he bends down like a captured animal. My brother's eyes are rigid. They're staring in some direction far beyond the horizon. He takes trips far away into other worlds. He travels farther than Australia. Nobody knows where my brother goes. Nobody can follow him. My brother stretches his hand out and points into the distance. There is nothing there. My brother smiles; he's happy. There's a light in the distance. My brother sees the morning star over Bethlehem. He sees the stable with the Christ child in the manger. Light is flowing from my brother's hands. God is speaking to him. God says, "Go home, take your coat and your Bible. Your sister will sew a large pocket in your coat where you can keep your Bible. Set out in the night hidden from all sight. Go eastward over the mountains where they need your words. Now go." My brother no longer feels any pain. His body is light and it glistens like gold. He goes home and does what God has ordered him to do. My sister sews a big pocket for him on the inside of his jacket. My brother puts his Bible in it for safekeeping. It's night and the stars are in the sky; it's winter and the land is frozen. My brother goes into the night. He walks up into the hills and toward the narrow part of the valley. He jumps over the streams and climbs up the steep slopes. The stars are gleaming above the mountains. The stars are his brothers and they show him the way. My brother goes toward the East where the huge frozen mountains stand. He has to climb these mountains. Beyond the mountains are valleys, rivers, cities and people who are waiting for the Word of God. My brother sinks deeper and deeper into the snow. Everything is frozen. It's winter and the land is lifeless. A hostile, cold wind is blowing. The animals are in hiding, living in solitude. A human being can't survive in the woods. My brother no longer feels his arms and legs. His nose is numb. He falls into a stream and feels something hard and ice cold; it's the hand of death. Now he's stumbling toward the valley and the lights of the city. He loses himself in endless stream beds; he comes to ravines without bridges. He runs, falls, stands up again. He knows that it's a matter of life and death. More dead than alive he reaches the city by dawn. He opens the house door and lies down stiffly in bed. It's hours before life returns to his arms and legs. My brother has forgotten God's Word.

The Office

Mr. Hammer and Mr. Funir are sitting at their desks. They're sketching plans with a big ruler. When they build a model of a house they stick a piece of moss in front of it that's supposed to be a bush. I like the plans. I don't understand them but there's a certain order in them. I have a briefcase. I draw spaceships and houses, forts and weapons with a ruler from the briefcase. I can even do perspective. Father praises me. I'd like to be an engineer someday.

Mr. Hammer has been in father's office for a long time. He's very quiet and smiles in a friendly way when I come into the office. He has a radio. The radio is playing so softly that no one hears it. Father said he had to play the radio so softly. Mr. Hammer does everything in the office. Mr. Hammer pounds nails into the wall, repairs a radio set, mows the lawn. In the winter Mr. Hammer shovels the snow off the walks in front. I think he likes to do that best of all. That's much nicer than sitting in an office and chewing an apple when there's no job to be done. Mr. Hammer is really only half an office worker. His other half is a mountain climber and bicycle rider. Every day he rides his racing bike ten kilometers to the office except when it's snowing. Then he comes with his gogomobil. His gogomobil has three wheels. The door opens toward the front. It's very funny when the tall Mr. Hammer climbs out of the front of the tiny gogomobil. One time together with another boy from the neighborhood I covered up the wheels of the gogomobil with snow. The motor howled and Mr. Hammer didn't move from the spot.

On weekends Mr. Hammer climbs mountains. He climbs with ropes and climbing gear. One time after the weekend Mr. Hammer didn't come to the office. Father was furious and called Mrs. Hammer. But Mrs. Hammer didn't know where her husband was. Mr. Hammer didn't even come to the office the next day and father said that Mr. Hammer was fired. On the day after that Mr. Hammer did come to the office; he had a burnt and frozen face. We were in the mountains, Mr. Hammer says. There were four of us. There was a huge snowfall along with fog and one of our party had an accident. The rest of us held out in bivouac and waited. We almost froze to death. Father doesn't let Mr. Hammer go. But neither does he send him home for a good rest.

Mr. Funir has hair like a hedgehog. Mr. Funir only comes to the office when there is a competition or an important job. Mr. Funir's voice

is like the voice of a hedgehog if a hedgehog had a voice.
When there's really a lot of work in the office a man with a leather jacket comes. He has long hair. At those times a big motorcycle stands on the front parking lot. Secretly I sit on the motorcycle and press the brakes. The brake light goes on. One time the man with the leather jacket arrives with a woman. He delivers some plans to my father and the woman waits for him. She has a leather jacket like he does. She's beautiful and I look her over. Then the man and the woman drive away on the motorcycle and their hair flies in the wind. I wish I could have a motorcycle and a girlfriend like that.

Father rules like a king in his office. What father says is law. Mr. Hammer obeys. And Mr. Funir and the man with the leather jacket obey. Father is king of the engineers. I put bills into a file. The bills are sorted according to number. I'd like to be an engineer someday. Now I'm going to play.

The Garage

Father drives the car into the garage with puffed-out cheeks. Father's eyes go back and forth as he turns the steering wheel. He sits straight up behind the steering wheel and is totally concentrated—nobody can disturb him now. Father's cheeks are always puffed out when he drives the car into the garage.

I puffed out my cheeks in school and the teacher told me I had to stop it. I really didn't want to do it any more but my cheeks puffed out all by themselves and the teacher screamed. Father may blow out his cheeks whenever he wants to and no teacher screams.

Our car is blue. It has a white sunroof. Father turns a little crank and the roof opens. The stream of air tickles your head. It's really fantastic to drive with the sunroof open. Mother is not allowed to drive. Mother got her driver's license a long time ago. She hasn't driven since. Father says mother can't drive a car. Mother sits silently in the passenger's seat. Sometimes she shouts out, calling father's name. Father defends himself. "Don't be so scared," he says.

Mother got a green bicycle when I was born. She comes back from shopping loaded down with heavy packages on the sides and a big box in the basket. The green bicycle is stored in the garage. Sometimes I ride on it on our street.

The House

There's an oily patch on the spot where my brother's red moped usually stands. My brother has ridden off on his moped in a yellow fur jacket. He's standing around in the city park with his friends. Father says it's bad company for him. My brother has kissed the prettiest girl in the city. He told me about it himself.

In the summer he rides with his friends to the river. Sometimes he stays the whole night there. My mother followed him there because she was so worried. He screamed at my mother in front of his friends. He told her to go away. My mother came home with her eyes swollen from tears.

The father of the neighbor boy wants to give me a thrashing. He's running behind me cursing. It's a hot summer day and I'm barefoot. I run into the garage and slip and fall on the large spot of oil from father's car. I hit my head on the stone floor. Dazed, I open the door into the house. There are cool shadows on the hallway. The neighbor boy's father doesn't come into the house.

The Cellar

My brother is in the cellar. He's standing by the potato bin and whispering. He's speaking with the spirits of dead animals. My brother lured a cat into the cellar. He put it in a sack and tortured it. Slowly, slowly, the cat died in spasms from the torture. No traces remain of the cat's death. But there are voices in the cellar, a whispering like outside in the bushes. And lots of mice have died at my brother's hands. My brother waited hours for them, lurking like a cat and then he struck— with a shovel, with a hammer or he left the killing to the trap. The mouse my brother locked up in the hamster's cage was gigantic and strong. He pulled it out of a hole in the ground and locked it up in the cage. He puts the cage in front of the house where we inspect the mouse. We leave the cage unattended. We come back and see the blood on the bars where the mouse squeezed through. We smell the mouse's blood and death.

My brother's eyes are in the cellar; opened wide like animal eyes they shine out of every corner. My brother is the king of animals. He kills them. He is a lion. His jaws are enormous. I feel my brother's breath on my neck when mother sends me to the cellar to get vinegar.

My Room

A large man stands in the doorway. His shadow is cold. The man has an iron feather in his hand. When he touches it the feather sings. It's a dead song. But there's a human voice locked up in the feather. The man's mouth opens and the feather sings. I try to tear myself loose, to stop up my ears but I have to listen to the feather's song. It's a terrible, cold song that's closed up inside the feather. If the man's shadow moves, the feather's song is distorted. It's like I'm wading in a marsh. I don't like the marsh, the feather nor the voice that's coming from it. The voice is a simile. That's it, it's supposed to be compared to something. But with what? I think about it and try to remember, but again and again white ground pushes itself under me. I feel the feather's pain that it's unable to speak. I'd like to put everything in order, to defeat the feather's enemy. But I'm confused and don't see the simile.

The telephone rings and my father's voice says I'm coming right away. I see the color of his voice; it's brown. My father has a voice like metal. I feel the dagger of his voice. Light falls on the face of the figure in the doorway and I recognize my father. I'm afraid. There's nothing that can stand up against blood. My father's voice. The feather whose simile is missing is his invention. My father wants to deceive me. He wants me to disappear in a feather, a door, a bed. But l recognize him. I feel his brown voice. l am written into this room. I want to get away. I don't like father. But I don't see any street, any river. Everywhere his reflected voice.

I open my eyes. It's morning. Father is phoning. He always has important business. I have to go to school. But I'm so tired. Do I really have the body capable of the journey to school? A voice is echoing in me—which one is it? Freezing, I slip into my clothes. It is still dark. Why do I have to keep to my daily schedule? Why do I have to do what others want me to do? Do I have to learn? Do I have to understand? I don't learn anything there. I get dumber and dumber. I forgot my name. I'd like to be a long way from here. A street to anywhere.

My Brother's Room

The hand dips the brush into the paint and leaves short strokes and dots on the paper. The colors rise like steps, bundle up darkly in the shadowy body of water, dissolve, and glow in the flood of light on the horizon where the sun is setting. The wing tips of two birds touch. Far in the distance a blustery lake breeze fills a single sail. My brother breathes loudly with each new attempt. He squints his eyes as if he wanted to see into the distance. He lights a cigarette and blows smoke into the picture. My brother paints the lake just like he carries it around within him. He paints it with colors that scream, colors that whisper.

My brother is sitting on the bank of the lake and casting for fish. For hours he sits motionless and waits for a fish. He is himself as silent as a fish. He pulls the bait slowly from the water. He reaches back and casts the bait far out into the water. The line runs with a loud whirring.

Then he sits there motionless. He doesn't say a word but just stares into the water. I'm impatient. I run around the bushes. There are lots of old campfire sites. Sometimes my brother stays overnight at the lake. He has a little bell on his fishing rod that rings when he gets a bite. At night he fishes for eels.

Early in the morning he comes home with two buckets full of fish. It's summer and father and mother are at the house in the mountains. My brother fills up the bathtub. He then pours the fish into it. Eels disgust me. The other fish are funnier. My brother fries a fish every day. The eels jump around in the skillet. Often I go into the bathroom and look at the fish. The water gets completely yellow. The fish know that they have to die.

My brother is standing in the mountain stream with his pants legs rolled up. He stares motionless into the water with his hands held at his knees ready for pouncing. The stream murmurs softly. My brother's hands shoot out—a bright flash—and he tosses a trout on the shore. We sit around the fire and eat. It's quiet in the forest; only the warm crackling of our fire. Somewhere a long way off, a cry. The shadows wander over our cheeks. My brother is an Indian. He knows all the animals and how you build a hut. He cuts down young fir trees with his friends and they build a hut. The forester comes and my father has to pay the fine for my brother. Later at this hut my brother tells me, "Give me your understanding!" I'm afraid.

He's sitting together with his long-haired friend in a vacation cabin. It smells funny in the cabin. His friend is a hippie and the others too. They have purple scarves around their necks; they're drumming and smoking a long pipe. I'm too young to be with them. But I get to come into the cabin and pet the beautiful red dog. There's a blackened spoon on the table. The hippies have strange voices. They're laughing and I don't know why. They're nice to me but I'm afraid of them. Father doesn't know that I'm at the house where the hippies are.

My brother is now living in his pictures. He flies with the gulls out there in the lake breeze. My brother no longer has any rest. He paints a picture so he can hide in it. He's nowhere to be found in the picture. He's everywhere in the colors that scream and whisper, in the dark water, in the blue hills in the distance, in the deep red evening sky. My brother is going off the deep end—I see his hand and its reaches out into the emptiness. I can't stop him.

My Sister's Room

My sister is screaming. My mother comes and lifts her out of bed. She puts on her leather corrective gear. My sister is bowlegged. She falls down. Mother holds her up by the arms. My sister dreams about the wolf. She's running on a large meadow. She runs and runs; the wolf breathes down her neck. She runs up a hill but the hill is steep and her legs are rubbery and she's not making any headway. The wolf gets closer and she smells its warm breath. All of a sudden the ocean. It's deep blue and there are whitecaps along the coast. A wave approaches—it's gigantic. My sister wants to cry out but she's silent. The wave breaks slowly and heavily. Its shadow lies on the houses. My sister is sitting on a swing and she flies over the ravine. She flies high up over the fir trees and the river. There's an aching in her stomach.

My sister is clever with her hands. She knits clothes for her dolls. She puts a dress on a bottle so that it looks like a poodle. She gives father and mother things she has made herself for their birthdays and at Christmas. Father would rather have socks, however. He's only happy about things he can use. Or he would like to have a bottle of red wine. He puts it on the living room cabinet and drinks a glass from it every evening.

My sister brings a book home that tells her how to lose weight. The new word at home is calories. My sister says there are calories in everything. I think it's something like a sickness. I don't want any calories. But my sister is always talking about them. Mother is reading the book too. Mother often talks with my sister about it. There are new products at home. These things are called muesli, molasses, beer yeast and the others I forgot. But my sister isn't fat at all. One time through a crack in the door I see her breasts. I get hot around the ears and have clouds in front of my eyes.

At night I wake up and hear little cries from my sister's room. I creep out into the hallway and stand by the banister. The cries come in waves, sometimes broken by laughing. Then whispering again. Someone is with my sister, a deeper voice. Quiet. Again the little cries. I stand at the banister, my hands on the cold metal. Someone's hurting my sister. I listen to her pleasure. I don't want someone with her. I don't want to hear her pleasure. I want her to come and say that it's not true. I want the man to go away. And I want my sister to go away. I don't want anyone anymore. I hate everybody. The night is like a huge sack.

The Room with the Large Table

A dusty broom stands in the corner. The shoes on the shelf are worn down. The smell of floor wax comes from a half-opened drawer. An ironing machine stands under the window. The ironing roller is scorched yellow at both ends. The coat hooks are crowded with coats, jackets and kitchen aprons. A towel hangs over the edge of the table. The table stands on two wooden trestles. The table top is wooden too. The dark area is a knothole. Under the table there are sacks full of old clothes and torn towels. When I move, the sacks crackle. I lie completely quiet with the musty smell in my nose. I stare at a single black, woman's shoe in the corner; it's mother's shoe. A sad old umbrella is leaning against the wall. It's quiet for a moment in the house and I hold my breath. A door is slammed shut. I hear my sister whimpering. Someone is running down the stairs. "Pig! You're a pig!" It's my brother's voice. A door flies shut, the key turns. "Don't always stick your nose into my business! You always take the children's side!" It's father shouting from behind a door. I hear crying; it gets worse. It's a sorrowful singsong. Then words are repeated again and again like they were being braided together in a wreath. Always the same words. I don't understand them. "What in the world is the matter with you! What is the matter!" father screams. My sister is still whimpering with sobs in between. Steps on the stairs. "Don't you even come near me," father shouts. "You pig! Pig!" my brother screams until his voice is drowned out. "What did you say, what?" father screams. Steps, then a stomping. A heavy object hits the floor. A door flies shut, then another one. A scraping like behind glass, a cry, then a plate clatters; once, twice, splintering glass, a falling chair. "Get out!" father yells, "Out with you!" A door is ripped open, then rapid steps; I see feet, a flashing and they're gone. The door to the garage is slammed shut. The garage door. The sound of the moped. My brother drives away. It's quiet. Somewhere there's swearing, a whimpering. My sister's whimpering. From far off, a sobbing, smothered by doors and handkerchiefs. It's mother. Steps and a door opens; another one and another. Father is walking through the house, swearing and mumbling. Broken glass. He steps over the shattered plates and curses.

My chest moves rapidly up and down. There's sweat on the palms of my hands. I breathe in the musty smell. The musty smell over and over, always here under the table of the room without names. I hate the sacks; I hate their smell. I hate all the dead things I see. I hate the ironing machine. I hate the cabinet. I hate the table supports and the table. I hate the floor wax. I hate the sacks I'm lying on. I tremble. I'm cold. I hate this house. I want to scream but I have no voice. My scream might help my mother and sister. Maybe it would tell them that they're not alone. But I don't have a voice. My mother's sobbing somewhere. Somewhere my sister's whimpering. Father's curses somewhere. The silence of the dead things. I'm almost as dead as the objects in this room. Then someone calls my name.

Translated by Francis Michael Sharp

Paralysis

Margarethe Herzele

THE horror of going in was in no way diminished. . . .
I adjust only slowly to the fact that this living corpse, Ulrich S., is my husband!
Adjustment, I call to mind, can be something positive! For heaven's sake, use the few days that you still have here! The baby *still* has a father and *you* a husband. Isn't that worth something?
Doctors and nurses very sympathetic! Whenever I want to, I can go to see him.
In any case, astonishment on all sides that—with all this agitation and my "mature" age—the birth went so well!
They do not know how much I had to clench my teeth (as if they were metal welded together) the whole time and even yet! Especially at night, when worries overtake me with their glowing arrows. . . .
Only (or already) twelve weeks since the terrible event. Longer? My calendar not here. Who should have gotten it to me! The scribblings in Ulli's date book not decipherable, and I don't want to ask either. Doesn't really matter anyway. . . .
There are patients—who, at best, they might tell me again—who remain in a coma for decades after an accident; and others who die immediately or after a few weeks. A few, however, and not *really* so few—their consolation—wake up again *after all*!
My first visit, accompanied by nurses! I still didn't dare even to look. . . . Later then *alone*. At first I held onto the ice-cold door handle, as if I were frozen to it, just in case. . . . As if it could suddenly happen that the person pretending to be dead would rear up, leap to his feet—like a giant, a golem—to take the child and drag her off with him to the deathly silent realm of nothingness. With the living doll in his arms then to grow numb in a terrible way, *both of them* . . .

Thus my thoughts tremble with fear.

Stupid, definitely stupid of me since he is just lying there unchanged—almost handsome and somehow noble! His sensuous mouth is peaceful, and the pale curvature of his forehead as if chiseled in stone.

STILL / LIKE FOREST WATER
REFLECTING NOTHING
EMOTIONLESS / FILLED WITH PEACE
IN A SPECIAL WAY *SELFLESS*
AS IMAGINED / IN MY DREAMS

Indeed, as if all these ideas of passivity and selfless dispossession, SELF-DISPOSSESSION, were exceeded in an inexplicable and awful way!

... AS IF DREAMS—
IF THEY LAST LONG ENOUGH—WERE
ANTECHAMBERS OF LIFE / PRE-PRODUCTS ...
DREAMS—FACTORIES OF THE *POSSIBLE*?

Turned around yesterday. Ran away. Lost a lot of blood again! Sometimes, however, and difficult to explain because so very contradictory—in any case, when the golden sunshine in the afternoon makes the long corridors (conduits) and even his hospital room (residence) on the fourth floor of the adjoining wing more human—me, haunted by a childish wish to sink down—like one of those princes in a fairy tale, who kiss the rose-petal mouth of his princess, enveloped in a death-sleep, until its mortal bewitchment is broken.... But, the reverse case—that a princess kisses a man who is numb and drunk with death, a pale corpse, back to life—*never* heard of it!

Are we girls, women such cowards? Are we afraid of this DREAM-PARALYSIS—this INCARCERATION OF THE SELF IN ITSELF? COCOONING? Or—are we gripped by the horror because we women are perhaps—more intuitive, more knowing?

Deep fright in any case in the presence of this helpless body-self.

... Fright to the point of becoming cold myself: SOLIDIFYING TO ICE! Ice that can sense only the coldness by which it is gripped, not the further coldness ... that's how I feel with him.

Of course, on other days my feeling-world is like a raging gyroscope—spinning first in one direction and then in another

UNTIL / THE FRENZY
—LOVE AND ANGER—
GOLD-RED GLOW
YEARNING BLUE / AND
METALLIC SADNESS

REDUCES TO
HELPLESS DELIRIUM

BUT TODAY *TODAY*
IT'S HATRED'S TURN

Another three days—the head doctor jokes during his visit—the whole family will be together under this hospitable roof! That's the most we can do for you!

He knows my plight, the financial debacle! And thus I emphasize my gratitude for his letting us stay here much longer than usual, a total of fifteen days!

And the little one already so heavy that I can hardly carry her along with her accessories—old-fashioned pillow, pink blanket, and all sorts of things! Or is it for other reasons that my knees are shaking? In any case, she is clearly the darling of the doctors and nurses, with her exceptionally sweet little face!

Because of that, the other mothers are livid! I'd like to tell them that *everyone* receives something good in this world. For their ugly children there is a dependable entourage of fathers, sisters, aunts, and grandmothers, while this oh-so-special-one ("VIPS" in cell 19, read: room) can expect *nothing* but unadorned loneliness. And that would be the case even if we were together with our husband and father, who
   HEARS NOTHING / SEES NOTHING / FEELS NOTHING

Please go to the billing office today, the head nurse calls to me from across the hall.

BILLING! I am alarmed. And the COUNTDOWN begins: three / two / only *one* day more . . .

THE BILLING

I try to make myself look nice—or what is considered to be nice! A touch of make-up, a little jewelry. Brush my hair until it shines. It reaches all the way down my back, as if to protect me: BLACK SILK VEIL.

Pumps instead of my slippers, and finally again, *finally*—a fitted dress! Over it loosely my new house coat, which, of clear turquoise, is beautiful and stiff like a sail. It propels me gently through the endless corridors, the one overheated, the other, in compensation, ice cold. Yes, propels me, as if on roller skates, going slightly downhill: I *am being* walked! For, although my physical apparatus is functioning, something important in me seems to be missing, or—as if behind glass!

As if my head were ahead of my body by years, months, or at least days . . .

ENCOUNTERS. Individual men smile at me. Appear silently from the basement and disappear into it again. Some are repairing the elevator—oh, would that it were still for a long time! . . . Visitors, and patients too, wink at me with their cigarettes. But *everything* is lost again by the end of the corridor—the people and their words. Only the fateful odors remain, as does the groaning from the rooms, as well as the many cigarette butts—stillborn hopes. . . .

Clearing my throat several times and smoothing out my loose hair, I enter the room. Hands ice cold. Circulation still not normal? In any case, I sit down in *such* a way that I have his forehead exactly in my field of vision (why, actually?). Further, I can make out the region of his heart and also something of his mute yellow hands, which were previously so warm and ruddy. . . .

Precisely, like a doctor (I've been learning stuff here), I imagine the condition of his kidneys and his liver, as well as certain points in his spinal cord, and also—ridiculously enough—the soles of his feet. As *if* all of these were interconnected by red, black, or even white threads.

You dog! You damn dog! I begin: Thanks to your boundless egotism and carelessness, you have done me out of everything! I am totally ruined! My castle, my beloved sloe bush, is gone! That wonderful old house—my second SELF, my SKIN, my HOMELAND! My entire pride, my protection, my dress! My past and my future! My dearest chamber! Oh, all my trouble and sacrifice in vain! Because—I fling at him—I had to *co-sign* for you! Because you forced me to! Indeed, you hypocrite, blackmailer, dirty pig! I can't express what you've done to me—now and before that too!

Bastard, murderer, thief! You've killed my life! And it's not enough that I've lost my castle, my home—but, because of you, I'll be reduced to the lowest possible level of subsistence! That means 1558 Schillings a month—for the child and me together! For years, decades to come!

As little or as much, if not several times more, as you used to spend in one evening for yourself alone, for *your* pleasure! And why is that, *why*, do you suppose? I'll tell you why! Because I have to pay for this here, your damned stay in the hospital, which, as anybody can seen, doesn't lead to anything anyway, absolutely *nothing*! Private room, of course! Because the fine gentleman was too lazy or too proud to get insurance for himself or his fucking car after coming back from Australia! But he had no trouble demanding that I co-sign, *that* he could do!

Indeed, every minute, every single day that they keep you "alive," as they say, here in the Intensive Care Unit, costs my lifeblood and that of your child—you living corpse!

What a wretched father! And abominable husband above all! I shudder to think back and tremble at the thought it could become—no, now *without* money—a hundred times worse!

You always pretended to be the strong man—at the expense of *others*! Had nothing but contempt for people who were weaker or more sensitive. But now you belong to that category yourself! You don't even know whether you should decide to live or die. . . . You've become exactly what *you* despised the most—a passive cripple!

You drive others to the brink of disaster but lack the courage to admit your own! What a miserable creature! Make up your mind finally for the one or the other. Die! If you still have a spark of decency left—*die* so that your child can *live*!

Doesn't the child need food, shoes, a winter coat! Or a bed? Fruit? How is that supposed to be paid for, if you please? If you don't want to get well anymore—*die*! Yes, *that's* how it is! Get well—or . . . I beg you! Every hour here costs money, it *does*!

Didn't your egotism use to grab everything it wanted for itself anyway? Girlfriends, even women from the street? Betrayed, squandered, wasted—what you had promised *only* to me in the most tender moments of sacred devotion! And then you denounced the woman who was deceived, robbed, and deprived as a snooper. . . . That's how bitter, how hurt I am!

So as not to be swept away by the flood of tears, my gaze is glued to the imaginary point between his closed eyes. Observe him very closely—nothing! No reaction! Just as his heart never showed any reaction to my sorrow or my anger. I have to cry. . . .

Think of your baby! I whisper and then present her to him in all of her helpless loveliness and sweet innocence. Cautiously, though, so that his deathly silence can't take possession of the precious darling ...

Strange to speak with someone who, even after the most terrible accusations, does *not* respond.

DUSK has fallen. Fills the room. Softens my mood. Violet-gray roses grow out of the whirl and snowy folds of the white blanket. . . .

... And it's *your* baby! I warble, gripped by emotion, while gem-like tears fall from my eyes.

Tender white feathers are suddenly growing out of the high altar of his bed. . . .

You and I—I breathe proudly—have given her life—a tiny, but wonderfully beautiful life! She is the most beautiful child on the face of the whole Mother Earth!

Just look—there is still a tender satisfaction in my hands from stroking her curls—that mixture of soft yellow straw and raw brown silk. And my breasts are still swollen from the most recent stings of our little honey bee—she's a wild biter! But oh, between my legs, which still hardly hold my weight, the BLOOD runs out—like the MONEY that you cheated me out of! Oh, a completely inverted Snow White—stuffed and plugged up with stiff cotton! Can't you see me walk? And don't you smell the blood? All the street dogs would follow me if I went outside! I'm AFRAID for the baby when I'm carrying her, and the BIRTH so very dreadful and full of pain: TEARING APART! MUTILATION! CHILD—ROSE OF MY PAIN ...

You see—*I* have already made my sacrifice for her life! Now it's *your* turn! We've been waiting for it long enough! We have to leave tomorrow, Dindia and I!

I repeat, *slowly*, concentrating on the point between his eyes: Get well or die!

If you make the SACRIFICE—I will tell your daughter only the very best things about you; about your courage, your sincerity, love, and intelligence. Understand?

... It will probably have become clear to you in the meantime—I continue then in a different voice, deeper and even velvety, the way one usually talks to dogs to quiet them—that a person, even if he is the strongest six-footer—will never be able to walk again with a broken back! Wouldn't life be a terrible torture for all three of us then? Or am I supposed to put the sweet little one up for adoption, which is what the midwife has been whispering day and night in my ear?

To give up the most beloved one—in order to take care of someone who has presumably taken more than his share of life?! *Never*! I'd rather die myself, starve, kick the bucket! Or—beg! But *with* my child! To warm myself in this cold world on her sweet honey breath . . .
    Dindia—my only ray of hope! My evening and morning star . . .
    And to continue pathetically: MY SAPPHIRE / MY EMERALD / MY GREEN MEADOW! MY WATER / MY BREAD / LIGHT AND SNOW / YOU RED BLOOD / THAT DISAPPEARS FROM MY CHEEKS / *WHEN*
    I'm feeling stronger already and bob in a satisfied way with my black patent leather pumps that sheathe my feet very neatly. And, when I turn a little, they even reflect pinhead-sized suns—the last shimmer of light in the room, which sinks in the dusk with the soft whistling sounds of the respiratory device. Am *satisfied* with my shoes and myself.

Sit down then at the foot of the bed and cautiously stroke the humps in the blanket, where his yellowed feet are presumably located, to provide them with something good as a farewell. And, a FAIRY-TALE VOICE, which is (not) mine, begins to murmur: Good heavens! I realize that it's rather pleasant to lie here

TO BECOME ONE
WITH THE HOUR
WITH THE STILLNESS
WITH THE DUSK
IN SOFT PAIN

FLOWING TOGETHER
BODY AND TIME—TO SPACE

Yes, only a few gentle noises now and then—scurrying steps, sympathetically lowered voices. Sometimes yellow narcissus in the window. No bothersome meals anymore, no brushing your teeth or difficult trips to the bathroom—only the soothing chugging and running of the machines that show you're alive! Nice, isn't it?
    For a DEAD PERSON, in contrast, the electronic leeches would be immediately discon . . . .
    I slap myself in punishment on my bright red mouth! But don't know what to do next—for, the minutes suddenly stand still: be careful! The minutes simply do not advance . . . come together to a mountain of unused time!

This SURFEIT OF EMPTY LEATHERY TIME—aren't you tired of it? I speak cautiously, and: still not satiated, no nausea? Or—my voice creeps around, like a well-camouflaged beast of prey—or—or are you so enormously AFRAID of dying?

I believe you. Yes, I believe you. . . .

Now it's sweet again, the voice, and trembles a little, my heart, like the inner workings of a golden alarm clock. Glad that I and not *he*, that he and not *I*, as one so easily thinks and even says in certain nights of love.

Die! I command harshly: you have to! Otherwise you will kill us all! You finally have to decide—by *tomorrow*!

It's best to die in the early morning hours—I continue more objectively. And my voice sounds as if it were forced through a pipe: between three and four o'clock! The best time, when day and night meet each other, and, flowing together, bid FAREWELL.

TIME'S DIVIDING LINE! Maybe your soul, which you don't believe in anyway, will depart more easily at that time. . . . Besides, it's less of a burden for the nurses then, with making beds and so forth. They already complain all day long. . . .

I stand up then solemnly to swear: With this *single* sacrifice in your less than glorious life you could make something great of yourself—one can only make *oneself* great. And we will love you for it, *love*! I'll invent the great LOVE MEDAL for you right now. Understand? But now, die!

From the word "die," a terrible scream emerges—for I suddenly become aware of the monstrosity of my command, my horrendous suggestion! And, with the scream still in my mouth, I wake up panic-stricken.

Or—haven't I been sleeping? I don't know. Bathed in sweat and exhausted, as if I had just been chased through mile-long corridors, or I had fought with white bandages that had wrapped themselves around my neck, and my thyroid gland were the blood-red entrails of a snake—so agitated and breathless, I'm sitting on the bed—unsure what is dream and what is reality—whether it is not *now* a dream, and I only *hoped* to be dreaming before when I demanded something so vile . . .

The blue emergency light makes the familiar clock into an eerie eye—but the *deepest* of all horrors is reserved for my own inner world. . . .

Still nighttime, hardly three-thirty.

The night nurse reluctantly fetches a fresh night gown, stiff, like white metal. The cart with the breakfast milk rumbles down the corridor, the babies cry.

Like piglets before you throw them their fodder, or they throw themselves to the butcher, it seems to me, *today*—

We are only just MEAT, all of us! It doesn't make any difference whether concealed under a night gown or disguised with an expensive evening gown. Yes, meat in nature's great theater: DIE AND BECOME!

For that, the day shift of the nurses so extremely nice at breakfast—that one pricks up one's ears, even becomes suspicious, waiting *eagerly* for every glance or gesture that they pick out of the air behind one's back. . . . Even the Professor, of whom one usually doesn't even get to see the coattails—appears personally. On a Saturday! The nurses tremble.

. . . An unusually regrettable case! And, although everything conceivable had been done—not only because your husband was a man of public affairs—today, at daybreak, God delivered him. . . .

No! I scream: I delivered *us*!

But my dear lady! . . .

I am not a dear lady! I killed him. *I* . . .

—Oh no, not this too! Schizophrenia, catatonic type! Quickly! Two ampoules Fluanxol, the strongest dosage . . . I'm sorry, you will have to stay here longer, ma'am . . . —

And the corpse *upstairs*. Or is it already in the basement.

Translated by Beth Bjorklund

Easter Stroll

Graziella Hlawaty

"**B**UT you can't just simply throw me out of this home for evacuees! Where am I to go with my three children?" asked Ilse's mother in despair.

"Throw you out?" repeated the director. "Nobody is thrown out here. The home is being turned into a hospital—the wounded soldiers have the priority! Bring the proof that you were bombed out in Vienna, then I can continue to help you."

"But I left my certification in Vienna. How could I anticipate that I would be needing it here in Salzburg?"

The director shook his head. "I can only transport the fugitives who have to leave the home when they possess the proper papers."

"And if I send my daughter to Vienna? To get the certificate? She should surely still be able to make it into the city."

"To send a fifteen-year-old girl alone in the direction of the front is of course risky," the director replied.

"Oh, Ilse will make her way through. But the question is whether she will still manage to get out of Vienna again before the Russians attack."

"If she leaves at once, it should work out all right. But she must go immediately! For one thing is certain: there will be a battle for Vienna, a hard battle!" The director drew himself up to attention, he suddenly stood very straight in his gray loden suit. And now changing to the victorious tone of the army communiqués, he added in conclusion: "Vienna will be declared a fortress. Vienna must not fall, and Vienna will not fall! We owe that to our Führer."

The mother looked somewhat disconcerted when she spoke with Ilse about her conversation with the director.

"Do you think you could do this?" she asked. "Can I really depend on you? As slow and dreamy as you are, it's possible that you won't be able to get out of Vienna again. Vienna will be declared a fortress, the director told me."

"Of course I'm sure I can do this. Why not?" answered Ilse. "And you can depend on me, too."

"Are you sure?"

"Definitely!"

"All right, I'll depend on you."

Now Ilse almost felt sympathy for her mother. How was it possible that her mother didn't in the slightest sense how gladly she departed from this place? Ilse tried to chase away this wish that kept becoming clearer and clearer: a wish never to have to come back at all, but to stay in Vienna. But then her mother would be left here without a document attesting to her having been bombed out, and the whole trip to Vienna would have been senseless and unnecessary. No, she couldn't do that. It would be a complete swindle.

But why pity? Why am I ashamed to wish that the "fortress Vienna" will close so tightly behind me that a return is impossible? Ilse asked herself. And how does mother suddenly dare to depend on me? On me, who is usually only "careless," "forgetful," and "undependable!" Did her mother have such a bad memory? When for coming home too late Ilse had once again been slapped in the face, slapped so hard that she saw stars in the sudden darkness, and when her mother spat in her face and called her a "whore," then Ilse had come to a decision. You are no longer my mother, she thought then, while she wiped the saliva off her face. And during the beating she became indifferent about whether she only thought this or also spoke it. She said it calmly and clearly: "You are no longer my mother." And she planned to stand by these words, to make them come true once and for all. For if her mother never wanted to believe the truth, namely, that she had walked her school friend home and then the latter had returned the favor, and if, moreover, it was impossible to explain to her mother that they had chatted on these walks not only about Wallenstein and the Burgtheater, but also about Socrates and Plato—if despite her explanation her mother nevertheless insisted she was lying, then she, Ilse, the one being punished for lying, the one being beaten, never needed to pay any further attention to her mother. And this eternal phrase after the beating: "Now everything is all right between us again. Tell me that everything is all right between us again!" Those were just words, nothing but words. Words, which one could hear, words, which one could say—but they bore no relationship to the truth. If her mother appeared not to attribute any great significance to such outbursts, well, that was her business. She, Ilse, after being spat on deflected every new scolding and all future blows onto a great pile of injustice. No, she was not forgetful, and absolutely never again would things between them be "all right." So, why pity? And why be ashamed?

"I hope you will get through quickly," said her mother. "Promise me that you will hurry. Not dally around!"

"Yes, I promise," said Ilse. She pointed out the window: "Look, the weather has turned beautiful. Everything will surely work out. The whole thing will be just a little Easter stroll."

***

The train to Vienna came soon, the cars were almost empty, there was really no lack of seats traveling east. Ilse walked through the cars until she came to a completely empty compartment. A jolt—the trip began. Ilse landed on the wooden seat even before she thought of sitting down.

And what a trip! Ilse lowered the window, on the curves she could see the locomotive. It smoked, puffed, blew thick clouds of smoke into the air, pulled the trail of smoke behind it. The train wound along the foaming Ache river, on both sides of the track the rocky cliffs rose steeply, blocked the view to the sky. It began to get cool, the engine tooted, a tunnel swallowed the train, then again came woods, cliffs, shadows, the Ache.

Sometime later, when she would have school and the prison of home behind her, when she could be free to determine the course of her life, yes, then she would often take such trips. Travel makes one free, thought Ilse, I'll try to never be sedentary, I'll try to always be underway from freedom to freedom. She began to imagine her travel wardrobe: a bulky silk coat with checkered lining and a toothbrush in the same color and of the same material. Everything that one needs, one takes along on such trips—to be free. But there should never be too many things, so one can always move about freely. To move freely and be underway, to travel wherever she wanted, without fibbing, without lies, without any promise, without any commitment. Then I'll stand at the window, just as I am now, I'll stand at the train window, lower it, stick my head out, and let the wind roar past my ears. And I'll remember today's trial trip, remember this first taste of freedom.

Salzburg, Salzkammergut. Open landscape, the mountains recede into the background. Meadows, fields, villages, cities. Now the train traveled in a straight line eastward, now it met the big east-west autobahn, ran parallel to it here and there, fenced in by barriers, interrupted by barriers. Did Ilse still want to continue dreaming about coming trips? About the great freedom, about finally having escaped from her mother? In glancing at the road she forgot all about her travel wardrobe, the beautiful coat, the leather gloves, the light brown suitcase, everything disappeared and was forgotten.

For suddenly the trip in the empty compartment, the fantasy trip, alone, by herself, out into a distant future, came to an abrupt end. Here, on the road, the present intruded, it waltzed toward the train, endlessly, mile after mile, an unceasing, uncontrollable stream: the route of the fugitives to the west. People on foot, ox carts, bicycles, handcarts, rattling cars running on gas produced from wood, ancient motorcycles with sidecars, horses pulling staked wagons. Everything was packed full of household goods, as one gathers them together at the last moment: bundles of clothes, suitcases, blankets, cartons stuffed full, tied fast with cord, dishes, pans, children's beds, chairs, carpets, pictures (paintings, with wooden frames, wrapped in cloth), what might they portray that made them worthwhile enough to be taken along: the guardian angel? Saints? Enlarged photographs of close family members? The son, father, grandson, grandfather who fell at the front? A landscape? A—memory?

And the endless stream pushed forward, step by step, everything and all bound together in the same slow pace, nobody rushed ahead, not even those who sat in vehicles, and they were mostly mothers, children, and old people. The stream moved quietly, united in a common rhythm, run by something like a central automatic system—like the wheels of an old, old mill that forever and ever methodically moves heavy stones in a circle.

A ghostly procession: no sound reached from it to the clattering train; the weary, even steps plodding steadily forward, the slowly turning wheels moving forward on their course, up hill, down hill the people trudged, the ghostly lines had no beginning and no end that could be seen. Whenever the train tracks crossed the road, then the long line of fugitives waited behind the barriers—reverently (this word popped into Ilse's head at the sight of the unemotional, patient, and exhausted faces). It was no great distance from the window of the compartment to those waiting behind the barriers. If the train had stopped, she could have asked them: "Have you been driven out?" Are you fleeing on your own volition? Where do you come from? Where are you going? The simple answer could be guessed: a shrug of the shoulders, the crack of a whip, a sigh: "From the east. To the west."

Twilight spread, the stream of fugitives was not victorious, everything was transformed into indistinct contours, into silhouettes, into shadows, which moved in lock step to the west, to the west . . . The darkness of the night came, the shadows contrived to move forward, the stream of humanity had no empty spaces, no end.

What might the fugitives be thinking at the sight of the train? Ilse asked herself. Mustn't they be astonished that there was a locomotive, a train, which transported people in the very direction from which they, step for step, tried with great effort to escape? No, they surely didn't think that, at most they were surprised at the fact that there was a train at all, and that it unfortunately wasn't traveling in their direction. They probably also regretted that they hadn't succeeded in crowding aboard one of the last trains west. But probably they no longer thought of any of those things, but simply walked, step by step, to the west, content to be part of a large group moving forward, and grateful not to be alone, not to have to confront this flight into uncertainty by themselves.

Ilse had felt pity during the day and also at dusk; pity, every time she picked out individuals amid the stream of fugitives. For example, the old woman in peasant clothes, leaning against the barriers: what circumstance, what providence had driven the peasant woman on this flight? "Providence," yes: that was surely involved somewhere, sometime. Once, in a pompous speech (had it been a speech of Hitler?—Ilse no longer remembered exactly)—this word had been spoken. Divine providence, the speaker had added, "Divine providence," which was granted to the German people, and which made it possible for this nation to embark on the course of the Thousand Year Reich—under this "Führer," who day and night on behalf of this unique and best of nations caused all other nations to worry. Perhaps—as said, Ilse no longer remembered all this so exactly, a thousand years is a long time, and now this era seemed to be drawing to its end—perhaps this very "Führer" had been speaking highly personally, thanking Divine Providence, which had given him this historical mission? Divine Providence, in any case! Had the simple peasant woman there, fleeing, been terribly impressed by the word "Divine"? Now, to be sure, she had to adapt to flight, driven out of her homeland somewhere in the east.

In the darkness, however, these individual figures merged, the stream of fugitives melded into a unity, into something whole, into a mass, whose submissive plodding grew into a mute accusation. This mass, this human procession became something powerful, something strong. It will teach us something, Ilse said to herself. I and my generation will hopefully never again give the slightest credence to words and phrases from above, no matter how beautiful and "Divine" they sound. No, she no longer felt any pity. Here, before her eyes, moved the remorseless procession of history. And hadn't Voltaire said that the history of humanity is nothing but a chain of deceit, crime, and intrigues? Yes, we have to be alert, she said to herself once, for we, the little people, we are the ones, who have to carry out the destiny of a nation, not the great people. And as long as we do not understand that, we have only ourselves to blame for our misery. At the same time, while Ilse, still standing at the compartment window, hardened herself against pity, her mind drifted off into completely different thoughts and feelings.

She didn't notice it right away, but wasn't a feeling of happiness rising up within her? Joy, of which she only now became conscious? Joy, very personal, very egotistical joy? A feeling of happiness that she owed to the sad, endless column of fugitives? For didn't the distant, quiet "valley of peace" in Salzburg recede into ever greater, insuperable distance, the further the train moved east? A human wall, a thick, tightly packed, majestic, ghostly procession of fugitives shoved itself in between, thousands upon thousands of people blocked and sealed the road, their road—back! To join this immense human serpentine of fugitives at the end of the column seemed even now to be an impossible task. How much more impossible would the departure from Vienna be on the next day or the day after that, after she had the desired document in her hand! Ilse felt confident that the fortress Vienna would snap shut. I will go to grandmother, she decided. And grandmother—she surely won't let me leave again.

And while Ilse leaned against the window of the compartment and continued looking out into the night, this great joy overcame her again: I'm free! I'm happy. I can now be myself. I am, so to speak, on vacation, on a splendid vacation. And with a sigh of relief, she said to herself: now, Vienna and war and Russians, I'll get through that. Somehow I'll live through everything, won't I?

Translated by Donald G. Daviau

Mr. Little's Last Days on the Job

Paulus Hochgatterer

Day One

IT is Thursday. This fact must be noted only because Mr. Little is convinced that it's Monday.

Mr. Little is eighty-two years old, about five feet eight inches tall, and weighs exactly 172 pounds. Everyone is weighed here at the time of admission.

Mr. Little is brought to us by his daughter who for fifty minutes recites the stock phrase that she just can't take living with her father any longer. All the people who bring their relatives to us recite the stock phrase that they just can't take it any longer. Our admitting physician is brief, as he always is when he can't expect relevant information either from the patient or from the person accompanying him.

Mr. Little had been living in town with his daughter ever since the death of his wife two years ago. Even before that he had shown signs of senility, the daughter says. Her mother was in much better health. She died quite unexpectedly from a stroke. Recently, in the middle of the night, he had knocked on the neighbors' doors and asked for a bottle of wine. He'd give them a decent tip, he had said. Twice that night he wet his pants. His daughter felt very badly about it, but she just couldn't take it any longer. She didn't want us to get the mistaken impression that her father had ever been an alcoholic.

That afternoon Mr. Little marches up and down the corridor at a speed and with a persistence that are remarkable when one considers his arthritic knee joints. He's looking for the Zurndorf train station. He can't imagine that no one can take him to the train station, and he is furious at the unanimity with which everyone insists they don't know any Zurndorf. He suspects a conspiracy.

Mr. Little's Last Days on the Job 113

Mr. Little has got to get to the train station right away so that he doesn't miss his train, because he's in danger of being late for work. Since he won't accept any of the rooms in his ward as the train station and grows ever more convinced of our maliciousness, he receives his first injection at 6:30 P.M. We allow the medication time to take effect. Mr. Little keeps looking for the Zurndorf train station and recognizes a fellow patient as the train dispatcher. The other patient denies it.

When the nurse on the night shift mentions that there probably is no such place as Zurndorf, Mr. Little flies into a rage.—"It's in Burgenland, you ninny!" he roars.

A second injection does the trick.

Day Two

Throughout the morning Mr. Little seems rather subdued. He urinates several times in the corridor, and after every incident he has to be put in a clean change of clothes. This doesn't keep him from continuing his zealous search for the Zurndorf train station. The head nurse, who was actually born in Burgenland, has never heard of Zurndorf.

In the meantime Mr. Little has become convinced that it's going to take him a little longer to get to work today. He has outfitted himself with a hard roll and a bottle of mineral water.

Under normal conditions the train ride takes twenty-one minutes, he says. He doesn't have to worry about being fired, his boss needs him. Nevertheless, we don't have the right to keep him from getting to work.

A nurse sells Mr. Little a tiny stamped slip of paper as a ticket. He shows it to every patient he thinks might be the conductor. A bit later he smashes the bottle of mineral water against the wall.

In the restraining bed, he yells for an hour, alternating two sentences: You can't mess around with me! and: Bring me a pack of twelve-inch spikes!

Day Three

When asked if he slept well, Mr. Little says: He who works a lot, always sleep well. He even slept well in the Siberian swamps.

Today our psychologist started his Reality Training. Mr. Little realized immediately that she didn't know where Zurndorf was and couldn't cope with his request for a pack of twelve-inch spikes and a two-pound sledgehammer.—Do you think doctors and nurses generally spend their time in train stations? she asks him.—The doctor from Zurndorf always takes the train, he says. Afterwards he complains that the cigarette girl wouldn't sell him his favorite brand; besides, she didn't have an appreciation for real work.

I ask him which company he's working for these days.—Gruber, in Eisenstadt, he says.

Carpentry work? I inquire. At first he looks astonished, then bawls at me: You think we're watchmakers or something?!

I am almost on the verge of apologizing.

When he gets the ground veal and mashed potatoes for lunch, Mr. Little empties it all in the wastepaper basket. That stuff is for toothless old geezers, that's what he thinks.

It's easy to recognize the Zurndorf train station by the two ancient grapevines that wind their way up the two columns of the canopy.

Day Four

Three twelve-inch spikes must weigh a total of almost two pounds. I finally found them in the fourth hardware store.—Are you a carpenter? the salesman asked me.

Took you long enough, Mr. Little says. Otherwise he seems to be satisfied. The wood for the rafters is basically sound, he won't need more than three spikes.

I ask him where the construction site is. He gazes at me for a long time, with consternation. These young apprentices nowadays just don't cut the mustard, he finally says. For a whole week now I've been going with him to the same construction site, and I still don't know where it is.—No work ethic, he says, no real interest in the job.

Then we're off to the Zurndorf train station. On the way we meet the psychologist. She is obviously impressed by the twelve-inch spikes.—Lethal weapons, she says.

Today's Reality Training lasts exactly ten minutes. Mr. Little is returned to the ward by two attendants.—Brainwashing! he roars, Siberia! In the psychologist's opinion, he doesn't want to accept the fact that he is in a hospital.

Does he mean the construction site in Bruckneudorf? I ask.—The city hall, he says, that was before the war. A beautiful roof truss, he says, six dormer windows, but the wood was green, just cut the end of

Mr. Little's Last Days on the Job   115

February, and hadn't even been seasoned for six months. We didn't have dry kilns back then.—A quick job, Mr. Little says, you know what I mean?

While he's sleeping, Mr. Little's face has an expression of concentration. He holds the spikes tightly in his fists.

Day Five

In cases of senile dementia, the brain shrinks, our Medical Director says. The colleagues who are accompanying him on his rounds nod their heads in agreement.

22, 24, and 26 Schüttel Street, Mr. Little says, second district in Vienna; three buildings in a row, an American bombing raid.—Were the roofs a total loss? I ask him.—Like Swiss cheese, he says, had to be completely redone.

Smoked tripe and radishes, he always eats smoked tripe and radishes on his afternoon break. It's nine o'clock in the morning.—Like a bricklayer, the Medical Director says.

Perhaps this is one way to achieve an improvement in his temporal orientation, the psychologist thinks.

After lunch Mr. Little asks me when the next train is leaving.

The handle on the two-pound sledgehammer is splintered, I tell him, I don't know what to do.—I'll have to report that to the boss tomorrow, Mr. Little says, he'll give me a replacement.

A new two-pound sledgehammer costs $25, I found that out yesterday.

Some demented people are happy in their little world, the Medical Director says.

Day Six

This morning Mr. Little kisses a woman patient goodbye.—It's going to take a little longer today, he says. The woman patient doesn't mind.

The doctors are considering changing his medication.

Mr. Little is now wearing incontinent briefs. It has become very dangerous for the other patients who might slip in his urine puddles and break their hips. The doctors are delaying the insertion of a permanent catheter. Even the weakest bladder ought to be given a chance, the doctors say.

Five-by-fives for the rafters, Mr. Little says. Of course it's the latest thing to just use four-by-fours for the rafters, but a five-by-five is just that much stronger because of the extra inch. Never underestimate the weight of the roofing tiles.—Viennese pockets, Mr. Little says, double roofing; if you're doing Viennese pockets, only five-by-fives'll do, and don't you forget it.

I could retrain as a carpenter.

In Physical Therapy, Mr. Little is supposed to paint a picture. He shreds a drawing pad and throws several jars of paint on the floor.—What makes you think I'm a painter?! he yells.—Completely maladjusted, the psychologist says.

Who's taking care of the block and tackle? I ask.—Well, do you think I'm just standing around here, twiddling my thumbs?! Mr. Little says.

Day Seven

I get Mr. Little out of the restraining bed. In the middle of the night he reportedly beat on the corridor mirror like a madman with a twelve-inch spike. No one has been able to find the other two spikes.—A lethal weapon, the psychologist says.

I ask Mr. Little what happened. A burglar, he says, a construction site thief, but he chased him away.—I've seen him before, he says.—In Zurndorf? I ask. He is amazed: How did you know that?

Mr. Little receives a visit from his daughter. What's she doing around here, he asks, can't she find anything to do around the house? His daughter is shocked.—He's living in his own little world, she says.—I refrain from asking her: Where else would you expect?—And you can just take those bananas back with you! Mr. Little says, since when do I like bananas?

In the Mini-Mental-Test, Mr. Little gets twelve points out of a possible thirty. Among other things, he cannot reproduce a drawing of two overlapping pentagons.—Significant loss of spatial perception, the psychologist reports. When required to follow the written instruction: Close your eyes!, he refused, arguing: And what's going to happen when I fall down?—As noted: significant loss of spatial perception, the psychologist says and anxiously wrinkles her brow.

Seventy-two hundred running feet of five-by-fives, I report to Mr. Little, according to our calculations, each between twenty-seven and

thirty feet long, material surplus already figured in.
He ordered the crossbeams himself, Mr. Little says, eighteen-by-twelve, practically without knotholes. In addition, he's going to lodge a complaint with the stationmaster about the rudeness of the employees. You can always recognize the Zurndorf train station by the two grapevines, he says.

Day Eight

Today Mr. Little is possessed by an unusual restlessness. According to reports, it all started at 5 A.M. when he got completely dressed all by himself, which he had not been able to do thus far.—Without incontinent briefs, of course, the night nurse says.

Did you guys also get enough six-inch nails? he asks me. Just being short of a couple of lousy little six-inch nails can cause big problems.—We've still got thirty pounds, I tell him.—That's cutting it close, he says.

Bowlegged, he runs up and down the corridor, swinging a bottle of mineral water in each hand.

Some days medication simply doesn't work, the Medical Director mutters.

He asks if I've double-checked the crossbeams. Asks if there just might be a splintered beam in the pile.—A cheap clawhammer, the handle gets bent, and next thing you know we're a day behind schedule, Mr. Little says.

The psychologist relates his response to the question: How many siblings do you have? He answered: Twenty-seven feet, eight inches. In addition, he thought she was a secretary and accused her of making a mistake and shortchanging him on his last paycheck; he'll have to take it up with the boss. He almost had her worried, she says and laughs.

You don't eat until the work's done, Mr. Little says and even throws other peoples' hotdogs into the toilet.

A nurse asks him if he'd like a bottle of wine.—I can't afford to in my profession, Mr. Little says, in my profession that can cost you your life.

When you're buying nails, you've got to pay damn close attention. You should only buy finishing nails. There's a cheap imported product that's covered with a horrible black grease.—You can save a couple of bucks, Mr. Little says, and lose all the pleasure in your work.

Day Nine

    Today is Friday. Mr. Little probably would have thought today was Monday. Mr. Little died early this morning, sometime between the last round of the night shift and the shift change. Up until midnight he was marching around, giving orders to imaginary people, the night nurse told me, he spent about ten minutes looking for the train station, afterwards he just lay in bed, completely calm.

    There aren't many causes for a death of this kind: stroke, maybe, or an embolism on the lungs. I think it would have been better if he'd fallen off some rooftop.

    I think today would have been our topping-out ceremony.

    While changing the sheets on his bed, we find two twelve-inch spikes in a corner of the mattress.

Translated by Todd C. Hanlin

WITH LOVE FROM INSPECTOR 19

KONSTANTIN KAISER

*W*ITH *Love from Inspector 19* was written on the small packing slip about the size of a calling card that some men found in the packs of their Egyptian brand cigarettes. There could be no question of an advertising gimmick; INSPECTOR 19 was printed in distinct letters in the middle of the little piece of paper, the salutation "With love" had been written above it in ink.

Several of the men hid the slips immediately because they feared having to give explanations. Others didn't even notice the handwritten addition. But there were also some whose fantasy was stimulated. The very fact that a package closed on all sides and sealed with a tax stamp contained a foreign entity aroused one's imagination. By unknown means it had penetrated through the paper sides and nestled amid the uniformly shaped objects—cigarettes. At this point a slight feeling of suspicion entered into the excited man's imagination, and he inspected the cigarettes to see if they contained regular tobacco. Once he had convinced himself of that, he came—after further consideration that took place, so to speak, in the back of his mind—to the idea that the little slip of paper must have been inserted before the cigarette pack was sealed at the factory. And he thought of the young girls who were enclosed inside the high, cold cement walls of the factories; he could feel on his tongue the peculiar taste of a strange, yet pleasant stimulus. A little slip of paper in a package became a symbol for a young, pale creature, with glances peering out from big dark eyes like hands stretched out through the metal bars of a gate of misery. And the number 19—wasn't it a girlish number, slender and strong and nevertheless rounded, different than the 8 in its all too opulent femininity.

To be sure the number had been printed in advance and was obviously used to designate a specific work station at the packing table, regardless of the person. But why shouldn't it be an indication of the sender's age? The most obvious interpretation could certainly coincide with chance. It was probably thoughts like this and others that caused our gentleman to make inquiries with the administration of the tobacco company.

Two weeks later came the answer. The matter did in fact involve a very charming girl with brown, curly hair who had allowed herself a little prank which one could overlook, could allow. She was a neat, pretty thing, representative, as one must imagine, of all the women who made up the army of tender fingers which packed the cigarettes. To be sure the act reflected individuality, capriciousness, which normally must not occur.... Yet the person concerned, who at the worst would have been given a warning, had in the meantime given up her job at the tobacco factory in order to follow her young husband to another part of the country, to the sincere regret of her coworkers and supervisors, who held her congenial, helpful manner in pleasant memory... Before she explained herself, the packer, who on the basis of her control number was questioned, had after a short conversation in the department head's office ("Why did you do that? Was this directed to anyone we know?" he asked, looked into her blue eyes that seemed to be covered by a shimmering veil, and asked no more.) gathered her few things together, turned in her blue work apron to the foreman, and bid farewell to her coworkers who looked up briefly from their work. The dismissal had been made effective at once. The productivity of the other women employees fell off quickly. By chance this woman worker came into our story. What should we do? And what about the "charming brown-haired girl?" Is she as a lie transformed into a ghost, still roaming through the spring boulevards? Perhaps she is now wearing chestnut blossoms in her hair, dancing with wisps of fog in the treetops—searching for the sheen of your silk tie?

Translated by Donald G. Daviau

ALMA

Marie-Thérèse Kerschbaumer

BARONESS ALMA JOHANNA VON EHRENFELS
Née Koenig, Pseudonym Johannes Herdan,
Alma Johanna Koenig
Born: August 18, 1887 in Prague
Deported: May 27, 1942 (Minsk Ghetto)
Missing since 1942

SO you say she has returned, Alma Johanna, from a long trip, you say; Alma Johanna is back. I saw a light in her apartment. A shimmer of light came through the kitchen curtains, through the window in the corridor. The bathroom is in back. Kitchen and bathroom were seldom separate in these old houses. Alma Johanna—it has been thirty years since then—they took her away when she was having breakfast (O. said), simply took her from her breakfast in the summer, in the early summer. No, it was winter, a cold, gray, winter morning. Johanna is in the bathroom. (There's a knock at the door.) Listen, footsteps. No, Anna was standing outside, the old woman. Or couldn't Giovanna finish her breakfast? She hadn't finished it (once in May), the pot of coffee, the rolls (actually there weren't any), bread, awful, gummy, expensive bread. She placed the wartime bread, the winter bread on her plate with trembling fingers, but they were probably not trembling with the cold in those unheated rooms with the high windows and the old stoves. There had been nothing all winter that Alma Johanna could have used to warm her soul. Knit mittens, knit socks, winter aid for Giovanna's trembling fingers. Who would have wanted to cover Giovanna's fingers in those days? Who had the courage to wrap their hands around Alma's frozen fingers? There was a war going on, and everyone had something to be afraid of. (Everyone?) Everyone. Even the janitor, the block warden, the watchman nods and points upstairs with his thumb, with his index finger. Everyone walks past Alma's door with its brass plate brightly polished, scrubbed clean. Who bothers to scrub things clean in these brown times? Don't you know? Don't talk so loud. Who wants to hear those things after all these years? Nobody wants to hear where they took Alma, during breakfast at five. A poet usually lingers over breakfast in the morning, with a notebook on her lap and the lamp—or was it a candle—in front of her. (Did they really have candles in those dark days?) It was winter, even if it was early summer, and in the cold hours of morning (of murdering?), with the laboriously scrounged, gummy, wartime bread between her teeth and her notes before her in her lap—to have written a book, to have planted a tree, to have given birth to a child (you accomplished only one of those things, Giovanna)—sitting at breakfast. (Were you lying down?) Were you on your knees, Giovanna, and did you pray half the night? To whom would you pray in the winter? Unheated rooms, much too high for war, much too dark for peace; with curtains and wallpaper that were much too stained. You spent your whole life in Vienna, in this city, your whole life in Austria, in this country, your whole life as a stranger among the people.

My Lord, what are you talking about? Neighbor, what are you talking about? You've been watching too much television. You've let yourself be brainwashed. You saw a film from that time. Sure, the war was going on, but the fashions, but the hats, but the music. (That was forbidden, stupid woman!) You heard music on the radio, listened to the news on the radio, received an important message on the radio. Be careful, Alma Viva. The stairs will not creak softly. (Boots do not squeak in the city.) No stairs, no steps creak—in the city stairs reverberate (and so do corridors with pounding footsteps) beneath the tread of the troops.

When I wake up at night, I always turn the light on in my sleep—I light the candle. During this blackout no light escapes into the night through the cracks, through the windows. And I pick up a notebook and write down the dream, the word, the thought, the fantastic dream image, the incomprehensible word. I make notes and lie down again on the bed, my resting place, my couch. (In the camp, did you say?) Which is it, bed or camp? I mean pillows. The bed sheets are tattered in this war. I make notes and close the booklet, the notebook, lonely in my bare, plundered rooms. (Plundered?) Oh, now and then you handed out something of value and politely said "You're welcome," and were courteous. You hid and you walked through the streets afraid, o Alma, Giovanna, Regina!

With her hair pinned up, her soul startled, while the siren sang, she followed the footsteps, went to the cellar. They made room. She said, "Excuse me," begged their pardon, remained steadfast. That's the expression; in all these things she remained steadfast. Breakfast! Just who would have had breakfast one last time? Who thought about breakfast in the tunnel, in the mountain, when they went into the mountain with bag and baggage and immediately fainted because of the lack of oxygen, because of the closeness of the many people, near the mothers, the sleeping (sleeping?) children. We thought of the heroes. (Really? did we think?) And didn't my son die, too, and didn't I wear the cross, the Mother's Cross around my neck? Neighbor woman, you never had six children, three at the most, so that they could be slaughtered all the faster. My good woman, have you gone crazy? A criminal, a ne'er-do-well, as he proved to be, was sent to the camp for rehabilitation. Now you remain silent, you're quiet and unwilling, you refuse to give information. Sister-in-law, if you had only remained silent, refused back then, having married into the family, having gotten pregnant, yes, pregnant, the way you did! But who still wants to talk about it these days, with all this abundance, with all the beautiful things, with all the beautiful colors, with all this beautiful stuff? When people are already talking about a third car, they don't talk about the ones who have nothing to say. "But back then, those were the days," he says, "when I fired my slingshot from the garden and hit the Jew's daughter in the cherry tree. Think of it, a stone with my slingshot! And the Jewish girl looked startled, didn't know what hit her, sitting in the cher-cher-cherry tree, the Jewish girl in the cherry tree, the Jewish girl during the war." Hit her with your slingshot, you say? The trees are no longer standing, the victims no longer walk. They built an apartment house in the Jew's old garden. (Or do you have something against that?) Back then a Bohemian tailor bought it. He's no longer alive, either. She sold the ground for a lot of money. Children were not permitted to play in the garden after that, still aren't, even now, only the poodle. And the tailor's widow had the walnut tree cut down because of the tax. And the way she broke the apricot tree, broke off the main branch, hanging from it with her face contorted! What a spectacle! After the war, the Jew's son visited us once more, very secretly. Yes, those were the days. "If I had hit her, the Jewish girl in the tree," he says, "think of the trouble it would have caused my father. He had just gone bankrupt. Great! Zing! The stone whizzed across the hedge where the concrete playground is now. A barber had just acquired the ground-floor apartment for a large fee. He was the owner of the two poodles that were permitted to play in the garden. Zing, over the hedge and into the cherry tree, where it hit the Jewish girl right in the neck." The Jewish girl is gone, my youth is gone, forever, gone forever. Moved away, Alma Giovanna. It says Sold on the door plate, Confiscated above the little plaque that was rubbed clean by hardworking hands. (Rubbed his hands? The Bohemian tailor rubbed his hands? And we?) And what about us?

She was always there, that good soul, Anna: Anna the cook, Anna the servant, a companion to her mother, Pepi, old Pepi, her mother's companion, old, half-blind Anna, she (with the characteristic article). Trembling, Anna, the half-blind woman, dips her red hands into the dirty rinse water. She cleans everything so well, she makes everything so clean. "How do you do that," I ask Anna, "when you really can't see well enough?"

"I feel with my fingers. I simply feel along the dishes with the tips of my fingers, to see if they are clean and smooth. That works wonderfully well."

Where was Anna when it was still dark on that morning in the late autumn, in the winter? No, it was the early summer. The rooms with their high ceilings were unheated. For days the atmosphere had been eerie on the streets, in the alleys, in the marketplaces of Vienna. For days, for weeks, for months there had been the endless freight trains, the long columns, the vehicles, the sealed freight cars. Where was Anna, her mother's blind, half-blind kitchen servant (blinded?), a nation blinded? Where was the aging maid servant? Yes, Anna, I refer to Anna. They say she came by at the time. They say she gave warning. They say she scurried by at five in the morning. "Child, what are you still doing here?" Anna supposedly said.

"Let me be, Anna. I haven't hurt anyone. Are you crazy?"

Anna was already dead by then. Besides that, she wasn't blind, but deaf. At least she was hard of hearing, completely deaf in one ear.

The doorbells in the old houses out in the country, actually villas with at most one family per floor—the privy councilor lived there. There was an old bell on a cord (with the cord? strangled?), a bell on a cord. On the pole a little bell rings, reminds us of monastery gates and similar places, an iron pole. The cord is pulled cautiously, the bell rings in the vestibule, a door opens. (Does it open?) The steps are mottled, mottled stone, mottled and glistening, not the kind of patterns they have in Vienna, or perhaps they are, if we are reminded of Roman villas, Carnuntum, Petronell, Anima Alma. (Ancora viva?) That was much later. Carnuntum was after the war and has nothing at all to do with Giovanna. That was another woman, and again and again we have these stereotypical, these typical repetitions of words. Otherwise there's nothing new. Oh yes there is, a renter. An older lady? It's hard to say. She's not really an old woman, but she's unapproachable. She lives next door, reminds me of somebody. I've seen her someplace before. That's right, you know, the poet on the fourth floor, on the left. It was during the war.

Just why are you whispering? Am I deaf? Who whispers to the deaf? To the mute, with voices, at most there is the whispering of doves, early in the morning at four, at five, when the others are still asleep in their beds. The doves whisper up high under the eaves: Where is Alma? I wouldn't call it whispering. By the way, she doesn't feed the doves, she's not one of those, old, but lonely. (Is that supposed to be a contradiction?) Yes, of course, a different type. Somehow it's peculiar to find such a renter in that house. Which house are you talking about, anyway? The one across the street? That's been gone for a long time. Of course, a renter without dependents; she washes her stockings daily, violently, and her other things twice a week. Yes, yes, unbelievable, the back room, with the corridor window, admittedly small, and with the unmistakable scent of the old, ornate rooms where old maids live in Vienna.

You say, the new woman is elderly and looks so peculiar? How so? Can't anyone explain that to me? What excites you, the similarity? And she has returned, she's back, and I'm supposed to believe that such a thing can happen? Should we change? What for? Weren't we all in danger? Didn't we all experience the nightly false—and then no longer false alarms, warnings, and the hiding from the air raids? Now I've had enough of that topic. And you also know she didn't go along anymore at the end, perhaps because we made it clear to her that we didn't want her. But what difference does it make? She sat up there alone, and out of pride she didn't tremble. That's all.

Proud decisions, back then. Just who could decide so quickly? It was hard enough, having nothing in common with them, robbed of any natural historical development and not good enough for the critics, and hardly mentioned in literary history. It was because of her youth. It was because of her childhood. It was because of her maturity.

Hidden up in the attic, living as a submarine—because form is not an idea but a thing (criticism can say a thing or two about that)—the poet has things in front of him, objects, realities, not ideas. He lives very concretely as a submarine in Vienna, and doesn't walk around too much, and doesn't drink too much liquid, and gives a friendly person something of value now and then, so that he can betray us all the more easily. But bourgeois criticism does not like it at all, because form arises from the content, and if we do not like the content, we smash the form, and thus we write about the officially accepted art that covers up all unpleasant contents with a hypocritical veil.

So Alma was alone and yet in the best of company. And nothing has changed about that to this very day. That's the way it was, yes, that's even the way it could have been.

After all, consider what we read, consider what we wrote, what then remained as—they call it sunken cultural heritage—which then haunts our vocabulary. We couldn't have known, we say, and we think that the others after us don't want to know. And because it was not honestly overcome but half-heartedly covered up, there was simply a chasm there, between the artists and historical reality, and sometimes reality caught up with the artists or called them home.

"Silence is complicity," said the deaf woman, the old woman, the woman up in the attic.

It's so hard for us not to be blind, Anna, not to be deaf, Anna. At five in the morning a poet crouched on bended knees with her notebook. She watched, she prayed, she wrote during the night. She was never silent.

Translated by Lowell A. Bangerter

MIDSUMMER NIGHT

ULRIKE KLEPALSKI

JOHANNA picks up the animal, its nose feels dry and hot, so do the pads of its paws. Since it is meowing in a low, plaintive voice, she helplessly lets it slide to the floor and decides to go to the Neunerwald; she puts on the red polka-dot shoes which supposedly make the earth tremble and whose soles defy gravity. Johanna arms herself with courage, the fear of encountering the fear, of counterattacking it. A beetle with a pageboy haircut assists her loud whistling with his singing about a Numero Nine. Johanna has to hike down some loops, a long incline, a fat little bend to the left, and she seems unable to find her way out of the cursed nine's encirclement, always returning to the starting point where there is an arrow carved out of a piece of bark in which the hardly legible hieroglyphics "Trail No. 9" are engraved. Thick black and gray rain clouds race across the sky, a strong wind starts to howl. Finally, she reaches the jungle. Dark lush green, moss-covered rock formations, vines hanging from dead giants present a flattering backdrop for the burned tree ruins, overgrown with poisonous mistletoe, threatening looking in their hollowness. Not only lightning has raged here. Wet and muddy dark brown paths, well-trodden by many horseshoes, direct her steps, the mud attaches itself to her shoes, making slurping sounds. Otherwise all is quiet. Suddenly two strange, wiry, little men appear from nowhere: their elbows and parts of their upper and lower arms are tightly bound with orange cuffs, from which tubes lead to compasslike instruments which the little men hold in their hands. Both move forward at an uncannily constant speed, making predictable, precisely calculated movements. Wires hanging from their ears are also connected to the cuffs. Johanna stops. She lets the two of them pass. They appear angry, hissing strangely. Johanna decides to rest a few minutes, to stay right where she is. Thirsty, she bites into the apple which until now has weighed down the left pocket of her jacket. Johanna loves to plow her teeth into big apples, like a mole through the dirt. The little men disappear around the bend farther down in the path. Johanna is alone, occupied only in eating her apple. Slowly everything around her disappears. She feels as if she will never want to, will never be able to get up again, let alone move on. Suddenly she hears women's voices, one, curiously hollow and deep, says: "The secret is in the documentation. Every being has its historicity. You can believe me there, my dear. I speak from experience. And my experience goes back a long, long way." During the last words the voice takes on a somewhat solemn tone. "But then you can't remember, of course, how could you? My experience dates back to a time when you weren't even in diapers!" At that point the voice sounded rather condescending. The other female voice, forcing back her impatience only with difficulty, was indignant: "Well, listen, my dear, you still can't do it like that. It will never work. All that theoretical fuss! And then, look, it may be decorative, but it is impractical, highly impractical. I tell you, one thing after another and short seminars, easily understandable guidelines for the general public . . . ." Johanna can't understand the rest of the sentence. She sees only the trace of a faded string, which seems to lead to a ball that the second of the two passing ladies is carrying in her right hand. But by then they have already disappeared. It must have been the goddesses Praxis and Historia. Johanna rouses herself to move on. When she comes to the bend in the road behind which the two little men have vanished, she notices an overgrown path, barely visible. She decides to follow it, and after a short time she comes to a clearing and a pond, mysteriously cloudy, but with shimmering water where white and peach-colored blossoms are swimming like open orange peels; strings of dust and silvery shining leaves lie softly and weightlessly on the reflecting surface. Willows with deep hanging snake arms are crying little lancet-shaped tears. Johanna carefully moves closer, but not without some trepidation. Not a sound, not even a breath of air is stirring. Could she catch such a blossom? But isn't that a shallop floating on the water there? Isn't it the mystery person from the park? Spellbound, she stands still and closes her eyes.

When she opens her eyes again, patches of sunshine are falling through the trees onto the silky grass, creating various tones of shimmering green. A swan family is bathing in a smaller pond. Protected by mama and papa, fluffy ducklings with eggshell-colored feathers are eagerly eating leaves. Reassured, Johanna sinks down. Very tired now, she is going to sleep a little.

Johanna's eyes look into a boundless sea of pallid blue that stare back at her in nameless loneliness. She is in a room in an old, somewhat run-down building in an exclusive residential district of a medium-sized industrial town in the west of the country. She has just washed herself at a washbasin filled with cold water and has dressed for work. Before she leaves the room by way of the steep, squeaky wooden staircase, she glances at the windowpane that serves as a mirror, halfway by accident, but also to make sure that the horses are still standing in the parking lot in front of the indoor swimming pool. There she notices a darting movement, a shimmering flash. Blinded and quickly turning away, she finally drives to the elementary school at the other end of town. The next night Johanna has a dream. Countless pasty, gray men's hands with long spiderlike fingers reach for her. Instead of fingernails they have suckers with lashes and blank pupils the size of a pinhead, which stare at her menacingly. She starts to shake wildly, wants to run, to flee, but cannot move, she's stuck. Her feet and legs are held in a vise, something pulling at her trunk starts to dig into her lower body. A babbling, tinny-sounding singsong can be heard: "Mrs. Meiiier, Mrs. Meiiier! She's wearing yellow underpants. With pink bows! Mrs. Meiiier, Mrs. Meiiier . . . " Desperately, Johanna gasps for air. She's in danger of choking. Bathed in sweat, she wakes up screaming and then lies there quietly for a second under a heavy quilt in a wide double bed opposite a window darkened by the night, which catches the pallid shimmer of neon light. Then she finds herself sitting in the grass beside a narrow path running along a river bend. Not far from her a man with a fishing rod sits motionless. From far away she hears the loud, drunken voice of Mr. Meier: "Ladies and Gentlemen! Our keg isn't empty yet. In the last fifteen minutes up until 3 PM a glass of beer costs only fifteen alpine dollars. A one-time opportunity! After that we shut off the tap!"

Does the fisherman come here every day? Even when it rains? While wondering what could be most important for fishing—the fishing rod, the water, or the fish—Johanna falls asleep again. Weighted down, she hikes up to a crossroad with great difficulty: a spastic man is riding on her back, beating her with a stick. Her limbs are hurting, her shoes are getting heavier and heavier, pulling her down. A red field poppy, wrinkled, not yet opened, persuades her not to give up. The refreshing smell of camomile and woodruff consoles her, revives her. But there is the mean, drunken voice again: "What an asshole! Did you see that? It's crazy. No need to talk about it. What an asshole. And now, yeaaah!

Gooooo!!!" Now the spastic is walking in front of her on a straight gray dirt road covered with shreds of paper shining in the bright sunlight. Bluish-purple shimmering train tracks run right down its middle. Beating the stick in a staccato manner, waving it in front, the man cannot run fast enough. After she catches up and tries to pass him, he suddenly walks very slowly. She should have stayed at the clearing, should have taken a bath in the friendly water. It smells like orange blossoms and oil of bergamot. Johanna blows transparent, shiny green and white bubbles in the air. The tomcat catches them with great delight, alternating between his paw and his black, wet shimmering nose, pushing them away or playing with them like a seal at the circus. A stern, thunderous voice speaks: "Are poisoned springs necessary, and are stinking fires and soiled dreams and maggots in the bread of life?"[1] "I don't know, Mr. Zarathustra. Please, don't be angry with me, I really don't know!" Johanna wakes up, it's night again. She had dreamed of grinning men contemptuously dressed in green and white, with shrill whistling pipes in their black-painted mouths, who were dragging a small, dark-skinned girl by her long, frizzy hair, rolling her out of an eggshell colored sari, laying her on a pile of wood to be sacrificed. All the while, the green and white men were spreading their fingers of both hands and were making guttural noises that reminded the little girl of the language she had learned at the lycée.

The next night Johanna had to run from a pharmacist with an excited cobra wrapped around his body. But she could not move. When the man in the white coat with the living belt, poised to strike, grabbed at her, he changed into a woman, a chemist. As such she was wearing a white coat. She said she was a sorceress. She grinned in evil triumph and pointed a long, thin cane at a grandfather clock hanging above her on a rope, ticking loudly: "This is my magic box!" Johanna started to cry. She continued to cry because the tomcat, Professor Corn Poppy, was lying in the street with a broken neck. His little heart pulsed red in his throat. He writhed and purred loudly: "It whispers and lisps and giggles, a lecherous scream echoes in the ether: 'I'm swimming in the sea and a stream of shit, a bulging rectum of packaged shit is approaching, floating toward me, threatening to drown me!' Fellow students lisp nasally through their upturned noses, like first year students, they shat

---

[1] Friedrich Nietzsche, *Thus Spake Zarathustra*.

their mothers from their bodies." Johanna understands his purry-purr and joins in a few beats later, her clear voice accompanying his throaty sounds: The raging, roaring, green and white foaming, storm-beaten sea is carrying the cargo ship loaded with a gray, clumsy mass of unidentifiable, immobile goods, visible only in a blur; sailors with Chinese faces, who turn out to be book- and newspaper binders working on giant printing presses, shepherd Johanna into the harbor of the medieval city. Many, many people in knee-breeches hurry by. Johanna is constipated. Professor Corn Poppy rises from the puddle of blood in the street, unhurt, and turns around the corner with his tail up high.

The next night, a murder was committed. A wild woman seized the stubbornly erect, obstinately raised head with its dented and stretched backside by short, gray patches of hair, tore and pulled on it, grabbed the stiff, stretched out, turning neck by her bare teeth, shook it and battered it, her saliva dripping, until the head finally separated from its torso. Blood was dripping from the retracted flews of the raging beast. Like a fury she trampled on the hated sphere, kicked it and hurled it to and fro. The face could not be discerned any longer; exhausted, she dug her twitching feet into the mushy mass. She crouched on the naked, cold earth, her eyes staring at the floor, at the horrifying mass; never again would she be able to look into eyes which are knowing and alive.

Not knowing how much time has gone by, Johanna sits, staring blankly into space. All of a sudden she knows that she isn't alone. Beings populate the space around her, beings who are known to her. Eight yellow-faced animals reach for her with countless tentacles, ridicule her with green lips, utter hissing sounds veiled in smoke from the canulas of their larynx holes. They swirl and wave their habits, enticingly lifting their tent-like robes. "Come, Johanna, come, a protective umbrella awaits you here with us!" In addition to the tempting promises, the animals throw little round white wafers at her. The wafers are grooved in the middle where they break and this white candy multiplies with great speed. Hesitant at first, than greedily, the woman in her numb desperation reaches for them, puts the white pieces to her lips, pushes the little sweets into her mouth by the handful. When Johanna attempts to swallow, a noose closes around her throat, her tongue starts to swell. An extremely bitter torrent rises up inside her. Her eyes are stuck in her throat, they burn like open wounds being carved up by sharp knives. She wakes up sobbing, rolling in a salty flood of tears streaming relentlessly from her eyes.

When she goes to buy croissants and flat bread from the Turkish baker, he points his finger at a man in the street, then points his finger to his forehead, making a tapping motion. Johanna shrugs her shoulders. The man who always stands in the street is standing in the street again. The black furry, primeval animal with shovel-like antlers stands beside him and sings a *laudatio* to the intellect of the men of the machine, to the invulnerable, unknown fighter whom nobody knows. The other woman joins in, her falsetto warbles an ode of joy to the spark of the halogen lamp. Johanna becomes catatonic, curses technology. The Council of Three conducts a debate:[2] the first man looks a little like one of the Three Musketeers with his slightly wavy, shoulder-length, dark hair cut in the style of a pageboy. He has a mustache under his nose, pointing skeptically downwards like the corners of his mouth—a line which turns into a plane, covering both sides of the lower half of his face. With half shut eyes, he says in French: "The soul is not located in the throat, but to the contrary, has its home in the pineal gland. Alors—thus, this gland is called the metaphysical gland." The second—a man with short, fair, equally wavy hair and a long beard, with the features of a reformed man, full lips, honest looking eyes, the Greek nose of a refined hedonist—says quietly and rationally: "Only moral behavior brings pleasure!" He adds with a superior smile: "Know thyself, knowledge is the way to happiness." A third man approaches. His gaunt face reveals itself as the face of a dying man. His arrival in the old-fashioned coffeehouse next to the pharmacy in the street at the foot of the earthen mountain seems to frighten the second man. Demurring, the newcomer keeps his hands raised and utters imploringly: "As long as I'm here, death is not here!" but then, contemplating, he adds, "And as soon as death is here, I won't be here anymore." The third man, the one with the face of a dying man, leads a little man by the hand from whom a ticking sound is emanating. The little man bows: "Allow me to introduce myself, my name is Enormon, my soul lives in my brain, tick tock." The man leading the little man by the hand looks at him sternly and admonishes him: "Behave yourself!" Finally, he informs the first and the second man: "Believe me, everything interacts! The mainsprings of human life function according to the principal of the human clock rewinding itself." Johanna is nearly convinced; the primeval black furry animal roars. And

---

[2] Descartes, Epicurus, Hippocrates.

Professor Corn Poppy is there too, chasing the little man. But perhaps they are only playing tag.

Translated by Helga Schreckenberger and Jacqueline Vansant

KING SEPP

WALTER KLIER

THEY filled him with schnapps until his face swelled into a bluish-red hemisphere and he was able to stand again, stuffed him into the Mercedes, and drove to Ausserdorf. On the outskirts of town the traffic jam, the concert of automobile horns, the pennants on the houses. We have three more villages today. Along the streets young people, small flags in the wind, jubilation, the little faces looking forward to the future—we will send you into the next war. This heat all the time, crazy. On the village square riflemen, a band, the silver television vehicles. The inconspicuous men in civilian clothing were taking pictures for their card index. The band played "The Old Comrade" and the Radetzky march. They heaved him from the car and stood him on his feet. Kien gave him the two thousand-Schilling banknotes. They were visible from a long distance as he held them tightly behind his back. He started toward the speaker's desk. A huge man with a black beard down to his navel, who looked like Andreas Hofer [the Tyrolean freedom fighter], grasped Sepp's free right hand and kissed it. Sepp bowed slightly and nearly fell over in the process. The pseudo-Andreas Hofer said, "Hello! Welcome to Haslach! So, have you ever been to Haslach before? I'm grateful and at the same time proud that you were able to come, with the schedule that you have." He shouted into the microphone, "We consider ourselves fortunate to have in our humble community today . . . ," and then he made a short speech.

The king stood on the lee side of the speaker, next to the young girl who would subsequently recite the little poem and hand him the bouquet of mountain flowers that she herself had picked. The band played the mountain-climber song; he hummed along to himself: "The world is really so large and wide." His hand wormed its way up beneath her dress from behind. He no longer sees very well, of course. She dropped the flowers and hid behind the band. The man with the full beard said, "Our community can look back on a proud and grateful collaboration. Just consider the ready-mixed concrete we're standing on here today."

In spite of his filled-up legs, he wobbled a little bit. A charming girl served him the schnapps. He said, "Well, it's about time," smiled broadly, and tipped the glass into his barely open, turtlelike mouth. Later there will be something to eat in the old post office. A soft burning moves pleasantly down his throat—the speeches all day dry out your mouth like crazy. Put the thousand-Schilling note in the hand of the right person. "We have three more villages. We're late," said Kluibenschädl, the loyal chauffeur.

Together they lifted him out of the car. The television people were already there. The mayor, in his well-filled Styrian suit, made his courtly bow and said to the people, "In any case, we consider ourselves very fortunate . . . " The band played "The world is really so large and wide and full of womenfolk." He grew old. The heat abated. The square lay in the shade.

He placed his hand on the lectern, so that the swaying ceased, and said, "This time I'm simply asking for your trust again, so that this beautiful little province can continue to flourish. I already know about your concerns and needs. As you all know, I've come up from the bottom, and I've remained a simple man all my life, and I don't forget the May devotions in honor of the Virgin Mary. We need a sensible highway with six lanes so that people don't drive out of the country going around Tyrol, and a reservoir, and a funicular railway like they have in Kaprun or whatever that place is called. The unborn child's life is a commitment to Western civilization. I've never lined my own pockets, as you very well know. I'm concerned about the spiritual unity of this province that has been divided for seventy years, and our brothers in Pflersch as well, and let's not forget the people in Vintschgau, and then there's the wine that we have to pay duty on at the Brenner Pass."

Applause. He paused. In front of him in the first row, the diadochi who always accompanied him patiently waiting for them to carry him feet first from his office—he would not leave the office otherwise. Behind them in the second row, already blurred because of his vision, the hippies, who were whispering and laughing and had gotten into a subdued argument with Kipfl, a provincial government official who was standing directly in front of them, the only woman among the devoted followers. He continued his speech, interrupted at intervals by applause and cheers.

"I was young once too. Who's going to pay for the pensions someday. My dear farmer's wife, give birth to the children that God sends to you; on earth you're sure to receive the Mother's Cross and in heaven a seat in the eternal confectionery. Free passage for all transport vehicles and other long-distance haulers. I've actually never been able to find out whether they bring the milk up from Italy or down from Germany. And the hydroelectric power from our mountains." That was the way he approached foreign policy. They liked that, their opinion was solicited, they thought. All of their opinions had always been the same and were the same as his. "The Greens protect every toad but not the unborn child. They even brag about that, those pacifists and murderers—the old bishop even said that, God rest his soul."

"But the unborn child, that will become the trip wire. They'll fly over that, I'll guarantee you," Doctor Heiter had said during the election meeting.

"I wrote an article in my farmers' newspaper, saying that they're worse than the Nazis and potential murderers, and they only use nature as an excuse."

"Let's not forget the Communists," Kipfl had always interrupted. "They're everywhere. They're only waiting for decadence, then they'll come, the Russians. Just wait. We'll see it happen."

Those meetings were always very boring. Much nicer the drives in the car with the license number "1," the speeches, bathing in the crowd, the clever little eyes that glistened like a clear mountain stream, the loyal voting cattle—he loved them more than any farmer ever loved his animals. He grasped the microphone tightly and croaked into the small metal sphere, "In order to preserve free transit and our personal friendship with the Bavarian prime minister, what's his name, we will, as we did back in the year 1809, and if the enemy comes into the country, even if it's the devil himself, you should know that, the Italians should know that, and just let the Viennese hear it, if they want to hear it. And if the bloated city dwellers think they can put their oar in our business with their environmental protection . . . " The rest was lost in applause.

Pfandl stepped up next to him, shook his hand, and said into the microphone, "For our friends here in town, I would like to add that we'll be meeting afterward in a small group at the Stag tavern to discuss Commerce Councilor Leibelfing's project, which would exceed the scope of this event. He wants to build his vegetarian executive recreation center in the middle of the Sonnwend Forest where the stupid wildlife sanctuary is. But we owe him our thanks for the comfortable jobs that he created for all of you in his crane factory. I'd like to take the opportunity to point out to you, dear citizens of Haslach, that I'm the designated successor, even if you don't understand the word 'designated.' I don't understand it entirely myself."

Shadows fell over the square. The asphalt exuded a calming warmth. High on the mountain tops, the last rays of the sun. The band played "The Frail Bones Falter." He will become an honorary citizen of Kaunz today. The last one before him was Hitler; now Sepp will virtually become his successor. His position is based upon broad approval. He was insanely thirsty. The schnapps at last. "It was a difficult time, the alpine fortress was giving way, the enemy was moving ahead on all fronts, the area commander had a new telephone number and couldn't be reached for weeks, the country was full of refugees that we had to get rid of, in April there were still the heavy snowfalls, and then instead of the Americans the French marched in. I thought I'd have a stroke."

We are in a hurry. Three more villages. He stuffed the title of honorary citizen into his pocket together with the mountain flowers. Unfortunately they had stayed in Haslach for a long time. During the speech Kipfl had begun arguing with the hippies. "The men with beards and the women with cigarette butts in their mouths and tight jeans and earrings made of red plastic," she recounted with horror in her voice as they drove on. "The plainclothesmen have them all in the card file; we can come sometime and look at the little pictures."

Raggedly lascivious, I must see that, Sepp thought, *in my time we didn't have that.*

Kipfl's voice broke. She had said it, they were Communists, had come from the city purposely to sow discord and to preach their environmental protection. Beside herself, she had screamed, "Wash yourselves first! Until you do that I won't talk to you at all! If you were my daughters, I'd slap you and send you home in those outfits! Wash yourselves first, or I won't talk to you at all!" But then she spoke after all. "You're always the ones who preach about the environment, and now you yourselves are throwing cigarette butts there on the ground. I'd sweep in front of my own door instead of driving out into the country where there are still decent people."

Schädelbitter, who was standing next to her, tried to pull her away so that they could drive to Kaunz before the air had gone out of Sepp, or before so much schnapps had gone into him that it was coming out his ears. Schädelbitter, another crown prince, much too respectable ever to be successful, has not grasped the first thing about politics, a nervous man, his background is in commerce: for years the fear of going broke, even the strongest man cannot endure that. He pulled the spitting Mariann away by the arm; she had froth on her chin and in the neck of her dirndl, and she screamed, "Go to work for a change, until then I won't talk to you! You still haven't paid a Schilling in taxes! You're the ones who are polluting the environment with your cigarette butts! Go away to where the pepper grows! We're the elected representatives of the people! Under Hitler we'd have dealt with you differently!"

He hissed, "Mariann, come on! It's all right. Everything's going to be all right. Calm down, Madame Representative. We have to go to Kaunz. We're late. The television people are already waiting." So they were in Haslach, not in Ausserdorf.

Kien had given him the two thousand-Schilling notes; he had given one to the choir director. The little boy and the little girl had recited the poem and had gotten it muddled and had begun to cry. The girl had given him the bouquet; he had put it into his pocket with the title of honorary citizen of Kaunz. General emotion. The tidy girl with the schnapps tray moved into his field of vision. He took a glass and tossed it down. Immediately he felt better, the gentle burning on his diaphragm, the ringing in his head subsided, his responsibility as governor of the state appeared clearly before his eyes—the welfare of the individual and the community—and so did the tits that were pushed up by the traditional bodice in front of his face. Wood by the cottage, they had said in his day. He stuck the thousand-Schilling note—it had been wadded into a little ball with corners sticking out—into her mouth and grabbed her bottom; her eyes grew as big as saucers and she did not say a word. He pinched her buttocks properly, a magnificent human specimen, child of this robust countryside. Kien spoke to him, something about an appointment with Steinkasserer for the day after tomorrow. "Can't you see that I'm busy?" In with the gray finger-sausages beneath the pleated skirt—where is the bush?—in with the fingers into the pleasure, then the wood by the cottage, displayed by the bodice like the fruit crates in front of Mühlbacher's store back when he was a child—was it still there today? He lifted out her left breast, quickly into his mouth with it, a hearty smack, the same treatment for the right-hand piece of wood by the cottage. "What a charming girl you are! Amazing that something so charming appears in such a one-horse town!"

She finally had the thousand-Schilling note out of her mouth, and like a flash she poured one schnapps after another into Sepp's toadlike mouth, until the tray was empty. His mouth remained open for a while, verrucose, purple, wheezing a little, beautiful memories of the old days, that authentic enthusiasm back then, after the war, when he had built up democracy again, riding his moped from village to village.

Kien, Schädelbitter, Pfandl, and Kipfl sat in the little Mercedes and waited. The faithful Kluibenschädl held the door of the big car open and shouted something like "Pastor's cook."

Sepp said, "Don't you see that I have something to do?" The girl had disappeared, his youth, the May devotions in honor of the Virgin Mary, the mild evenings in the chestnut grove behind the church, the pinching of Mariedele's bottom when leaving the church after Mass, getting properly drunk was still something special. Now any common laborer can afford it; we have the morality to match. The band played "Tyrol Is One." The young men of the town surrounded the Communists, who would have second thoughts next time.

Kluibenschädl helped him into the back seat and said, "This heat."

Sepp said, "Just get me a schnapps in a hurry. I'm dying of thirst. These speeches dry out your whole body like crazy."

The people from the city were forced off behind the Black Stag tavern. Franz held the one with the glasses tightly from behind; Karl tore the glasses from his face and stomped on them and said, "Go to Russia with your environmental protection." Then he gave him an uppercut.

Felix and Bertl had taken on the small woman with the glasses and the red hair. They gave her glasses the same treatment. "We'll give you a beating, you rotten whores," screamed Felix, beside himself with excitement. He had never before participated in an election campaign.

"In the old days before the war there was a different punishment, anyway we treated the Reds differently," growled an old citizen who had come behind the building to urinate. "They're all bloody whores," he said approvingly. "I'd have liked to screw one of them myself, but who dares to go into the city at my age and the way I look?"

A second senior citizen stepped up next to him; the Black Stag has had a toilet for a long time, but only the tourists use it. "You did all right," he said to Bertl, "but if this were a real war, everything would look different later." Bertl bashed in the nose of the tall man who was being held by Franz and Hermann.

The older citizens went to the Golden Crown where refreshments

were prepared for them.
    They had finally pulled the jeans from the thin woman with the red earrings and had twisted her arms behind her. First of all a few slaps, then some hair was ripped out. Felix casually fingered her pubic hair as if all of that did not matter to him. He would like to fuck a woman like that thoroughly in peace, but at home, not here on the dunghill behind the Black Stag where the old men are pissing nearby. The tall man cowered on the ground and spat blood and parts of his second set of teeth; he would need a third set, assuming that they let him go.
    The television people were gathering up cameras and spotlights. They have to go to Kaunz where the last appearance of the day is supposed to take place. There is a traffic jam in the lower village; the square is closed because of the mass rally; the policeman runs around like a piece of shit on a hot plate and tries and tries to direct the traffic, but everything just becomes worse.
    "We're terribly late," said Kluibenschädl for the hundredth time, but that did not move them ahead faster either.
    Felix screamed, "Bugger!" and "Jewish sow!" He did not know his way around yet very well. And then he had his epileptic seizure. The small woman took advantage of the excitement over the man who was lying there with a blue face, tore herself away, and fled. "We'll find her, she's hiding in the woods, we'll tip off the hunter, the blood trail is easy to see in the snow, make no mistake." The snow remains on the ground here until the middle of summer.
    The three black limousines, followed by the silver television vehicles, drove into Kaunz. The band played "The world is really . . . ," then "The Old Comrade." They had filled Sepp up with schnapps again. He said, "I've got to piss."
    Kien said, "You can't do that now, the appointment book is full, we're too late." Pfandl and Schädelbitter heaved him up onto the platform and leaned him against the speaker's desk with the sweaty, crumpled thousand-Schilling note in the hand that he held behind his back.
    Once his mother had sent him across the street to go shopping at Mühlbacher's store. Ten Schillings had been a fortune, clasped in small sticky fingers, so afraid to lose it, and then it was gone in spite of that, the fuss at home, nobody can imagine that poverty any more. "Just wait until your father gets home, you damned dirty little devil!"
    Blows, screams, tears, his father in the evening, the same treatment all over again, blows in the face, on the back of the head. "Ten Schillings!

I'll kill you!" his father had roared.

Then little Sepp had decided to become a politician, had fled to the neighbor, who had screamed at him, "If you hadn't thrown away the money, you stupid brat! Maybe you just stole it! Go home! I'm not going to get in trouble with Hans because of you!"

Sometime during the night he had crept home. His father had been waiting for him. The same treatment all over again, blows on his belly, in the face.

"That never hurt anybody," Kluibenschädl said tersely.

With Pfandl's and his own help, he lifted himself out of the car, moved the few meters across the gravel-strewn square and past the riflemen who were standing at attention, suddenly foggy in the head, a little petit mal seizure.

"Where am I?"

"In Kaunz."

"Who am I?"

"Sepp." Something about a king . . . from the bottom at the back . . . one of you since I was little. The band played "The Old Comrade" and "The Grand and German Master." He slipped a thousand-Schilling note to the band director so that everyone could see it. The band director broke out in tears, kissed his hand, fell to his knees before him, kissed his shoes, clumsy brogues that were suited to the weight of the office, dusty after the day's appearances, whimpered, clasped the knee stockings and arthritic knees.

"I'm not going to live much longer, but they'll only carry me out headfirst."

The band director pressed his head between the legs that even Sepp himself, with the greatest effort, would not have gotten apart; from the middle of his body down, everything was rotten, swollen. With inconspicuous kicks, Schädelbitter forced the band director away, the girl with the good breasts in traditional costume presented the schnapps to him, he tipped the glass, the tightness subsided, he stepped to the speaker's desk. The people had streamed in from the highest isolated farms to see him and hear him speak, a toast to congeniality, the legendary personality that made you forget all your ailments, the flabby mountain of flesh, the festering middle of the body.

"Everything full of water," said Kipfl with her hand in front of her mouth. "He won't last much longer."

But it was schnapps, the dark blue face, the little purple blood vessels in the almost silvery skin that was filled almost to the bursting point, the dark red claws that clutched around the plywood edge of the speaker's desk while he began to speak and said, "So God created man in his own image, he created them male and female. Be fruitful and multiply . . . ," and spoke on and on. Since the war it had always been the same speech. The diadochi cramped their jaws in suppressed yawning; he spoke: "Behold, I give you every herb bearing seed, which is upon the whole earth, . . . "

Kien jostled Schädelbitter and hissed, "Shit, that's the Protestant version. He's putting us through the wringer. That's the beginning of the end."

Schädelbitter, with the fidgety musician in the sweatbox, whispered, "Calm down. Nobody will notice it."

Pfandl gave the choir director a signal; they sang "In Mantua in Fetters" and "The world is really . . . " After that Sepp came to the next point and said, "Today, principles are disappearing because nobody dares to confess them openly any more, and because we're governed by Vienna these days. Let's say it: Federalism is dead."

Kien hissed up at the podium, "Dialect, dialect!"

Sepp said, "Because the ones that shy away from work these days and loiter around in rags in the city and make demands and have never done a lick themselves and don't pay a Schilling in taxes, and our soldiers fought in vain in Stalingrad, and we're not building the highway in vain, and may the devil take them, those who begrudge us those few hard-earned Schillings . . . " He fell over backward in the middle of the sentence; he was already speaking to the top of the pavilion when he said "hard-earned Schillings." They played and sang "In Mantua in Fetters": "The faithful courtier was in Mantua, the enemy host led him to his death, . . . "

Sepp said, "It is finished!" The top of the pavilion tore apart, the sky grew dark, he wanted to scream, but only a soft humming burst forth from his breast. The band director freed himself from Schädelbitter's grasp in the ensuing confusion and ran howling down the Kirchgasse on all fours.

Old and young screamed, "Bravo!" and clapped.

Sepp gasped, motionless on his back. He said, "Let me die, you filthy dogs!" to the four loyal followers who dragged him over and heaved him up into the back seat with their united effort. His head slid from the seat. Kluibenschädl lifted him up. The whole mountain of flesh slid down behind the back of the front seat. He whispered hoarsely, "How easy it is for me to die, I'm not even crying."

Kluibenschädl said, "Not now or ever. Wait, I'll help you out of there."

Sepp croaked, "I'm stuck. I'm done for. Get Pfandl or a priest."

Kluibenschädl said, "I'll help you get out of there. Can you possibly pull your belly in?"

Pfandl stepped to the microphone and said, "In any case, we consider ourselves very fortunate. We'll continue with all our might to pursue the policies that we've followed up until now. It's a question of the whole nation in the fight for German capital, of our farmer's and chair-pusher's paradise, the worthwhile jobs that the honorable Councilor of Commerce has created for all of us . . ."

Kipfl heard the word "capital" and screamed at Pfandl, "You're a Red! I knew it all the time! Come down from the podium, you pig-headed Red!"

Schädelbitter held his hand over her mouth and said, "Calm yourself, Madame Representative, everything's going to be all right." He had to twist one of her arms behind her back and slap her a couple of times in order to get her to keep her mouth shut.

Kien jumped up onto the podium, pushed Pfandl away from the microphone, and while doing so yelled, "I'm a candidate of the Center, the free peasantry, the free Tyrol north and south of the Brenner Pass, a new Tyrolean state, the oldest continental democracy, the alpine fortress to the last bullet."

The faithful Kluibenschädl tried to lift the king onto the seat and said, "Can't you help a little? I can't lift you."

Sepp said, "Now I've got to vomit, now, now."

Kien punched Pfandl in the stomach, who acted as if it did not bother him and said, "We'll defy the objections to a different Tyrol, as we defied the Reds in the year 1934. Somewhere there must be an end to tolerance, otherwise it cannot be defined as such." He turned around quite suddenly and kicked Kien in the shin, then he rammed his knee between Kien's legs.

Kien slumped to the floor with the words, "I'll make you pay for that, Pfandl." The band played "True friendship must not falter, even if it is far away." For the aged citizens a light meal had been prepared in the new post office.

Sepp gasped, "Now, now." Then he vomited.

Pfandl had the mayor, the policeman, the priest, and the postmistress kiss his hand. The band played "Girl, you'll feel good on vacation in Tyrol." Around the square the German guests applauded.

Kluibenschädl went into the post office for beer and goulash, his favorite food. He had done more than his duty, really everything that was humanly possible.

The people of the inner circle were sitting in the back room at the Stag, and Pfandl was explaining the deal with Doctor Leibelfing.

Darkness fell over Kaunz. A side window of the large Mercedes was open; a thick soupy liquid, as if liverwurst had been stirred into schnapps, flowed out and formed a lake on the evening-warm asphalt. The band director ran up barking and began to lick up the liquid with the long tongue that dangled from his mouth.

Translated by Lowell A. Bangerter

THE PLUNGE

ULRIKE LÄNGLE

PAUL put his book down with a sigh. The hero of the Altar of Tirol had just had a fatal accident. The Altar of Tirol was the Serles, a mountain south of Innsbruck; the hero had been bewildered by an inextricable conflict of conscience, and therefore the author had him suffer the fatal fall down the mountain side. The author was a Catholic clergyman who had written the book in question with the attractive title, *The Light of the Mountains*, in order to propel young men into the lap of the Church. Paul had followed the fate of the hero with feverish interest: the protagonist came from the country—like him; he went to the big city in order to study there—like him; this hero would almost have succumbed there to the charms of a so-called "flame"—like him; but he had restrained himself just in time, unfortunately also like him. This same protagonist ultimately returned to his village, and there a serious older priest had made him aware of his true calling: service to the Church. In order to find clarity of mind, the protagonist had taken off on a climb up the Altar of Tirol, perhaps even on a search for an edelweiss—the author was silent about that—and on this climb he had met his death. Whether the edelweiss that he wanted to take back to his sweetheart was to blame—in addition to the "flame" he naturally also had a simple village girlfriend who loved him—whether his inner discord had torn him apart, or whether the older priest had intentionally sent him on a perilous path, that remained open.

Paul was twenty-two and Swiss. He lived in Kerns in the canton Obwalden, one of the very oldest cantons, and he studied philosophy in Zurich. His astrological sign was Taurus, but he was still a virgin. He was basically a sacrifice of the book; during his entire youth he had become satiated with reading à la *The Light of the Mountains* with the result that he preferred to stay away from the feminine sex even in the sinful big city. He withstood even the temptations of an emancipated red-headed philosophy student who had chosen as her ideal the ladies of the eighteenth-century salons and who wanted to relieve Paul of the burden of his innocence. Paul believed that, precisely in such matters, he owed it to even his most ancient Swiss ancestors to make nothing but a responsible decision. The first step can be decisive for everything else; therefore he preferred to let calm consideration reign, although the "wild blood of his youth," as it was so nicely labeled in *The Light of the Mountains*, i.e., the "sting of the flesh" that pursued even Saint Paul, didn't make it easy for him. It was possible that he simply was afraid of the first time.

Paul reached for the *Luzerner Neuesten Nachrichten* and paged listlessly through the newspaper. The year was 1969. Besides football there was nothing special, but there was something else there after all; Paul was taken back. The "Days of Viennese Culture" with the "Vienna working group motion" were announced in the "Chaise Lounge." Paul had no idea what that was, but he went there anyway. At the Chaise Lounge three architecture students from Kerns had created what was then called an alternative cultural center. In the semi-darkness Paul squeezed in between two visitors on a narrow wooden bench and listened. A man sat on the stage and read from the *Luzerner Neuesten Nachrichten* with a quiet, scarcely audible voice: "Soccer results: the Lucerne Soccer Club beat the. . . ." Then Paul understood nothing else, since someone from the audience yelled: "Can't you do anything but read the newspaper?" The actor, unmoved, continued to read in his soft voice: "And it also says: Exchange rates. . . ." The audience became increasingly restless; the man on the stage persisted in his monotone: "And it also says. . . ." until the uproar became too loud. Then came the scene "Meal for Biafra." The actors sat on the stage, consumed a delicious meal, and threw the bones into the audience. Then they went through the rows of spectators with a collection box. The pastor said: "This is hyprocrisy!" Paul didn't know what to do. Then a fat man with a beard, whose name was Rolf Schwendter, appeared with a drum. He sang a song entitled "Evening Prayers of a Child who has read Wilhelm Reich". The last stanza was: "Give me power finally to break up the corporations. Give us today our daily solidarity. Lead me through hostile surroundings without ulcers in my stomach, and give me a girl so that I can pray more effectively." The refrain was: "Dear God, make me rigid so that I'll soon be ripe for love. Dear God, make me pious so that I'll have an orgasm."

The preacher jumped up and shouted: "This is blasphemy!" The fat man left the stage and left Kerns on the same evening.

Paul learned later that the pastor had instigated a complaint against Schwendter for the perversion of religion, but the latter was already beyond the borders of the country. Paul had enough of Viennese culture and went home. That night he had a strange dream: he lay in bed, he was about seven years old, and he was praying. Suddenly an angel with wings made out of the *Luzerner Neuesten Nachrichten* swept into the room and lay down beside him on the bed. The angel was a female. They prayed together, then the angel ordered Paul to climb up the Altar of Tirol and to pick her an edelweiss. Paul climbed over jagged rocks and crossed a field of snow, then he saw the edelweiss. He stretched, his foot slipped, and he fell into the depths below. He awakened bathed in perspiration and his ears were drumming with: "Dear God, make me holy." His sheet was moist. Paul reached again for the *Luzerner Neuesten Nachrichten*; while reading a report about the annual meeting of the citizens of Appenzell, he fell asleep again.

The next morning—Paul was now on summer vacation—he went into the village to a second-hand bookstore. There Pastor Franz Josef Joller stood beside him and was paging through an old edition of the *Examination of Conscience*, in which transgressions against the sixth commandment were described in fastidious detail. "Unbelievable, those Viennese," he said excitedly when he caught sight of Paul. "Such filth and in one of the original cantons!" Paul nodded hypocritically; after all, those obscenities had helped him come to the dream of the angel with the *Luzerner Neuesten Nachrichten* wings. "The Austrians were always our enemies, Paul, think of the Rütli oath; that was also directed against the Habsburgs. And today they infiltrate us with sex literature. William Tell would have. . . ." The Pastor's voice cracked; he didn't know what else to say. Paul remembered that the psychologist Reich's first name was also William and he preferred to say nothing. Everyone in the village knew that the Pastor had once been a professor in a cloister school in Austria, but because of transgressions against the boys was given a disciplinary transfer to Switzerland. The Pastor's favorite companion was his sexton Emil Benzer, who, on his solitary walks, liked to carry a switch with him and to beat the air with it. Paul said: "I don't know what's the matter with you. That was a nice evening." The Pastor almost choked out of indignation; Paul left the bookstore. He felt like William Tell after he had shot the apple.

Paula chewed her fingernails and looked at the flower vase on the living-room cabinet. Since she had taken Freud's *Interpretation of Dreams* out of the city library, she could no longer look at any flower vase without embarrassment, nor at other long or hollow objects. She and her friend Pia felt like the avant-garde in the provincial Austrian city in which they grew up, Bregenz on Lake Constance. They wore long black maxicoats, miniskirts, and broad-brimmed slouch hats on their heads, like Garibaldi; Pia wore a white one, Paula a black one. On Friday afternoons they were forced to go to dance class together with the boys from the high school. The year was 1970. Proper clothes replaced the miniskirts, and they had to wear gloves in order to reduce the effects of unpleasantly perspiring masculine hands. The twist was considered sinful and was therefore forbidden. The dance class lasted from October to December so that the girls wouldn't lose the rhythm of their school schedule for too long. Paula had to be at home at seven-thirty.

Peter, her first love, was the shy son of a policeman and didn't get any further than a kiss under the street lamp. Paula and Pia fled into the world of books and read the texts of the Vienna Group, Freud's *Interpretation of Dreams, Lady Chatterley's Lover,* the *Man without Characteristics,* and *Ulysses*; Pia was in addition a specialist in Virginia Woolf. In the Capuchin Cloister an anti-abortion film, *Phöbe*, was shown, in which the heroine named in the title was seen becoming sick in the shower. After the film there was a discussion during which a young couple, still in school and known in the city, sat there hand-in-hand and declared that their parents would surely not object if they were already to have children. Paula was torn apart. On the one hand, Freud; on the other, the Capuchins. At the bottom of her heart she was resolved to preserve herself for the one with whom things became serious, although the temptations were enticing. She was hoping to meet Peter at "Flint," the folk festival that was to take place, like Woodstock in small format, on the grounds surrounding the fortress ruins. Her hopes burst, however, when the authorities declared the area a wildlife sanctuary a few days before. Instead of Flint, a burial of Flint took place at which a coffin was carried to its grave accompanied by a litany sung against the provincial government. Shy Peter, who had absolutely no self-confidence, gave Paula a record of Rolf Schwendter, *Songs for a Child's Drum,* on which he had marked the song "Ballad of the High School Graduates": "No mentors for many an intellectual soul. They must do it themselves if they want to relinquish their hole. Most graduates must play the masturbator's role." Thereupon Paula gave Peter his walking papers and turned to her book, *Tales of a Thousand Nights*.

In 1989 Paul and Paula met for the first time. Paul had become a philosopher, Paula a writer. Paul had not yet permitted himself to be ignited by a "flame"; Paula had already broken her oath, but the right man had still not been found. They sat beside each other at a literary gathering and started talking with one another. In the afternoon they hiked to a country inn and sat there until nightfall. Paula remembered that there was a path from there through the woods to the city, but in the dark they did not risk taking it, although Paula had already taken it before, but, to be sure, during the daytime. Paula imagined how she would discreetly stumble over a root and Paul would have to catch her, or how she might lean against the trunk of a tree in the moonlight and Paul would not be able to resist kissing her. In May this forest at the edge of the city was a favorite meeting place for couples who had no other place to go. Paul insisted, however, that they take the bus. He did not once reach for Paula's hand on the ride home; he spoke only about a book that he had written. Paula was disappointed and did not even phone him the next day as they had agreed. She rode home and wrote a wistful love story in which she had everything happen that had not happened in reality. But it did not help at all. Literature did not have the effect of a magic potion and the distant Paul did not succumb to the magic of the written word. He did not move. Paula had the text published in a magazine and hoped that Paul would read it. That hope, too, remained unfulfilled. Finally Paula took a trip to Brazil and requested a good husband from the dear Jesus of Bonfim. Who it should be—whether Paul, whether someone else—that she left up to heaven and relaxed on the fine-grained sandy beaches of northern Brazil.

Paul could not get Paula out of his head. He liked her with her clown hairdo, as she herself called her black hair that stuck out from her head, and her enterprising spirit. Unfortunately he had a Swiss temperament and he had not dared to seize the opportunity by the hair. He had not even risked a shy approach. Nothing, simply nothing. The absent, yet present Paula inspired him to write a philosophical treatise with the title: *Only Expenditures. Unexpressed Declarations of Love and Their Consequences*. With the title he was referring to the price of the bus tickets. In this work Paul demonstrated what consequences concealed love had for the individual's being. Since he had naturally little illustrative material at hand, he shifted the focus of his work on the construction of categories of unexpressed confessions of love and on possible groups of results. The type *alpha*—he had a preference for Greek letters for classifications—the type *alpha* was the declaration that was neglected out of shyness; the type *beta* was the declaration not made out of consideration for the other; the type *gamma* out of fear of the consequences, and so on. Paul's perspicacity produced the finest categories. His work gave him particular pleasure with the chapter on the consequences of unexpressed confessions which extended from philosophical formulations of a problem—to what degree does that which is not said influence that which is said?—through magical ideas up to the practical effects on the work behavior of the non-confessor. Paul came to the conclusion that unexpressed love was a factor at least as important for the development of humanity as are customarily hunger and love. His work was published; he received a prize for it and was in all the important newspapers. Since Paula was in Brazil at the time, she heard nothing about it and naturally could not write to him either. Paul now conclusively believed that he belonged to the non-confessors, type *epsilon*: confession of love undeclared out of the secret conviction that the second party does not want to know anything about the confessor. He tried consequently to forget Paula. The primary consequence of his non-declaration was the book, the secondary result was an intensifying inability to work. There was nothing left for Paul to do but to retreat to the mountains of his Swiss homeland. He bought a ticket to Saint Moritz in order to live there in the best hotel, since he now had enough money through the success of his book.

After a few months Paula came back from Brazil. In the meantime her wealthy aunt had died and she could live on the interest accruing from a considerable fortune. After the tropical jungles and loafing on the beach, she was longing for fresh air and thus decided to take a vacation in the Swiss mountains. In Saint Moritz her aunt had owned a vacation home into which Paula now moved. On the day after her arrival, accompanied by a mountain guide, she climbed up the Piz Nair and, after some effort, reached the summit, from where one could see as far as König Ortler in South Tirol. While climbing down, she slipped and fell into a field of rubble. The guide had to watch passively as Paula disappeared into the abyss. Since he had had the impression that she was a skilled mountain climber, he had not fastened her with a rope for the less precarious portions of the descent.

On his way to Saint Moritz, Paul made a stop in his hometown Kerns and found *The Light of the Mountains* in the attic of his parents' home. He read the story once again and then decided to go into the Alps to seek edelweiss. If in the process he were to plunge from the heights or not was a matter of complete indifference to him in his state of mind at the time. On a cool spring morning he left his luxury hotel in Saint Moritz and swung himself onto the cliffs of the Piz Nair. He was a practiced climber and had already accomplished many a climb with a difficulty grade of seven. When he extended his hand toward the edelweiss, his mountain shoe slipped on a slab of rock and he lost his hold, unfastened as he was. While falling, he suddenly thought of the angel with the *Luzerner Neuesten Nachrichten* wings. It had Paula's eyes and was bent over him. Just as they were about to kiss one another, Paul lost consciousness.

Paula's plunge into the depths ended at the foot of a rock wall. When she came to a stop with scratched hands and knees, something from above fell on her. She lost consciousness. When she again became conscious, she felt something soft on her mouth. It was a man who was kissing her. She pressed him to her and then away again in order to be able to see him, and she recognized Paul. In the last meters of his fall Paul got stuck on a dwarf pine which broke the force of his plunge, and thus he landed on Paula with diminished impact. He was still holding the edelweiss frantically in his hand. During the fall his past life had flashed by him; now he was considering his future with Paula. She seemed desirable to him and he thus decided to write a new book with the title: *The Unhoped-for Often Occurs. Possible Situations for Declarations of Love*. He embraced Paula as passionately as was possible with limbs battered from the fall and said with a firm voice and the slight accent of interior Switzerland: "I love you." Paula looked at him for a long time and then whispered: "Moi non plus."

The honeymoon trip led the young pair through Venice, where they saw a performance of *The Abduction from the Seraglio* in the Teatro La Fenice, to the water falls of Iguaçú on the border between Argentina and Brazil. They stayed at the luxurious Hotel das Cataratas. In the intervals between the bliss of love and the long walks through the landscape mottled with butterflies, Paul perfected his tract on declarations of love while Paula was absorbed with her new cycle of poems, *Tumbling Waters*.

Translated by Margaret T. Peischl

Long Time No See

Robert Menasse

WHEN I see an abstract picture, all I see is an abstract picture. A Rorschach test merely makes me identify it as a Rorschach test. If I see a virgin floating in space, then I see a woman who appears to be floating due to a magician's hidden technical procedures. The magician is paid for artfully creating the illusion of floating, so that even in this case I can trust my eyes. And considering the eternal plausibility of the small world in which I live, no one could ever have thought that I might not see correctly. I do not know all the things that are possible. But when I do see something, I know it to be real. The idea of seeing something and not to believe it feasible is therefore just as alien to me as the idea of closing my eyes to reality, merely because I might see in it quite different possibilities, perhaps possibilities that have occurred, and that I cannot bear.

All of this is not true, of course, as I had to realize. Not only because, for once, I saw something with my own eyes that I should never have considered possible. But this is how it began.

As I've done every night, I walked around the block with my dog. Countless times during my evening walks I would pass the Queen-of-Spades bar, without the idea of going inside ever even having crossed my mind. Why, however, I suddenly entered that evening to have a beer I don't know. Perhaps at that moment my diffuse longing for life was stronger than my fear—my fear that on principle takes disappointment into account and therefore avoids it, especially when all this means is passing by a dubious suburban Viennese pub, even though sounds of laughter reach into the street.

I must have made the impression of a blind man when I stood in the pub with my dog, staring helplessly with wide-open eyes through the fogged lens of my spectacles. What I saw as through a slowly lifting mist and could not believe for moments of eternity was a horde of drunk and brawling men standing around a table—a table on which Lechner danced. Lechner, Maria. I knew her from school—we were classmates—as the embodiment of honesty and integrity. She never let anybody crib from her work for fear that this could diminish her own scholastic standing. During the final exams, which of course she passed with honors, she still had two pigtails. Immediately after the exams, half of the class went into town to celebrate. We were surprised that Lechner wanted to come with us, but not for long, as she was the only one who refused to take a joy-ride on the tram; we had to wait for her forever, as she intended to go someplace to buy advance tickets. All she drank in those days was soda with raspberry syrup. We thought Webora wicked because she always drank sweet Martinis; then, suddenly, she disappeared with Kaiser, who had habitually been ordering Uzo.

Later I sometimes ran into Lechner by accident, but up to age thirty she continuously remained like the ten-year-old who did her homework like a good girl should. At age twenty-four she had finished her law studies, at twenty-five, after her year at court, she passed the qualifying exam for becoming a judge, and four years later she passed the exam that actually allowed her to assume the position of judge. In her case everything always proceeded smoothly, without conflict or distraction, according to an ideal time plan, and then she was a judge and I had lost track of her. And now, approximately five, nay, almost six years later, I saw her again, drunk, screeching and laughing while dancing on a table from which she almost constantly came crashing to the ground; meanwhile she contemptuously warded off the hands which reached toward her, under the pretense of steadying her.

The music that filled the small dim space of the bar came from a radio, I noticed, for when the song had ended it was followed by news. German Democratic Republic. The work to tear down the Berlin Wall had begun, the announcer said. The postwar order was dissolving. Once more, through the shouting and laughter, the word postwar order was clearly audible from the radio. Maria stood on the table, her hands on her hips. Suddenly she saw me and burst out laughing, either because she recognized me or because the men who helped her get off the table—no, because she had indeed recognized me, for she came to me immediately. She had this brilliant, fixed gaze, like glass eyes stuck in a soft mask that is about to melt any minute. She stumbled, almost fell shrieking upon my neck. Hello, Holzer, she said, long time no see. My dog began to bark, I began to sweat, my eyeglasses, which had seemed almost clear again, turned foggy once more. We must celebrate, she said, but not here.

I can still remember the tight pink sweater of the waitress who suddenly stood before me, the thought that momentarily came to mind of a woman's body made of glass and filled with soda and raspberry syrup, the big black briefcase of the waitress that opened like a dark abyss, glittering at the bottom, an arm in a blue-white striped shirt that came from somewhere and was cast aside, I don't know how and by whom, so much movement directly surrounding me, and I was benumbed. The dog whined. Be good! said I, and: That's right! Six-hundred-and-fifty Schillings! Fortunately I had taken my wallet with me before going on a walk. In the street Maria linked her arm through mine. Tell me what's new! I suddenly had to laugh. I had nothing to tell.

The way I've lived my life so far, the only thing worth mentioning about it was that, with a strange consistency, it never was worth mentioning. Once, when I started to feel a certain pride that my life was sensational, I noticed soon enough that the banal cause of this pride was nothing but silly and insignificant student pranks. When, once again, I believed that I was justified in thinking that I was about to live in a more militant and intensive fashion, I noticed that I had attached almost too much importance to inconsequential student skirmishes. When I terminated my studies, I started working in a bank, where I am still today. Even more so since then, my life can be fully described in shamefully few words: punctuality, friendliness and that diligence which sees its objects multiply with the same harmonious rapidity with which it disposes of them. I have no desire to write an autobiography, but the thought really irritates me that if I had such a desire it would be accomplished by the mere purchase of paper because the entire biography would have to consist of empty pages. This discontent is incomprehensible, because I have no serious cares. But it is understandable, because I've never been happy.

I take after my father. He is a correct man, friendly without excessive exuberance, with an eternally anxious wife, my mother.

I should have preferred to take after my grandfather. In 1968, when I had just turned fourteen, he told me about his life for the first time. In February 1934, as a Social Democrat, he had participated in the workers' rebellion. Later he fought in the Spanish Civil War in the International Brigade, then he emigrated to England and returned with the British Army as a liberator. That wasn't a victory either, he had said. Why? Just look around you. Well, you'll find out what I mean. And no one ever gave us any credit for what we did, all the years of struggle, not even for a proper pension. Today it's just enough to sit on a bench in the park. Should I perhaps feed the pigeons? Such disgusting beasts.

When grandmother became seriously ill, the two of them together swallowed an overdose of sleeping pills. I was seventeen years old then and almost flunked in school.

My self-esteem at that time surely stemmed from the contempt I felt for all those in whose life everything always proceeded so smoothly, unproblematically and harmoniously that they could always think of the right answer but never of a question. Thus I despised almost everyone, and of course Lechner, too. I was surprised how much I enjoyed meeting her again. Now, at age thirty-five, she was suddenly an eighteen-year-old in whom the simple exaltation one might feel when one is first permitted to smoke appeared grotesquely exaggerated. But it had a suction that swept me off my feet, since I, anxious and tense as I was then, was vaguely excited thereby. And when, after a spree through several bars that almost exceeded my strength, we went to bed together, I felt as if Maria had been the first to make a man of me. I mean this in reference to the ideal images of masculinity and femininity that exist in society, and which culminate in a sexuality idealized as lust—a lust I knew only from pornomovies, but which seemed unattainable to me in my own life. While I myself was able to trigger the most amazing ecstasies in Maria, she served me lust in such a fashion that I—I cannot put it any other way—was suddenly another person.

And I also saw the world now with other eyes. Surprised, I asked myself how it was possible that I could take her so much for granted without question, and that what she offered me could have sufficed me. This orderliness, which became so indefatigably exhausted in itself, this smooth functioning, which as a rule was not rewarded with pleasure . . .

Of course I immediately developed a certain addictive pattern toward Maria. We were two straight-laced humans who had suddenly discovered that the lusty exuberance and buffoonery of a carnival, which I had never experienced lustfully, could be produced any time without harmful consequences. How many bars, restaurants, nightclubs there were in the city, and how many pleasures we could afford . . . And how many places for love. And one never had to say: I love you. And one never needed to conceal: I don't love you. Because we were no pair of lovers, but, so to say, colleagues, who took care of a common interest, namely, the production of exceptions.

Exceptions that became the rule. We agreed on excesses according to the calendar of her cases, consumed pleasures that were offered on a market subject to calculations as precise as those of the businesses of the bank for which I'm working. And suddenly all these stimulants produced only new longings: for a vacation, for health food and fruit juices, for a good TV program.

When I woke up in the morning, my face was bloated and my eyes were swollen. Taking two aspirins against a headache soon became as much of a habit as it had once been to have an egg for breakfast. I hardly ever succeeded anymore in reading the paper before going to work; I glanced at the lines without understanding what I read.

When I strolled to work through the Stadtpark, I had anxieties of choking in the rush of the pigeons that swirled, like giant gray flocks, around the old women with their paper bags filled with food. Last Friday night, when I picked up Maria at home, she wanted to watch the news on TV before going out. It's crazy, she said, nowadays something surprising happens every day. Soviet Union, German Democratic Republic, Czechoslovakia. Look at it, she said. She appeared tired and run down. During the local political news she began to tell me of the incredible case, as she put it, she had had to deal with in court that day. An imposition, she said, what she had to contend with. It concerned a procedure for appointing a guardian. I asked her what that meant. Put simply, she said, to put an adult person under the control of a guardian or trustee. It meant appointing a guardian, based either on the judge's proposal or on some other official procedure, for a person suffering from a mental illness, or mentally handicapped, and unable to handle matters without the danger of putting himself at a disadvantage. All right, so now imagine this: an eighty-nine-year-old blind man repeatedly walks around in the center of town; he jostles people, stumbles, almost runs people down, in brief: he causes public annoyance. The man became known to the police because there were complaints, even denunciations of him at the police station, or because altercations occurred on the street during which passing police officers had to step in, etc. The problem was caused mainly by the man not identifying himself as a blind man, say, by wearing an armband, and also by his not using any aid that would enable a blind man to move around independently on the street, such as, for example, a white cane or a seeing-eye dog. Such a guide dog is very practical, as you know, since you have one yourself, she said grinning. The long and the short of it is that it turns out the man isn't even blind. He has no credentials to prove he is blind, and when interrogated by a police officer in the inner city, he confessed that his vision was unimpaired except for some farsightedness caused by old age. He was warned, but subsequently, as it says in my dossier, continued the pretense of being an invalid, which led to regular disturbances of the public order. Thereupon the police made the court start proceedings against him. Since no fraudulent intent could be proved, such as the wangling of disability benefits—after all the man did not even beg from people in the street, on the contrary he had run them down—there were no grounds for a criminal trial. Suddenly I find the dossier on my desk in guardianship court and am supposed to clarify whether it is necessary to appoint a trustee. With such hair-raising nonsense I must spend my time, said Maria.

I asked her why the man pretended to be blind.

Exactly, she said, that's what I wanted to know too. So I set a date for a hearing, and that was today. You know, the man is simply not mentally competent, I believe. Besides, he is querulous. You know what he said? I know, he said, that being an invalid is the most desired privilege in Austria, and thus every Austrian's goal in life. But he did not wish to pretend to be an invalid, nor did he desire any other privilege. And certainly no alms. That's also why he had not accepted this so-called complimentary gift, those four-thousand Schillings which the Republic of Austria had bestowed last year on the Jewish survivors of the persecution. It was simply, he said, that he could no longer bear to see all that one witnesses when one passes through the streets with open eyes. Therefore it was a natural and healthy reflex to close one's eyes against this.

I asked him what was so terrible in what there was to see. Upon which he told me about his life in excruciating detail; I tried to interrupt him, but he just continued talking. He should answer my question, I said. That's exactly what I am trying to do, he replied. I asked Maria what he had told her.

I'm not sure, she said. He talked and talked, he wanted to tell me his entire life story; you can imagine, I mean it's well known that things were very difficult for this generation. But I no longer can stand these old men who even today like so much to talk about the war, or the civil war; I....

Which civil war, I asked, the First Republic's in 1934 or Spain's? What do you say? Oh yes, Spain. Yes, I believe he also wanted to talk about Spain; you know, I really don't know, it's just that he fought a lot, and so I asked him again: what is the terrible thing that you see? Is it the images of the past that you cannot shake?

The television set was still on. Now began the competition between the weather report and the cultural news. I was extremely irritated and would have liked to get up and turn off the set, but I was afraid to interrupt Maria. No, the old man said, it's the images of the present. I don't understand this, I replied. He should be happy that there is peace now and we no longer have political confusion and terrible poverty. And imagine what he said now. He said: so don't you see it now, Your Honor?

No, I said, I don't see it, what is supposed to be so terrible?

Then he: you see, Your Honor, now that I'm getting older I would like to fit in better, that's why I am closing my eyes, so I won't see it either.

Is that what he said? I asked.

Yes, said Maria, the man is sick in the head.

And what did you do?

Nothing. All I had to do was to determine whether the premises for a guardianship existed. They don't. After all, I cannot give him a guardian as a seeing-eye dog. The man is probably running around town again right now, like a blind person. A little crazy, what can you do?

I sat leaning back, my eyes closed; in my head echoed Maria's voice and throbbed a detergent commercial.

Can't we turn off this damn set, I asked.

No, wait, she said, I'd still like to see the cultural news.

I was no longer able to exchange a word with her. She noticed soon enough that something had been severed, although she obviously did not know why.

We went out to eat but didn't say a word except to order. I drank faster and more than usual. Maria looked askance at me. When she finally asked what was the matter with me, I didn't understand her right away. My senses were not all there. I had expected, when she spoke, to see the text in print, as in a cartoon, to have to read what she said and not to hear it. But I couldn't see the sentence. What's the matter with you, she asked again.

    I didn't reply. When a rose vendor entered the restaurant, Maria bent far across the table toward me, touched my arm, and said: Buy me a rose and leave me alone!

Translated by Eva Dukes

THE DEATH OF ODYSSEUS

INGE MERKEL

LAERTES had died already some years ago. Shortly thereafter Eurykleia followed him.

The old woman was only a bundle of clothes, her face shriveled like a winter apple, her body beneath her robes resembled the rustling shell of a cricket. One day the people missed the tapping of her cane, which had so often provoked them. She had always been the first one to rise in the mornings. After all, she barely required any sleep. Then she hobbled through the house and with her stick she knocked against the doors of the servants' quarters, so that the servants and maids were startled awake and swore at her. One morning when that did not happen, they missed it. They looked for her and found her on her bed. A pile of covers from which her body barely distinguished itself. Tiny and flat she lay there, on her features a rigid expression of combativeness.

Odysseus was called. He closed her eyes and kissed her on her sunken mouth. He wept profusely. She had always been his "dear nurse," no matter that he himself was aged. She was buried with all honors beside Laertes. At his right lay Antikleia, the lawful wife. At his left, his heart side, they placed Eurykleia, the daughter of Ops, for whom he had given twenty cattle and whom he then never had touched after all.

Telemachus had now finally become a man. It was he who headed the household and commanded over Ithaka and the surrounding islands just as his father had before. His prudent and concerned aunt Iphthime had found a suitable girl for him in Sparta, lovely and from a good family, cheerful and diligent and also provided with a handsome dowry. Already a few children were crawling around the house. It was livelier and noisier than it had been for some time.

Penelope's hair had now turned completely white. It contrasted well with her brown face. Still she held herself very erect and busied herself around the house, especially with her grandchildren. However, she tired more quickly than before. Whenever she walked up the steep path to the stone oak, she had to stop from time to time to catch her breath and rest her feet. The children however—the youngest one she usually led by the hand—kept her alert and in good spirits.

Odysseus too was still working around the house, sometimes even in the fields. But his sea-gray eyes had become dull, and he was also much more taciturn than before.

Often he sat for hours down at the beach between the cliffs, his chin propped in his hand, gazed out upon the sea, watched the ships leaving or entering the harbor. He was dreaming.

The fisher boys liked to gather at his knees and torment him with requests for tales. He did not speak of Troy but rather of the horrors and wonders behind the sound barrier of reality: the story of the Cyclops and how he had escaped with his companions from the man-eating monster, clinging to the wooly bellies of the sheep. He warned of the lovely-voiced sirens and how they stood ankle-deep amidst the carrion of those who let themselves be seduced by their song. The children also liked to be told about dogfaced Skylla and the terrifying gorge of Charybdis squatting in the depths, and how he, Odysseus, clinging precariously to a swaying fig tree branch, had stared into the horrors of the abyss.

When he grew tired of telling tales he sent the children away and silently looked out upon the changeable sea with eyes that reflected dread and delight. A strange longing drew his gaze and his thoughts to distant lands and often he felt an aching nostalgia for the unsteady ship planks, for the hard clattering of the sails, the smell of fish and seaweed, the cries of sea gulls, and the wave-jumping of dolphins. Above all for the moonlit, starry summer nights on the sea. When the surface of the sea was stormy he believed he saw the moist silvery hips of the Nereids in the foamy waves, from the surf he heard the ardent conch calls of the Tritons, and the glassy clear waves mirrored to him the greenish cool breasts of Galatea. Then too he thought of the grottoes on the islands lying beyond the ship routes, charmingly overgrown with wild climbing plants, which recalled the flower-bedecked hair of women.

Often Penelope had to dispatch one of the boys to the beach to call him home when the evening grew cool. For now he suffered severely from rheumatism, the illness of sailors.

Penelope sensed how Odysseus gradually was slipping away from her. Not that he was seriously contemplating a sea voyage. Whenever

Telemachus put out to sea, he no longer demanded to go along. He slipped away from her inwardly. Back into the decades in which she had played no part. It was painful for her. But she understood. This curious nostalgia that inhabited his bones and beguiled his cooled-off blood had nothing to do with merry sea voyaging and seeking adventures. Nothing with craving knowledge and curiosity about never-seen wonders which the sea and the islands had withheld from him. It was curiosity about death.

All his adventures, after all, which had befallen him behind the sound barrier of reality and which he had sought out, had dealt with death. At that time he had not known it. Not until now did he gradually realize that. All the grottoes and caverns, which had irresistibly lured him inside, were enclosed with trees of death. The alders and cypresses on Ogygia, the black poplars of Persephone, the willows of Circe. What, after all, had the seven years with Calypso been? Not merely a place for amorous pleasures. Seclusion from real life, stagnant years in the calm monotonous serenity of death. He had been curious about all these grottoes, about all these women, who clutched tightly in the strangle hold of their charms, which was also—simultaneously—a strangle hold of death. Then already he suspected and therefore he had rejected immortality. When he decided to return to Penelope he returned to reality, to life. Of these things he now was thinking often, but he kept them to himself out of a shyness inexplicable even to himself.

One late afternoon he was brought into the house on a stretcher.

A ridiculous quarrel with beach robbers. Sailing close to the shore they had eyed a couple of young women who were rinsing nets. No men nearby, only the old man leaning his chin on a cane. Easy booty to be profitably bartered at the next slave market. The women resisted and shrieked. Odysseus could not look on idly. He gesticulated wildly with his cane and scolded and threatened with a weak old man's voice, but as glib as ever. Because the old cripple annoyed them, one knocked him over the head with the oar to make him be silent. The men of Ithaka who came running to the shore upon hearing the ruckus dispelled the rabble, to be sure. For Odysseus, however, it was too late. He lay contorted in the gravel with a bleeding head wound, which didn't even look that grave. But he was unconscious. They lifted him cautiously on a stretcher and brought him into the house to Penelope.

Now they were all standing around his bed. The servants were weeping and wringing their hands. Telemachus was staring at the ground.

The Death of Odysseus 163

A sobbing of rage and pain shook his breast.

"You're not to blame, child," Penelope said with a gruff voice; "why did he have to get involved!"

She did not cry. She turned to the moaning men and women and spoke harshly: "Go outside, all of you. I want to be alone with him." They obeyed her timidly; Telemachus too left. He knew his mother. Outside the wailing and whimpering resumed.

Penelope was oblivious to it. She sat at the edge of the bed. The bleeding from the forehead wound had stopped. It had not gushed forth. Old age blood. His beard stared steeply and pointedly in the air. His eyes were shut. The cheeks yellow and sunken. Penelope took his cold hands into hers, as if she could warm them up.

It grew darker and darker in the room. Suddenly his blood-drained lips moved. Heavily his eyelids lifted above his blurred eyes. His mouth, which seemed to intimate a brittle smile, whispered: "I know! . . . I should have kept still until the others came . . . I could not let it be . . . talk at least . . ."

"Quiet, be quiet, dear one. I know you never could let it be when it came over you."

"It's probably over now . . . I feel it . . . come very close to me, I don't have much strength in my voice . . . the coldness . . . it rises already up from below . . ."

Penelope bent over him, her ear very close to his mouth. After a while he spoke again.

"Tell me, Penelopaion! . . . did I give you a lot of grief? . . . Troy . . . and then the sound barrier . . . you know what I mean."

"That's so long, long ago, dearest. I came to understand it. You could not do otherwise. But tell me, if it's not too strenuous for you, tell me one more thing: Did you ever love me?"

After a long pause, during which he kept his lids closed, he moved his lips again. She leaned even closer over him to understand his indistinct whispering.

"You know! You were a good talker in spite of your loose tongue—and that business with the oar was your masterpiece—it never was boring with you."

"That's not what I want to know. Odysseus," she whispered imploringly, "I know that I'm clever. That doesn't matter to me. But tell me just for once, now that you are leaving, tell me: Did you, not always, but some time or other, did you ever truly love me? You know, *how* I mean it!"

He was silent. But pain can make one clear-sighted, and so she noticed that it was not merely the weakness of death that rendered him silent. She waited. Then suddenly he opened his eyes wide and there was still an extinguishing spark from his former slyness. He spoke suddenly very clearly: "What more do you want? Don't probe!" Then he died.

Penelope gave a very deep sigh. From the very depth of her being, as if she were finally sighing forth—once and for all—an old hope and expectation, which had remained up to now within her heart.

She pressed Odysseus' eyelids closed over his rigid eyes. Heavily she rose from his side and knelt down beside the bed. Squatting on her heels, her empty hands limply on her thighs, she looked into his face. She did not lament and moan. She also shed no tears. She spoke with dead Odysseus: "And now you have left me for the third time!"

"The first time was shortly after one year. The commotion over Helena, the unfortunate expedition to Ilion. You could not miss that. Your little game with the salted furrows I saw through at once, no matter that I was young and inexperienced. It was thanks to Eurykleia, not to me, that I didn't make you any scenes then. All that I did not understand until much later. Not until little Telemachus did I learn what it is to be a man.

"That he needs to prove himself. He could barely hold himself erect on his two wobbly legs, when he tore himself loose from my hand to startle a swarm of pigeons. And when they flew off he shouted and showed off with pride. And there was not a hole into which he did not squeeze himself out of curiosity. And always full of fear. But then, when he was tired and roughed up he crawled back into my lap.

"Then, Odysseus, I understood why you left me. You have to get involved in every adventure and thereby forget all around you. Full of curiosity and full of deadly fear. For at the end of the adventure there is always the wondrous or death. And one never knows beforehand which of the two it will be. Not until you have managed to escape, roughed up and every bone aching, do you remember that somewhere someone is sitting, who will take you into her lap and offer comfort and not hold a grudge except for a little grumbling. But by then you have fallen asleep already, a cozy humming in your ears. That's how you are, you men. From childhood on. You can't help it.

"When word got around that Troy had fallen and you were among the survivors, yet did not return home, it became clear to me that you had left me a second time.

"Before Troy you had 'proven yourself' among men, shown them what a fellow you are. Now it was the turn of the grottoes and gorges. Now you were after discovering what women are. Not the kind who sit at home and wait. You were after the glassy grottoes of delusion: the wondrous, or a snatching gorge? Often both. Also the game with death. With one's wife—if one has made the right choice—this thrill is missing. She does not want to consume and digest you and make you her slave, who whimpers at her feet. She happens to love you. And love is not out to possess. She gives and does not calculate what she gets in return.

"Not even Eurykleia could tell me about you men and the grottoes. Not until much later did I come to understand that. Then there was nothing left for me but to wait, a vague suspicion and a mixture of burning jealousy and cold fear for you.

"So now you have left me a third time. Surely you were not out to fight with the pirate riffraff. That you couldn't hold your mouth—that I am more willing to believe. But that too was not the real reason. I have sensed for a long time that something was troubling you. As if ants were crawling over your brittle bones. You no longer felt good in your skin. No one had to heed your suggestions any longer. Our Telemachus only listened to them out of goodnaturedness and respect, but with suppressed irritability which did not escape you. He is, after all, a man, head of a family. He needs you no longer. And so the last longing for adventure tormented you: the curiosity about death. You had been down there already as a guest. But only for a glance through the entrance. That was wholly sufficient for you then. You saw to it that you escaped unscathed. What death really is you never found out. This discovery still awaited you; a great discovery: craving for wonders mixed with fear."

Penelope was silent for a while and brooded. Then she began anew and spoke: "I'll follow you soon, Odysseus. I'll stay for a while yet up here in the light on the green earth and look on how Telemachus' little ones are turning out and how he himself is getting on. Perhaps I'll have to help his young wife too if one day it comes upon him and he has to set out to 'prove himself.' You'll have to wait for me a little bit as you can see. Perhaps you'll understand then what it means to wait. But down below even suffering most likely is only faint and pale. And I don't even grant you true suffering. Only a little understanding. Because down there you will be dependent upon me alone; your half-goddesses in their glass grottoes vegetate, after all, up here in desolate immortality.

"But there is one thing I still don't understand.

"You know, my Odysseus, who are now lying here silent and immobile, with beard pointing upward, and your cheeks becoming yellowish and sunken so that the cheek bones protrude, your eyes are closed, your changeable, roguish sea eyes which, from the very beginning, had done me in. Do you know? Did you ever know what made me suffer most bitterly?

"Not that you left me after a short year and did not return as soon as it would have been possible. Not the grottoes and gorges and all the endless wasted years when I lay fallow like a forgotten field.

"Gradually I came to understand all that. One can understand everything if it concerns someone you love. One wants to understand it, after all, for then it is less painful.

"It is something else that still grieves me in this our last hour. Something very foolish, but it has been tormenting me to such an extent that not only my heart has suffered but at times every limb in my body, every drop of my blood has hurt so that I could have screamed. Whenever I wanted to begin to speak of it you always avoided me, suddenly had something pressing to perform. Now you can no longer avoid me and you have to listen: Why, Odysseus, did you never—not even in the first months of our being together and not even now, on your deathbed, say: I love you, Penelope!

"My ears are resounding with these words which you will have whispered and stammered and shouted to all the others. On the walls of their caverns they are still clinging—your declarations of love. You always had a glib tongue if you wanted something. Why did you always suppress it with me? Yes, suppress it! Why was that? Perhaps it was true, after all, that you never did love me but merely liked me. But if that were the case, you didn't have such a delicate way with the truth and you were always good at lying. Why could you not force yourself just once to say: Penelope, I love you, I desire you!—You told me again and again that I am clever, that one can talk with me, and rely on me, and that it's never boring with me. But not a single time did you say: Whenever I think of you, Penelope, whenever I look at you, I go weak in the knees.

"Of course I know that I was never as beautiful as Helena, not even as pretty as Calypso with her batting of eyelids and her silken tresses. But Odysseus, you know people, you know women. Did it never occur to you how much I longed for these three cheap words, which no kitchen-maid is denied: I love you! Most likely I would not have believed you. But at least I would have known: I'm worth a lie.

"Did you never ask yourself—you who seldom miss anything—why I raved on and on about the suitors? How they gaped at me with open mouths when I descended and stopped for a moment at the entrance to the hall and looked around: made up with care and skill? Did I even tell you about the kind of glances that Antinoos cast toward me and that I even made an attempt at returning them a few times. Odysseus, you never looked at me the way Antinoos looked at me. This glance you reserved for others.—Did you also never ask yourself why I never contradicted people's whisperings and grumblings into your ear that I had slept my way through all the suitors? You remained quite cool and unconcerned when they pricked you, and you laughed at most. Were you so confident, did you take it so for granted that desire couldn't seize me or that someone else couldn't have desire for me? Or were you indifferent? Were you never tormented by jealousy of me?

"I know jealousy, Odysseus! Between fear and jealousy my being was torn back and forth for ten years, during which I knew not whether to weep for a dead man or hate a vagabond. And even after you had been back for quite some time and gradually all your adventures had been told, I was still seized now and then by the crawling beast of jealousy, and its reptilian bite poisoned my blood and limbs. In my head and in my heart I no longer bore you a grudge. But it could happen that a dream at night would burst forth into light the old torment from the depth of forgetting and understanding, and the torture of jealousy plagued me as if you had just left me now, young, in the bloom of your strength, abandoned and cast aside for the sake of another, who possessed something I lacked and which transported you into an ecstasy such as you never experienced with me. When I could bear it no longer and spoke of it, you began to talk of something else or went outside. You see, my eternal beloved, who now lies before me with numb lips, unable to reply, what tortured me so terribly and hurt me was that you were never jealous of me. That you never at all bothered to bring yourself to utter the lie: Penelope, you were the best of all I have known in the course of my vagabond life, you alone I have truly loved and for your sake I have returned from all the shimmering grottoes, because longing and desire and jealousy tore me to pieces. Today I am old enough to know that love is more than the delusion and the desire for well-shaped limbs; that in the long run it is not a matter of a few high bounces in bed or in the grass, but what matters is the support one gives to each other toward life and toward death, which the Gods have imposed; toward their childish senseless whims.

"I gave you this support, and you relied on it and you returned because of it, when the glorious adventures began to tire you somewhat. It was then that you realized that a feeling of security without all the to-do of the wondrous is what keeps one going and is essential. That's when you returned home.

"But look, Odysseus! Does one derive happiness from the essential, does one make a living from the essential? To be sure, it strengthens the spine, it helps one to an erect posture and keeps the pulse at a regular rhythm. But then let's not forget the foolish, love-obsessed heart! And mine too—just like yours—longed for the 'unessential' now and then, which offers happiness and confidence, faith in life, and a little pride in the dear, transitory flesh. I don't mind a sated lie, if only it can disturb the regular rhythm of the heart beat, make it miss a beat and then race wildly. That feels so good. One doesn't feel alive until the heart misses a beat, Odysseus. You experienced it, after all, and indulged in it ignoring reason and responsibility, which told you: Go home.

"I don't hold a grudge any longer. But it hurts me, I had so hoped and longed for words, for lies, that would have brought sweet disorder into my heart. What good is it for a woman to hear words of recognition about her cleverness, her prudence, her reliability and fidelity and be told that one can talk and laugh with her, and that she understands a man and makes no scenes when he strays a little.

"O, my Odysseus! How I have waited to be taken in by your words that you loved me because of some charms that have nothing to do with intelligence and decency but cling to the naked exterior, to the dumb skin that withers so quickly. To be taken in just once: that for my sake you were tormented with burning jealousy and had bitten into the earth, just as I had done for your sake.

"Eurykleia wanted to convince me that you had slaughtered the suitors out of jealousy because one or the other had slept with me. But you killed them only out of fury and rage because they laid hands on your possessions, and I too was a part of your possessions. It may well be that you would not have harmed a hair on their heads for Calypso's sake but ordered everything peaceably through negotiations, but you would have been jealous. The idea that she could have betrayed you would have infuriated you.

"You see, my old Odysseus, who have roamed so much and so attentively among people, it never occurred to you that I too, 'circumspect' Penelope, would not have given a damn for all my cleverness and would have taken pride in being for you, whom I loved, nothing but a woman who could bring your blood to boil, could drive desire into your flesh. Perhaps I was even successful at it occasionally. But why did you, who were so glib, never say it, why did the words never cross your lips? Was it so difficult for you? For me it was never difficult to say: 'You dearest, only, wonderful one!' even if you weren't always so wonderful but left me sitting high and dry. It was especially then that you needed to hear my words.

"But what's the use now. It's over.

"I can't torment you any more with questions or elicit any answers. I can only give my own answers, why everything was the way it was: Why you never looked at me the way Antinoos had looked at me. Why you never told me that you were jealous of me. Why you even withheld from me this very simple word: I love you, Penelope, in your flesh.

"I think you were simply too clever. It had nothing to do with me and with how seductive I was. You were not willing to endanger your nest. And if one treats one another in such a way, the bed becomes a cesspool in which you moan and wallow with lust but then is filled with dread and one never wants to see it again. It can't be a nest any longer. That was the reason why you satisfied these desires elsewhere and not with me. And I, who experienced the same desires, I denied myself their fulfillment. Not because of decency or because of your honor but because of the honor of my flesh which a woman only yields if love is involved and affection and mutual care and respect.

"It seems to me that we women cannot yield to the longings of our sex in the same way as you men can, without scruples and also without harm, because this place is not only a garden of pleasure but we also conceive and bear children there. And you, whom we love, we also always carry you around there somewhere, and you look not only for joy there but even more often seek refuge and a security deeper than thick walls and iron armor are able to offer.

"And therefore we have to take care that this dumb lascivious flesh not become tainted, nor loiter shamelessly and free itself from the supervision of the soul, which forces it to guard its honor and defend its dignity as a nest for husband and child. The clever man does not build a house in the mire. And, my Odysseus, you have always been clever.

"Could this have been the reason why you never told me, I love and desire you, Penelope? That it was not out of indifference that you withheld this word so stubbornly from me but rather shyness? Fear? A kind of preventive magic? If I don't articulate that you are desirable, then you aren't, and it will occur to no one to look at you with thieving eyes!

"Poor Odysseus! You could rest easy. No one disturbed your olive tree bed, even if it had not been so deeply embedded in Ithaka's hard soil. You could sleep very soundly and enjoy yourself in the loosely made beds of your half-divine trollops. You were well taken care of, nonetheless, in my lap, even though you roamed through the world and crawled into every grotto. I surmised and even knew much of all that. I neither hanged myself because of it nor did I betray you. Your nest stayed unblemished. Not because of my virtuousness—don't pride yourself on that—but because of my incapability, which I hated from time to time. The threshold to your nest was not crossed by any stranger because your face stood in the way, your mocking eyes.

"By now the staff of Hermes is probably shooing your poor soul like a lost bird's down into the deepest grotto, into the black lap of the earth. Your familiar body is still lying here on our communal bed. But yellow already, as if made of parchment, an emptied shell. Soon they will carry you away from me. I myself will still wash you and anoint you and wrap you in soft robes so that you won't be so cold in the earth. Then this house will be empty, as it has never been empty before, when you were away. Because when you were roaming through the world there was always some of your warmth left within these walls. Therefore I never quite could believe that you were dead, because I felt this warmth, which settled over the thyme in the hour of Pan, when the fauns were rutting.

"But now you are dead.

"During the last years our being together was merely a habit. All our stories had turned lame. Each of us knew from the very first word which story, which adventure, which fun, which farce was now being ground out, and we were happy whenever a stranger came to the house who had not yet heard it. Every word we knew by heart, every phrase. Often it grated on our nerves, and our goose bumps rose up on account of so much irritation over so much intimacy.

"Once you were the crown of my heart, Odysseus. It has been such a long time. Then it was gradually revealed that the crown was full of

The Death of Odysseus 171

thorns. They were sharp and tenacious and dug themselves deeper. And then came a time when the thorns turned dull and brittle and I no longer perceived a crown. But now that it is gone, I realize again that it was here; because I am freezing. There was a short spring for us both, my husband, my Odysseus. Then storm clouds were gathering and erupted, hurling lightning bolts and echoing thunder far and wide. Afterwards came a damp fog and turned everything gray and vague.

"But after they will have carried you outside and it is irrevocable and forever, then it will be again as in the first weeks and months of our love, when we still had so much to say to each other and tell one another and show so much love for each other. It will be as in the days when the broom bloomed, when my heart skipped a beat just at hearing your step outside on the path and then it blazed up when you entered through the door, so that I had to place my hand on it because I thought it would burst with amazement that you were existing and you were mine. You will stand before the eyes of my heart and live in my veins and in every fiber of my body as in those distant days, and all sorrow, all resentment and all despair and also the bleak habituation will be extinguished, as if they had never existed. Only your image will remain and above it the phantom wings of the never again.

"Now I am still talking to you so calmly as if you were sitting across from me and listening. My heart too is calm and so is my head. Now it seems as if I could bear it and survive it that you are no longer here and go on living quite normally. But it is merely an artificial numbness. The fright when they brought you home on the stretcher has anesthetized me for a few hours. But slowly this deaf coldness will thaw, my heart will beat, my nerves will begin to feel.

"Then the vault of heaven will be torn asunder, light and darkness will be suspended. It will be very silent in this non-light, and something will pass by me in this stillness. A dread that will face me deep into the withering marrow of my bones, a dread whose gaze says: Odysseus is no longer on this earth. Then may the Gods be merciful to me."

It was totally dark now in the room. The moist wind from the ocean had died down and stillness clung to the olive trees and cypresses outside. Penelope struggled to her feet from her kneeling position. Her limbs had fallen asleep. She sat down once more on the bed, leaned over the face of dead Odysseus and laid both of her hands on his cheeks now grown cold. His familiar face was surprisingly small, angular and rigid. She ran her hand once more through his reddish-gray curly hair, which felt like hay and withered leaves; his shut eyelids beneath the high-arched brows, which still seemed to retain something of his critical vigilance. She stroked his naked shoulders, which were still warm and not yet rigid. Then she sank down upon his hollow chest, shaken by a sobbing that was soundless and did not dissolve in tears.

"Farewell, my Odysseus," she whispered, "my greatly beloved, you scoundrel, you philanderer, liar, and dreamer. I succumbed to you. I succumbed to your sea-green, changeable eyes, which revealed all which you then let me see anyway. Nonetheless! I regret nothing. And today still, now that I know all that's in store for me, I would jump again into your carriage and hold fast to your shoulders and not look back at my father's house."

Once more she took his cheeks into both of her hands and kissed the cracked, bloodless lips. Then she pulled the sheet over his face and rose very erect. She had the feeling she was straightening out her bones, as if the rusty joints were grating. Then she walked to the door and called the servant girls. Her voice had a jagged sharpness when she commanded:

"Remove from the house all of your master's belongings. The clothing, utensils which he used, and the sandals, above all his sandals. Remove them from my sight, so that I no longer see any of it.—And from now on make my bed in the room where Eurykleia slept."

Then she left the house with quick, long steps and walked up to the stone oak and further on through the thicket of thorny shrubs and blackberry bushes, so that blood was running down her calves. And all the while the servants followed her with their astounded and disapproving looks, having expected an orgy of weeping and grief and now whispered maliciously that the mistress was incredibly unfeeling.

Translated by Renate Latimer

TO THE EDGE OF THE VILLAGE

FELIX MITTERER

MATTHEW has gotten worse again. For some time now, he's been acting peculiar. With bowed head he pushes his cart along, talks to himself, and slinks off into his room in the evening. Recently the old school principal happened to say hello and asked how he was. Matthew, startled, looked up and said: "I ain't talkin' to you! I don' know you." And he hurried on. After a couple of steps he stopped and yelled back: "Anyways yer a Pisces. That's fer sure. But I don' know you, no way. I can't know everybody, can I? It's gettin' to be too much!" The same thing happened to other people Matthew had known for a long time. And then the episode in church. Matthew is kneeling in the first row of the gallery, his eyes closed, saying the rosary. And all of a sudden he jumps up and shouts toward the altar: "Oh yeah, you know why! You know why, don'cha?" The people in the nave down below turn around and look up. The chalice slips off the salver the priest is holding. One of the farmers next to Matthew whispers: "Hey, man, sit down." Matthew sits down, and buries his face in his hands. The farmer lays a hand on his arm, tries to think of something to say; he is embarrassed because Matthew is crying. But the thing that most disturbed the village old-timers, who had been sympathetic to Matthew's plight for years, was that he no longer recognized many of them, and even refused to talk to them, insisting that he didn't know them.

Up until then, the most amazing thing about Matthew had been his uncanny ability to tell a person's exact age. Right down to the month. He used to stop total strangers in the street, look them over carefully, and say: "Yer a Taurus, right? Born in '26, right?" And he was always right. Matthew enjoyed widespread respect on account of this gift, although there were those who said he just got the information ahead of time. But even these skeptics could not deny that he had an exceptional memory. In any event, at one point or another he had told everyone in the village their exact age.

And another thing: Matthew no longer entertained the young people of the village with songs he invented. In the past, when a group of children met him on the street he would put his broom and shovel in his cart and sing his songs. No one ever understood the lyrics; he made up the words, too. The songs were very beautiful, but also very sad. People called them Russian. And the children weren't the only ones who liked Matthew's singing. The farmers, too, liked to stop when they walked by, listen, and nod their approval.

Now Matthew doesn't sing anymore. Hardly even speaks anymore. Is obviously frightened. And he doesn't know why. He just knows that the village isn't what it used to be. That something is out of kilter. That is why there is something out of kilter with Matthew. And it keeps getting worse.

Still, for a while there, it had looked like the danger was past. For years everything had been fine. When Matthew returned from Hall, more than twenty years ago, everyone was kind to him. That made it much easier for him to readjust to the village community, to ease his way back into a life of freedom. Yes, people felt a little awkward when their paths crossed his, to be sure. But it was the kind of awkwardness that would be brought out by any person who has experienced something very unusual and extraordinary. It is the same awkwardness you felt in the presence of the young farmer whose hair suddenly turned snow-white after an eerie experience. This farmer had gone out to cut grass one summer morning. His father had been away, up on the mountain pasture, for three days, because one of the hired hands was in the hospital with a broken leg. Suddenly, so the young man's story went, he saw his father walking toward him out of the morning fog. He was moving very slowly, as though something were holding him back. But then he was right there, a couple of feet away. The father stretched out his right hand and seemed to want to say something. When he—the son—spoke to the father and took a step toward him, the father vanished again in the fog. And he—the son—knew immediately that his father was dead. And indeed he was: two hours later a farmer came with the news that the old man had died earlier that morning. The villagers talked about that strange episode for a long time. Yes, you felt awkward around Matthew, just like you did with the farmer's son. No one ever referred to the place where he had spent the last seven years. He, too, never mentioned it. The village commissioner, who had visited Matthew a couple of months before his release, once mentioned something about shock treatments to his cronies in the local tavern. And about a therapeutic water bed. The people didn't know what that meant, so those words made them feel uneasy. Matthew's extraordinary serenity seemed unnatural to the villagers. His melancholy gentleness was downright disquieting.

The first thing Matthew did when he got off the train was to head straight for the cemetery. The commissioner wanted to go along, but Matthew asked to be allowed to go alone. The commissioner agreed, but followed Matthew at a discreet distance. Finding his father's grave was not difficult. He stood for a while in silence, then knelt down and said: "Hi, dad. They jus' let me out. I got here quick as I could. Ya don' hafta be afraid no more, dad. I won' bother ya anymore. Forgive me. I didn' know what I was doin'. Forgive me, dad!" Matthew began to cry. The commissioner approached him and spoke some soothing words. Just as he had done seven years ago. When the terrible thing happened that caused Matthew to be sent to the mental institution.

Matthew's father had been having pains in his belly for several years. But in the country, people don't pay much attention to pain. You only go to the doctor when it seems absolutely necessary. It didn't seem necessary to Matthew's father until the stabbing pain had gotten so unbearable that he wasn't able to sleep for a week. The local doctor feared the worst and sent the man to the hospital in Innsbruck. There they operated, and sewed him right up again. Terminal cancer. Nothing to be done. He was sent home to die. Suffering terribly, he lingered for seven weeks. His body started to rot while he was still alive. The stench drifted out of his room and spread through the whole house. It was unbearable. When they told Matthew that his father was dying and wanted to say goodbye, he refused to set foot in the room. He ran away and hid. His father died on a Thursday evening in August. No one was with him. Not even the priest. While he was administering the last rites, he had to run out to throw up, and he didn't come back. Since the body decomposed all the more rapidly in the midsummer heat, the funeral was set for Friday. In the meantime someone had found Matthew in a barn. They told him his father was dead, but he refused to believe it, he wanted to see his father. In view of the circumstances, his request was denied. Anyway, the coffin was already sealed. Matthew insisted that he would not allow his father to be buried alive. He grabbed an ax, ran into the room where the body was laid out, and tried to open the coffin. They held him back. Had to knock him out. Then the burial. Matthew pale and trembling at the grave. The commissioner puts his arm around his shoulder, comforts him. Today is Matthew's sixteenth birthday. No one remembers it. When the coffin is lowered into the grave Matthew jumps in after it, embraces the coffin tightly, cries out for his father. They drag Matthew out, bring him home, and lock him in the cellar. Early that evening they let him out, and he seems to have calmed down. He doesn't say a word or eat a thing. Goes to his father's room and lies down on his bed.

About two o'clock that morning the sexton is awakened by a strange noise. He walks to the window and looks down into the graveyard. Sees someone with a shovel, digging. He gets his flashlight, goes out, and finds Matthew digging up his father's grave. When the sexton asks what in God's name he is doing, Matthew hits him over the head with the shovel. The sexton takes to his heels and knocks on the constable's door, yelling for help. When the two get back to the cemetery, Matthew comes toward them. He is carrying his father's body in his arms. When the constable retells this story in the tavern, he always says that the whole graveyard was stirring. He had never been afraid, not even in the war, but that night his hair stood on end. He wouldn't wish anything like that on his worst enemy. When Matthew sees the two men he lays his father tenderly on the ground and says "My dad is not goin' to be buried alive, let me tell you. Let's get that clear right now. 'Cause if it's not, I'll give it to you. Just you try that again." The two men try to explain to Matthew that his father really is dead, but it doesn't sink in. Matthew takes out a pocket knife, opens it, and says: "Get lost, or I'll cut ya real bad!" The constable walks up to Matthew, talking all the while, deftly catches him by the wrist, twists his arm behind his back, takes the knife away. Then with the help of the sexton he hauls the desperately struggling boy to the village jail. The next day Matthew is picked up and taken to the mental institution.

Now, seven years later, Matthew is home again. Begged his father's forgiveness and was welcomed by the villagers. He had no close relatives, so the community assumed responsibility for him. They gave him a job as a street sweeper and a small room above the area the band used for rehearsals. Matthew began to feel at home—began to forget, even went to the tavern now and then for a beer or two, watched the people playing cards and told them when they were born. He took care of the farmers' paths and received in return milk and eggs and, now and then, when they slaughtered an animal, a nice piece of meat. Once, when the very pregnant wife of a sawmill hand for some reason or other threw herself in front of a passing express train, and both the grave digger and the constable refused to collect the scattered pieces of the woman and the baby, Matthew immediately offered his services. He meticulously picked it all up with his bare hands and carefully put it in the plastic bag. From then on they always called on Matthew for tasks like that. The people said: "He's somethin' else, ain't afraid of a damn thing. He's on a first-name basis with the Grim Reaper." And that undoubtedly added to his legendary stature.

The years passed, and Matthew seemed to be normal. But then something happened that confused Matthew, disoriented him, destroyed the normal pattern of his life. The outsiders came. Of course, in the past tourists had come through the village. But there weren't very many of them. You scarcely noticed them. Now they were coming in droves. They attacked like swarms of locusts. The streets of the village used to be fairly quiet—with the exception of market day and various festivals. Matthew was able to go about his business in peace. But now the traffic kept getting worse and worse, the streets were full of parked cars, and often hundreds of people were strolling through the village. Matthew felt like he couldn't do his work. Felt disturbed by these outsiders who spoke a language he could hardly understand. And Matthew came to the disturbing conclusion that the village was changing, and the people along with it. The villagers were always in a hurry. They had to build rooming houses and make beds and sell souvenirs and pick up guests at the railroad station. Scarcely anyone stopped to say hello to Matthew or to have him guess their age. The only people who hadn't changed were the farmers from the mountains. As always, they would chat with Matthew in a friendly and respectful manner when they were in town to take care of something or other.

Now it has gotten to the point that Matthew is completely disoriented. He doesn't go to the tavern anymore to watch the people play cards. Not that they play cards much anymore. The young men have become ski instructors and have to devote their evenings to the guests. They slip into their *Lederhosen* and learn what are passed off as folk dances to the tourists. Matthew can't even recognize most of the taverns any more. They were remodeled, expanded, modernized. The menus feature things he has never heard of. Matthew doesn't feel comfortable in these places. And twice now they wouldn't even let him in. One day the owner of his favorite tavern said to Matthew, he shouldn't be offended, but he just could not let him in with his muddy boots. He hadn't installed a new floor just so Matthew could trample it with his dirty boots; the chairs, too, were new, and he didn't want Matthew and his filthy pants sitting on them. In another tavern they complained that he always slopped up the tablecloth, and you can't expect the guests to put up with that. And anyway, they didn't need his business. After all, he sat there all evening with a single beer. Matthew was deeply hurt. Was ashamed of himself. Didn't understand why the people in the village had changed so much.

Matthew's reaction was totally in character. Now he has turned the tables. He retreats into himself. He loses his memory. His ability to recall the past. The old commissioner, long retired, is one of the few to whom Matthew speaks. Even though the commissioner's responses do not register. "Ya know," Matthew said to the commissioner, "Ya know, I used to know everybody here. Every one. Even if I didn' know their name. Weren't no strangers back then. And it won' be long now before I don' recognize nobody. They're all disappearin'. I don' know where they're goin'. They're dyin' or somethin'. I don' know. Every day there's less an' less of 'em that I know. Don' see nothin' but outsiders. An' they don' like me. Nobody likes me. No one likes me no more. They're all outsiders. I jus' don' know my way around no more. Stuff is hap'nin' behind my back. Stuff. If I only knowed what."

Matthew is also doing things he hasn't done for years. In church he scratches his face until it bleeds, and when someone asks him why he is doing it, he answers: "The good Lord had to suffer a whole lot more."

The word also spread that Matthew stopped keeping his money at home, but was burying it in the forest instead. He marks the places with rocks and branches, and then wanders around in the forest for days because he can't remember where he buried it. A real epidemic of gold fever broke out among the children.

Then the story of the gamekeeper. He told about the time he was in the forest and ran into Matthew, with a noose in his hand. And when he asked him what he was going to do with the noose, Matthew hid it behind his back and said: "I ain't talkin' to you. 'Cause I don' know you." Then he—the gamekeeper—unshouldered his rifle and said in jest, "O.K., man, jus' climb up on that stump there an' I'll shoot ya. Beats hangin' yourself." And Matthew ran away.

Matthew can't stand the brass-band music now, oddly enough. When the band has a rehearsal, he goes out and doesn't come back until the last musicians have left. He used to be very fond of lying in bed and listening as the march tunes rose from below. "I don' need no radio at home," he would say. "Twice a week I gets a free concert."

Now Matthew always starts sweeping the streets at three o'clock in the morning. Then he's by himself and no one disturbs him while he's working. Matthew spends most of the day at the edge of the village. He sits for hours on a little hill and looks out at the little town where he was born. He has become an outsider. He feels like he has lost his home. Forever.

Matthew stands up and screams his despair down into the village. But no one hears him. They are busy building rooming houses, making beds, selling souvenirs, and picking up guests at the railroad station.

Translated by Jerry Glenn and Jennifer Kelley

Villa Dolorosa

Barbara Neuwirth

CATALINA was sitting behind the whitehorn bush, repairing her boom box.
"She's a strange child," she heard her mother saying to Aunt Oggi.
"She's entering puberty."
"No, that's not it. We went through that with the other two girls. They lied, were stubborn and sassy, didn't wash—you know, the kinds of behaviors you can deal with. But Catalina . . . "
"She's just precocious."
"Oggi," Catalina knew that her mother was shaking her head now, "sometimes I find her really eerie. Yesterday, for example, she was coming home from school, and the mailman was following her. He was stumbling along behind her like a sleepwalker and didn't even notice me. And she was smiling."
"He was probably drunk."
"Not at all. When I started talking to him, he shuddered and then 'woke up.' He was—well, like he was really under a spell."
"Are you jealous of your daughter?"
"Catalina is fifteen!"
"That's not an answer."
Then she refilled the teacups. Catalina put the last diode in, screwed the housing back together, shoved the little mirror between the two tracks that she'd mounted on the back herself, and tried the on-button: " . . . had no support from his teammates during the game. What a shame!" the loudspeaker croaked. Catalina got up and headed for the house. She didn't pay any attention to her mother's horrified face nor to her outraged: "Were you hiding there listening to us?" She just carelessly waved her aside, raised the radio to her ear, balanced it on her shoulder, and hinted at a few dance steps in time to the music.

Catalina's mother's face turned red, more from shame because Catalina had heard the accusation of jealousy, and then she started hissing at Oggi: "There, you can see what she's like."

Oggi smiled: "Actually, she's quite normal for a fifteen-year-old. Don't get yourself upset over nothing."

"That's easy for you to say. You don't have any kids."

"I wonder why not," Oggi said dryly.

Catalina took the old, crumbling ballet costume that her Aunt Oggi had bought at a flea market in the capital out of the trunk. While she bent over to tie her shoelaces, the stiff, frilly skirt reaching for the ceiling, she hummed: " . . . oh Lord, won't you buy me a Mercedes Benz . . . "

She brushed her long, brown hair over her head, then tossed it back with spirit and smiled at herself in the brass-framed mirror. Then she shouldered her radio again. She used the kitchen door to leave the house because she didn't want to walk past her mother again, and although Aunt Oggi was nice, "Don't trust anyone over thirty."

The forest began behind the kitchen garden. Although at this time of year, in September, almost nothing blossomed in the shadows along this path, wild, overgrown green caught the eye everywhere in the tall, unkempt bushes, overburdened shrubs, and thick, fat grasses that edged the path. The rain from the last thunderstorm had washed out deep gullies, but the farmers had patched them again a few days later with white gravel from the river, and that's where Catalina performed her dance steps, swaying forwards and backwards, wagging her round rear-end and her narrow hips, twitching her shoulders one after the other, closing her eyes for fractions of a second while she sang, and concentrating fully on the agility of her slender body. She placed one foot in front of the other, pulled her head in slightly towards her neck, danced a half-step back, and saw a baby carriage rolling out around a corner of the forest path.

Only when she recognized the woman pushing the carriage did she start moving again, prancing in time to the music. She didn't want anything to do with this woman, didn't want to recognize her presence here. She saw Susanne, the pharmacist's wife, every day when she waited across from the pharmacy for the bus after school. And every day the pharmacist came out onto the sidewalk and looked over at the children;

he answered the schoolchildren's polyphonic greeting, and then his eyes sought Catalina's, and they stroked her with a calm gaze. But this velvet stroking bored something into Catalina's brain, a screw that was tightened a little more every day, causing her an unpleasant pain that was reminiscent of something forbidden. More than anything else, seeing Susanne everyday poured a sticky feeling of wrong and shame over this pain, Susanne with the little brat whom the community had greeted with satisfaction, the brat who made the pharmacy dynasty secure once again for the time being. Wasn't it irksome enough—in Catalina's mother's words—to have to see an outsider marry his way into town in this generation?

Then it was pushed past her, this child, this drooling, whining baby who today, for a change, was lying in the carriage in the shade of a tiny parasol with a contented smile on its face, fast asleep despite the rattling ride on the uneven ground. Susanne was only ten years older than Catalina, but now, when she saw the girl in her pink costume, when she watched this young body floating along, she got a pinched expression on her face. The nonchalance with which Catalina moved, although she was already in Susanne's field of vision, outraged Susanne. She herself was walking behind the carriage in her unimaginative tight skirt and gray-blue silk blouse, the top three buttons of which she had seductively, she hoped, left open, and this ill-mannered girl with her mocking smile on her soft lips was jumping around in front of her.

Catalina grinned straight into Susanne's face, and Susanne pursed her lips because it was this girl's obligation to say hello first, and because something in the girl's expression scared her. Susanne thought about the gleam in her husband's eyes when he came back into the pharmacy after watching the school children. Susanne worshipped her husband— they'd been married for barely a year. The suspicion that he might be watching one or the other of the schoolgirls with lust had already cost her many a sleepless night. And then this brat showed up, stuck her well-rounded backside out—it was an unheard of incitement to let your gaze glide across this young body, to watch her tiny, but awfully noticeable breasts and her slender waist. And on top of that, the girl had smiled and had done so in a way that suggested she knew a secret that had something to do with beauty and craving. Susanne walked faster. A cold fury dug its claws into her belly. She gave the carriage a shove in order to get home quickly, find her beloved husband, and put her arms around him. The baby in the thoroughly rattled carriage woke up and began to scream in discontent.

From the distance Catalina heard the child screeching. She laughed, taking pleasure in Susanne's pain mostly because she didn't like her, this unfriendly Susanne who deposited a torrent of hate and death wishes in Catalina, an allotment of evil wishes that Susanne's burning gaze sent forth from behind the window of the pharmacy's perfume department, flooding Catalina's soul until Catalina felt *guilty*.

Catalina was on her way to the ruin. Although a number of schoolchildren lived within a radius of a few kilometers, the ruin was almost never visited. Because the path was badly overgrown, Catalina had to take her radio off her shoulder: The bushes kept greedily reaching out into the path and touching her body. Catalina twisted and turned playfully to avoid them. It was shady here because the September sun couldn't force its way through the filter of the hazel bushes until the afternoon, but further into the forest—the ruin lay in a ravine—it became noticeably cooler.

A first glance at the ruin didn't reveal that it was situated directly on the slope of this steep ravine, for overgrown white beech and alders concealed the abyss, and only the terrace, a free floating arc that the architect had rammed into a crevice in the cliff, indicated an abrupt, unbelievable depth. From the badly damaged walls of the villa, steps led on the right and on the left to the terrace, but of the exterior walls on the south side, only a few stumps were left. The height of one section hinted that the building might have had two stories, and the completely preserved mosaic floor showed the former wealth of the place. From the terrace, a vaulted entryway into the cellar could be seen diagonally under the rooms, but it was situated so inconveniently in the section of the villa that clung to the slope that one could no longer reach it, unless, perhaps, by means of a rope.

Catalina loved the solitude of the place, the decay, and the sad boldness of the terrace over the gorge. She came here almost every week, set her radio down on the oval terrace and danced to exhaustion, finally collapsing dizzily onto the ground, where, in her laboriously produced trance, she felt a power flowing from the walls into her, a burning that began in the soles of her feet and took possession of her body until she felt a slight, momentary release from the misery of her pubescent confusion. The brick surface had in the meantime been wiped clean by her dancing, as clean as the covered terrace in the courtyard of the pharmacist's house. Catalina had seen it at the wedding, to which half the town had been invited in order to meet the young, recently graduated pharmacist who had married into the pharmacy. He had been bought with the business, Catalina's mother had said back then, but her father had only shaken his head in irritation and said that Susanne was certainly attractive enough to find a young man who wouldn't see the pharmacy floating over her head like a permanent halo.

Swaying to the beat of the music, Catalina climbed the steps to the terrace, placed her radio on the hip-high balustrade, and leaned against it. Thickly overgrown, the gorge was now an iridescent green sea gently rising and falling in the afternoon's breath.

Someone spoke.

The fright caused Catalina to stiffen. Behind her stood the mailman with an overheated, red face. Catalina held tight to the balustrade with both hands.

"Listen, I've been following you," he stammered.

Catalina's hand felt its way to the radio and turned the music off. Now she was surrounded only by the rustling of the leaves in the trees, and somewhat further off, in the gorge, the short cry of an oriole.

The man was breathing heavily. His hand with the wedding ring was resting on his belt. He opened his blue pants and lowered them slightly, his gaze directed fearfully at Catalina's face. He presented Catalina his half-stiff penis.

"That's you," he attempted to explain to her.

Catalina squinted at the tangle of his lowered pants. Under her disturbed eyes, his penis grew larger and jerkily stood upright. A kind of rage gathered in Catalina's face, and her lower jaw moved back and forth and ground out a sound from her upper jaw. Her eyelids twitched.

The sweating mailman stumbled one step closer to her, and Catalina could tell by looking at him that he was about to reach out to her in the next moment. And then something began to rise out of the cold brick; it flowed into the soles of Catalina's feet, slowly filled her body with a raging coldness, and flooded her brain so that she gasped in shock for a brief moment. Her face became completely calm again. Only her eyes held an empty and terrible expression, and she said: "Sit on the balustrade."

Under her white gaze, the man staggered toward the balustrade and sat astride it; his erection towered ridiculously among the folds of cloth.

"Now turn to face outwards," Catalina ordered. The mailman ponderously heaved his legs over the small wall, his shining face turned toward Catalina. For a moment Catalina looked at him, and she wondered if she should give him a shove; he deserved to be pushed off the balustrade to punish him for his repulsive behavior, but then she looked at his fat red fingers, at the wedding ring that separated the finger from the hand like an incision and thought about what he had just done with this hand. She looked at her own small hands and suppressed the wish.

Instead of that, she spoke directly into his face, swollen with expectation: "Now jump off."

She bent forwards to observe his fall. The approximately twenty feet to the first crash went quietly, then the red head smashed on a rock, the mailman's brains spurted out, and while the limp body continued to fall, touching on several trees and finally disappearing in the green thicket, his blood and brains smeared the stones. Catalina took a step back from the abyss and stood for a moment before she yanked the radio violently from its resting place and pressed it to her breast. She breathed heavily, turned the music on, and began to nod with her upper body. Then she turned the music on as loud as it would go, put one foot in front of the other, put the radio down on the red brick next to her, shook all her limbs, threw her long hair over her head, and stamped her feet on the ground.

The children were yelling and shoving each other at the bus stop. Only one of them stood silently, her head tilted to the side as if listening to something.

Catalina looked over toward the pharmacy. Susanne was standing in her white lab coat in front of the perfume counter and staring angrily at the girl with the book bag, replenishing the screeching pressure of the previous day and supplying a new contingent of hatred and pain where all the old feelings had been consumed by the energy exerted against the mailman, and Catalina absorbed the hatred like a sponge. *If you feed that to me long enough, it'll make you choke.*

The young pharmacist appeared at the door. He approached his wife, followed her gaze, saw Catalina standing delicately in the midst of the scuffling children, and then looked intently and questioningly into her eyes, and when Catalina's mouth began to smile, he placed his hand around his wife's shoulders and led her away to keep her from recognizing that she had unmistakably been forced into the role of the loser by Catalina's smile. But as he turned away, he spoke to Catalina with silent lips, telling her that she had penetrated his heart. Catalina couldn't quite grasp the meaning of this message because the school bus came driving up and blocked her view of the pharmacy. And as she looked out the bus window at the imposing old house, there was no longer anyone to be seen in front of the shop.

The excitement caused by the mailman's disappearance was restrained in Catalina's family. Since another mailman now delivered the letters, the disappearance was treated only as a local sensation, not like anything really unsettling. Catalina's mother told anyone who would listen that the mailman had seemed abnormal to her as long ago as the previous week, and she described in detail his clumsiness, but she regularly neglected to mention Catalina's presence during this scene because everything had taken on a new meaning, as she carefully explained to Oggi.

"Well," said Oggi and glanced at Catalina, who was tormenting herself with her Latin homework, "how many children did he leave behind?"

"Do you think he just ran off?" Catalina's mother asked in outrage.

"In some sense, of course," Oggi answered and again looked over at Catalina. And when she started thinking about going home, she asked Catalina to accompany her for part of the way.

"I have to study," Catalina attempted to fend her off, but her mother insisted she go: "You sit in the house day in and day out. You're going to get fat that way if you never get any movement."

Oggi studied the slender girl at her side as they left the house.

"Your mother has problems with your growing up. With the other two it was obviously the daughters who entered puberty, but now it seems to be your mother instead of you."

Catalina didn't answer.

"Do you know the Villa Dolorosa?"

Catalina looked up in astonishment at her aunt.

"Yes, that's the villa back there at the edge of the ravine. It may seem absurd to you, but I saw it before it was destroyed, when it was still being used."

"That ruin?"

Oggi smiled because Catalina had revealed her knowledge of it.

"It was the most beautiful villa in the whole area. An English couple had built it as their retirement home. It was a sensation, to put it mildly, when the building was completed. The owners were hardly ever here.

They owned a large cloth business in London, and the woman visited the villa only twice. She never loved the house, not like he did . . . and then she had it torn down."

"That can't be true. Some of it is still well preserved."

"She contracted for its demolition, but died before the work was completed. After that no one was dumb enough to spend any money finishing the job." Oggi paused to coax the question as to *why* from Catalina, but Catalina was obstinately silent until Oggi took up the story again. "It's a strange place. Several accidents took place within the space of a year. People lost their lives."

"It was probably some old witch that was at fault . . . "

"You know about that?" Oggi was truly amazed.

Catalina shook her head. "Know about it? It's just that it's always the same thing. Whenever something frightening happens, whenever men flip out, it's always the fault of some woman or other, preferably a beautiful one, or even a very ugly one, and it's especially awful if she doesn't look much like anything at all."

"Where did you get that from? Certainly not from your mother."

"I read books."

"What? What books? Who's giving you books like that?"

"Gives? Who gives me anything?"

Oggi looked at Catalina carefully: "When I was your age, I thought that eleven tenths of humanity deserved to be wiped out; that's how embittered I sometimes was about the unjust ways of the world. So don't be too proud of your cynicism."

Catalina again looked up at her aunt, and this time her eyes were smiling trustfully at her.

"Since then I've become less harsh. But there are people I wish dead."

Their eyes were rooted in each another for a second; then Catalina said curtly: "They're nothing but words for you. You don't feel anything when you say that."

"Do you feel it?"

Smiling contemptuously, Catalina shook her head: "You're much too even-tempered; next to you I don't feel anything."

A paleness crept into Oggi's face. "Sometimes it's good to know someone who's even-tempered," she said and reached out to Catalina.

The next afternoon Catalina again went to the villa. Since she'd heard

Aunt Oggi's story, a shadow had fallen on the ruin, and Catalina felt a slight shiver when she entered the building. This Englishman—he'd loved the villa—isn't that how Aunt Oggi had put it? What might he have looked like? Did he also come to a bad end here?

She had brought along a cassette with heavy, dark bass riffs, recordings off an old record by Led Zeppelin, and moving her body in time to the music, she felt that she lost a little bit of her horrible despair each time she struck the earth. It was a gloomy afternoon, and heavy thunderclouds approached from the north, spreading a sulphur-colored filter across the horizon; then a fresh wind arose, grew, and whipped the branches against each other so that the leaves were shredded off the trees and sucked out of the forest by the roaring hurricane. Catalina's hair became disheveled, whirled upwards, and blew into her face. She jumped on the terrace with the power of a Rumpelstiltskin; sweat ran from her temples, and she placed her hopes in the shattering, dissolving force of the rain, but the hurricane came to a sinister head and hurled the radio, which Catalina had again placed at the foot of the balustrade, across the terrace, only to shrink back into a normal storm without bringing the redemption of rain. It only became dark; night returned to the villa, and down below the blood and brains still were still stuck to the cliff.

Lying in her warm bed back home, after the darkness had swallowed the storm, the first drops fell on the roof, and a gentle rain began.

The next day the pharmacist was waiting at the ruin for her. Even before she entered the building, she saw his large frame standing on the terrace. He had his back to her and didn't turn around until she was already standing next to him on the terrace. When she saw him, she turned off the radio, but she knew that he must already have heard her and that he had turned his back to her in order to leave the decision on their meeting up to her.

His light blue eyes stroked her forehead: "What's to become of us?" he asked.

Catalina didn't know the answer.

"I've come here even though you don't need me, and I really should be somewhere else. I married into the pharmacy, and I'm now accepted in town. I can't and won't endanger my position. I can't deceive Susanne. I don't want to hurt her."

Catalina thought, *why have you come? What's to become of me?*

Why are you hurting me? but she didn't say any of those things. Black pupils consumed her green iris, and she stared into his adult face like a small rabbit facing an evil python. Down in the gorge, a male blackbird began singing a wonderfully beautiful song—it was the first time since the postman's deadly fall that a bird sang there, but Catalina wasn't thinking about him. She was trembling in the face of the feelings that this man had released in her, this yearning that made her knees weak, this aching that was destroying her stomach and all her insides, this vacuum in her head that made her dizzy. Would he try to touch her? She knew that she would let him do anything to her. He had followed her into her secret realm and filled her with the language of yearning.

Half unconscious with agitation, she waited on the sun-flooded terrace for him to help her step out of her childhood, but he only shook his head: "It's forbidden. It's also not right. I'm more than twice as old as you. It wouldn't remain secret . . . I'll have to do without you . . ."

Catalina didn't understand. Had he come here to see her embarrassment and then to turn away? Perhaps it was even just to coax a look of love from her and then to ridicule it. She would have liked to scream, to slap his face, but touching him was completely impossible after he had so easily rejected her. The only correct deed now would be to harm him, and for a moment she searched through the hatred and the fear that Susanne had deposited in her until she hit upon a segment that carried the treacherous label *vanity*. In the aggression that was meant to conceal her pain, she yanked the radio high into the air, turned it toward the man in such a way that his gaze fell right onto the little mirror; the blinding glass tipped slightly to the side and Catalina saw the reflection of his eyes, which seemed to bore into hers by way of this detour, and he saw her pupils, gigantic with agitation. With a quick movement of her hand, she pulled the mirror off the radio and bending over the balustrade toward the house, threw it into the open slit of the basement vault. It didn't get very far inside before it shattered.

The pharmacist stared at Catalina. Catalina had destroyed his image. Filled with indignation, his self-esteem rose up against the girl's rejection and his refusal. Without thinking, he jumped up onto the low wall and then, hanging above the abyss for a second, down into the dark vault.

Catalina suppressed a scream when she saw the pharmacist disappear into the maw of the cellar. He would never come out of there again. She grabbed her radio and ran off. The compulsive branches grabbed her from all sides and slapped against her body. Disoriented, she staggered back and forth on the path; she stumbled in the absurd fear of meeting someone *now* and turned back in the direction of the villa, but she didn't return there—would he be calling for her from down below? Where should she go now, where should she push this horror that blocked her view into the distance. And while she ran fitfully back and forth, a monster broke out of the underbrush behind her and raged along the path. Catalina turned toward the cracking branches, and one of them hit her in the eyes. She covered her burning eyelids with her little fingers, sobbed, bent her body against the ground, and pushed against upstretched hands. From between her fingers she saw the monster, the pharmacist, her lover on his knees beside her.

Had he risen from the cellar vaults, from the realm of the dead, had he been able to leave this dungeon with the whiff of decay clinging to him in order to follow her at a rapid pace, to catch her here amid the green isolation, to punish her for her disobedience, for her brazen rebellion?

He grasped at her fine bones, tried to speak, but only blood dripped from his lips. With a horror grown to incomprehensible dimensions, Catalina saw the fragments of the mirror glinting in his half-open, slack mouth, and she understood: he had been prepared to swallow anything that could hurt him for her sake.

As penetrating and powerful as this message of devotion was, Catalina, her teeth chattering, kicked the pharmacist's hand away, ran through the twilight forest, and swallowed her screams, although she thought she heard the bleeding man's death-rattles behind her; she ran, ran, ran until she collided with a person who held her tight.

Aunt Oggi. Catalina looked into her aunt's wide open eyes. Then she shook her head, trembled on her aunt's breast until her aunt began to sob, pressing the child to her body and trying to console her: "It's not your fault. I had to do it too. I had this terrible power too. But it never grows independently in us; it needs someone to place this hatred in us— and someone to pull it out of us in this terrible place. It's this house at the abyss." She stroked Catalina's head. "You loved him, didn't you?" and she whispered into the tremblings of the slender body: "You don't have to tell me now who it was. I'll find out soon enough. Be calm—it's over now. I killed four men before the one that I loved came. He was the fifth, and I was just fourteen years old. Their skeletons are probably all still lying in the cellar. I lured them all there when I no longer knew how to keep them off me. It's unlikely that anyone has discovered them;

it's a dark place. I only got to know the owner after I had been going in and out of the house for ten months. At the owner's wish, a chess club had been set up there, as a kind of present to the mayor who had kept one eye closed when they issued the building permit. The leading men of the town gathered there every Thursday, and Mr. Kleinhäusler played the role of porter. He guarded the house in the owners' absence. Most of the schoolchildren weren't good enough to be accepted into the old gentlemen's chess club, but they were gracious enough to accept me. The four who later died all approached me, one after the other. How they repulsed me. When they then killed themselves at my command, I never really suffered. But then I killed him too." She spoke over the top of the girl's head, more as if to the forest. "He was thirty-five years older than I. Every fiber of my body and my mind was fascinated by him. He was, of course, married and not prepared for me to return his love. The first time I met him, the fourth man had just killed himself at my command by pressing a knife into his chest. I had ordered him to do it. But this man, he knew nothing about the dead men in his cellar, and he lusted after me without a doubt, but he was much too timid to touch me. He released feelings in me that he then took great pains not to see, but he wasn't fair enough to really keep silent and go away. I killed him because he *didn't* touch me. I was so desperate when I killed him."

She found herself again with the crying child in her arms. "Your mother knows nothing about it. No one will figure out what happened to the mailman and your—the other one."

She shook Catalina a little bit away from herself and looked into the girl's reddened eyes: "Catalina, if you ever loved him, your power has vanished. No one can ever fill you with such hate and repugnance ever again that you can manipulate others with this power. Now you really have to watch out for yourself. The two men have disappeared, and no one will ever ask you about them. But if you want to forget completely what has happened, then follow my advice and never return to the Villa Dolorosa."

Translated by Michael T. O'Pecko

Vico

Martin Ohrt

He sat on a bench at the curb and thought about whether or not to go over to the building on the other side of the street. He watched the streetlight that was suspended by wire between the rows of houses as it swayed back and forth. Neon light, green. Neon green, he thought to himself, a green with which he was quite familiar. Operating room green.

But quickly his thoughts brought him back to where he was. Forget it, he said to himself, you're here now, in this city, in this country, a plumber by trade, the nights outside are getting cooler and cooler, forget about everything else, don't make any mistakes. They can only use you here as a plumber.

He was holding a piece of paper in his hand. An acquaintance, no, actually someone whom he had happened to come to trust, a Romanian, just like him, had slipped him an address. He had met him at the train station. They had spent a night together there in a railroad car on the loading track. Until they suddenly came, with their dogs: "Let's go, you lazy riffraff, get out of here before we call the police."

He lit a cigarette and, as he continued to hold the slip of paper in his hand, considered whether he should go over to the hotel across the street. He had been told that the boss there was a Romanian; perhaps this was finally a chance, perhaps it was *his* chance. The main thing was to do something, he thought to himself, just give in before the nights outdoors become unbearable. He had often heard that there were jobs for waiters. And in the meantime he had been studying German, at the refugee camp, for three months. Besides that, he had already worked a number of odd jobs as a bus boy, earlier on, during vacations, while he was a student.

He opened the door. The sureness of his stride was only an act. He felt himself overcome by the anxiety that each step could be a false one, a step into the abyss, which would mean rejection. Without any papers everything would go quickly.

He thought he could feel every look that was cast at him. They are surely sizing me up carefully, he thought. They must be able to tell that I don't belong here. Not in this hotel in which everything is so orderly, not in this country where a person can assert himself without having to use his fists, assuming he only has the right papers.

He walked up to the man behind the bar. "Good day," he said, as he leaned self-assuredly over the counter.

"Good day. What can I do for you?" replied the waiter.

"Want to speak with boss."

"Really?"

"Looking for work."

"Aha, Yugoslav?"

He blushed as he felt himself caught. And he had tried so hard to sound like someone who already had complete control of the local language.

"Romanian," he said curtly and coolly.

"Aha. I understand. I'll go get the boss." With that the waiter disappeared behind a door.

"So, you want to work for us?" the boss, a dark-skinned, hefty type, asked the stranger as he scrutinized him.

"Yes."

"And you've already had experience in the hotel and restaurant business?"

"Have already often done work as waiter."

"But it's not your profession?"

"Was trained as plumber."

"We can always use help around here."

"Matters not to me. Do anything."

"Your German is not bad," the boss then interjected in his native tongue, "pretty good for a Romanian."

"We can speak more in German," the Romanian said, proud of his knowledge of the language.

"We don't want to complicate things more than we have to," the manager replied in Romanian. "What city are you from?"

"From Bucharest."

"Oh . . . Bucharest . . . I haven't been there in quite some time now . . ."

"Are you from there too?" the foreigner asked, trying to show interest.

"No. From Klausenburg. A beautiful city. That is, it was. Everything's in ruins. While the people in Bucharest were building themselves palaces.—But now I'm an Austrian. Austria is good. Everything's perfect. And there's real money to be made working here. I don't want to go back. Romania! It doesn't mean anything to me anymore.—Who sent you here anyway?"

"I just heard that you had work to offer."

"Who told you that?" the manager asked with curiosity.

"I don't know his name; I just met him, at the train station."

"Train station. Hmm. So you've been sleeping at the train station?"

"Haven't found an apartment yet, without work . . ."

"And your papers?"

The man reached into the pocket of his jacket, pulled out his passport, and handed it to the manager, who took a quick look at it.

"We know that you are from Romania. But where is your work permit?" the boss persisted.

"Don't have any papers yet. But at the police station they told me I would get them," the Romanian tried to say convincingly.

"I know, that's what they all say. And then all I get are problems with the police, because of illegal employees."

"But I'll get the papers, for sure."

"Yes, of course, I know," he waved him off.

"So you have work for me?"

"Well, we'll give it a try, a few days, a few weeks perhaps. But if the police come and ask for your papers, you'll have to leave. Disappear. I don't want to have to pay a fine on account of you. Do you understand?"

"I'll disappear like a mole if they come."

"Fine. Then you can begin, at the bar."

"Right now?"

"Right away."

"And what will you pay?"

"Five thousand schillings a month, cash. Room and board included."

"That doesn't sound bad."

"This is a serious-minded establishment."

"Then I'll go get my things—from the railroad station."

Well, at least it's a start, he thought to himself, as he made his way to the station. Five thousand schillings and a solid roof over my head, three good meals a day, a good start. And the boss is Romanian, like you, you can trust him, perhaps he might also be able to help you to get your papers more quickly.

"Well, what's with you? You're late today!" said one of the men who had gathered around the food wagon in front of the train station for a couple of sausages and bread.

"Nothing. I've got something better to do," he said, happy that he no longer belonged to this group that had to be satisfied with two pieces of sausage and bread for the whole day and a couple of sips of tea at night.

"Oh, our friend's starting a career!" mocked one of the men who had come from the former Yugoslavia.

"Leave me alone," he grumbled as he continued walking. I've had enough of all of you, he thought to himself. You always want to be first. You line up for your food as if you were the bosses, even when things continue to go badly for you. You're the first to be taken along for hourly work, and now you are getting care packages thrown at you by the ton, so that you can continue to bash one another's skulls even longer. But I'll show all of you what a Romanian head is capable of.

One last time, he said to himself as he turned the key in the locker. One more home that you are now leaving, as once before, in Bucharest. How quickly things become final. He took his bag out of the locker. Illona. How long has it been since we've seen each other? Christian. How big he must have gotten in the meantime. Maybe I shouldn't have given up so quickly, he thought. The break. Perhaps it was only now that he felt the impact of this separation, this irrevocable refusal. Maybe things would have worked out some way or other. He rubbed his eyes, which were suddenly moist with tears, as he left the railroad station.

He sat on the edge of the bed in his hotel room and thought about whether he should go down to the office. He had made up his mind that he wasn't going to stay here any longer. He had already worked for ninety-five days without having received a single schilling. Except for the few tips that the guests had left on the table and that he immediately swept into his pocket as he cleared them.

The rage within him welled up. Why had he let himself get involved with a Romanian? With one who certainly had experienced the fact all too often that the world was divided into two classes: the cheaters and the cheated. And now he was standing on the side of the losers. If Illona could see him. She would wring her hands in agony. What kind of man are you, he said to himself.

He packed his things hurriedly. He stuck his bag under his arm, as he ran down the staircase.

He gave himself one last bit of encouragement as he walked up to the office door. You goddam bastard, you. I'll kill you.

With a forceful tug he opened the door. The manager flinched momentarily behind his desk.

"Can't you knock?" the hefty man shouted at him.

"I need to talk with you," countered the Romanian coolly.

"You can see that I'm busy," the boss parried.

"You will hear me out, now!" the man said impatiently. His voice became more and more threatening.

"Come back in half an hour," the boss said, trying again to fend him off.

"I demand an explanation. And right this minute!" He began to make a fist with his hand, but he continued to restrain himself.

"Okay, fine. What is it you want," the boss asked with feigned composure, as his eyes nervously registered every move of the man, who was now standing right next to him.

"For ninety-five days I've been breaking my back for you, and I haven't seen one single schilling yet! And every time I ask you, you just keep saying, 'Later, later.'"

"And I would just like to see your work permit!" the boss interjected.

"I've done good work. Everybody has been satisfied with me."

"And for weeks I've been standing with one foot in jail because of you."

"I only want what's coming to me."

"Okay, fine. I don't want to be that way. Not to a fellow countryman." He reached into the drawer, took three thousand-schilling notes from the cashbox, and handed them to the Romanian. "Three thousand schillings. That's it."

Hastily the Romanian grabbed the money. "Three thousand schillings for two months' work? You promised five thousand, for one month!"

"You should be grateful to me."

"Grateful . . . ?" The Romanian was at a loss for words.

"Where do you think we are? If the police get wind that you are here, you'll cost me more than the most expensive chef would!"

"You promised you would get the papers for me."

"Who do you think I am, the immigration authority?"

The Romanian suddenly lost his patience. "Damn it! Hand over the money, you cheapskate!" He grabbed the man by the collar. With a gesture of contempt the boss tried to push away the threatening hands. "Listen. You're not trying to threaten me, are you?" the boss said with an air of superiority.

Immediately the Romanian gained control of himself, withdrew his arms, and backed off a few steps. Don't make any trouble, he thought to himself, just no police. This guy isn't worth it. His face was still flushed, as he said calmly: "We'll talk about this again. Some day." Angrily he stomped out of the room and slammed the door behind him.

He sat down on a park bench. Have a cigarette first, he said to himself. You've got to think hard about what you're going to say to the others there. As he puffed on the cigarette, he took the slip of paper out of his jacket pocket with his other hand. He unfolded it. Luckily I still have the address, he thought. It was the address of a shelter for homeless foreigners.

The Croatian recognized him right away. "So our friend hasn't forgotten us after all!" he announced with a derisive tone to the group that had gathered in the community room to play cards and drink tea.

"Hello," the Romanian said casually as he entered the room somewhat dejectedly.

"Admit it. Even we haven't done too badly." The Croatian took Vico by the arm and led him into the adjacent factory wing that had been converted into a temporary dorm. In it the beds were so close to one another that there was not even enough room between them for a chair. It reeked of men's stifled sweat. The Romanian hesitated as he read the sign on the door: "No foreigners allowed." That was exactly what he had experienced over the last few months. The best response that he had heard was the refrain: "Sorry, sorry, sorry . . . "

The Croatian continued his presentation undaunted: "Thirty-six beds. That means there are thirty-six of us who don't have to sleep outside in this cold and who get at least one meal a day.—Not everybody is as lucky as you are."

Vico was silent.

"Well, you're not very talkative today, are you? Come on, let's go have a drink in our salon." With a fatherly grip he took the Romanian by the arm and led him into the community room. Vico merely followed without protest. Nothing much mattered anymore. The main thing was that it was warm inside, nothing else mattered now.

The others, who were mostly from Poland and from former Yugoslavia, only looked up briefly when they saw the Romanian. Embarrassed, Vico sat down at the other end of the table, while the Croatian took a bottle of schnapps from his storage compartment on the shelves. The walls of the small room were lined high with shelves on which the residents could store their personal belongings. Every compartment was clearly labeled with a name. The meager two square feet of space was therefore protected all the more carefully. Anything a person let out of his sight might disappear in a flash. The lighting was typical of an abandoned factory: bare neon lights suspended between wires from the ceiling. No daylight came into the room because the rolldown metal shades to the street were kept closed. This green light once again, thought Vico. Once again this ghastly light that tires your eyes so quickly.

Mistrustfully the card players stared over to the stranger as the Croatian poured him a drink of his schnapps. "What's he doing here?" they seemed to be asking. "He just wants to get in good with the foreman," said a good-looking Bosnian.

"Oh, leave him alone," replied one of the Poles, "a person who comes here must really be in the shitter."

Vico acted as if none of this bothered him and wrapped his hand around the glass of schnapps.

"So, tell me. What are you doing these days?" the Croatian asked curiously.

"Got into a dispute with my boss," Vico answered curtly.

"So he threw you out?"

"I left on my own."

"So. On your own? Even you don't believe that," replied the Croatian.

"Three thousand schillings for two months work. What is that?"

"More than most of us have."

"I was cheated."

"Look, come on now: you're living here, without papers, as a nobody, you can be sent back at any time, but you think that the whole world should be at your beck and call!" the Croatian tried to educate him.

"Oh, leave me alone. We've already had that lesson," Vico fended him off.

"I was just trying to help," said the Croatian, once again striving for a fatherly tone, and poured Vico another drink. "Come on, have another shot. You're my guest today. But only until 10 PM."

"Today's our boss's day to be generous," joked one of the men at cards.

"He acts as if he owns this place," added the good-looking Bosnian.

"Clothes do indeed make the man," said one of the Poles. The Croatian was actually the only one of them who wore a custom-made suit most of the time.

"Yeah, you, you're all just jealous because you don't have any class," the Croatian defended himself.

"We have just as much class as you do," retorted the Pole.

"Come on, don't get excited. We're all stuck in the same shit hole," a fellow countryman tried to pacify him.

"And shit is always brown and stinks . . . " the Croatian added. "And what are you going to do now?" he asked as he turned to Vico.

"I don't know."

"But you have a bed for the night at least, somewhere, right? You must have some friends who can help you?"

Vico sensed that the Croatian was attempting to keep his distance from him.

"I'll find something," he said as he tried to get out of the situation. You don't have to bow down in front of this fellow, he thought to himself. Don't lose the last thing you still have: your pride.

At this moment Paul entered the room. He was the one who had slipped Vico the piece of paper. When Vico recognized him, the tension in his facial features over his plight eased for a moment. Paul walked closely past him, as Vico looked up at him. "Hello," he greeted shyly. It had been such a long time since they had seen one another that he wasn't sure if he could still trust him.

"Well, it's really a surprise to see you again," Paul said with pleasure at seeing a fellow countryman. He slapped him on the shoulder as a buddy.

"I've had to work a lot; ten, twelve hours every day," Vico said as if making excuses.

Paul sat down next to him.

"Want a shot too?" the Croatian asked the Romanian.

Paul sensed that it was just arrogant politeness coming from him, the put-on generosity of someone who feels superior. "No, thanks. I don't feel well today," he declined.

Carefully the Croatian put the cork back in the bottle and wrapped it in a plastic bag as he stood up. Silently he walked away from the other two.

"Just like two Romanians who are after his good bottle; it's just too much for him," mocked the Bosnian.

Deep in thought, Vico stared down into his glass.

"It's all just talk. Just for fun. You shouldn't take it seriously," Paul tried to cheer him up.

"I'm not in a laughing mood today," Vico said dryly.

"Full of jokes you're not," Paul agreed.

"When a man loses his bed and his work, what else does he have left?" asked Vico.

"So you quit?"

"You could say that. Or would you break your back for three thousand schillings for two months?"

"Well, in Romania you'd be king!"

"But here in Austria you're just the lowest shit."

"Come on, don't exaggerate! I once worked for weeks in construction and didn't even get a sandwich out of it. Our boss just skimmed off all our wages."

"Yeah, with us they know exactly what they can get away with."

"Oh, damn it, let's have a smoke instead," Paul said and took an open pack of cigarettes from his jacket pocket.

"Some day we'll show all of them," Vico attempted to build up his courage.

He had often heard himself say these words. So often that he himself didn't believe them any more. Just somehow get through the winter, this damned cold that constantly creeps under your coat, in the summer the world will look different again, he thought to himself, as he took the cigarette and lit it, one more year and then you will be closer to your goal. Money, first money, as much money as possible; then everything else will take care of itself. Your own house, or at least a good apartment, in which you can live with a woman. Being alone, that was even worse for him than sleeping for a night in the railroad station. These doubts that were eating away at his thoughts and seemed to gradually devour his feeling of self-worth. "A nobody is what you are," he said as Paul puffed silently on his cigarette.

"Come on, don't go getting philosophical," Paul rejoined, "at least there's this place here, for us."

"Yes, I know: one meal a day, a bed for a night—and what does that make you?"

"It's not forever," Paul replied.

Translated by Paul F. Dvorak

The Benefit Concert

Elisabeth Reichart

I

TO sneak away . . . when he took their measure, the old exemplars snapped closed more quickly, looking on with amusement when he tried to deceive them. Perhaps he hadn't sneaked away from the party at all; perhaps he had just been tired, which would be understandable at the end of a concert tour. He was walking along by the city wall, which was crumbling in his face, which he could pull down with his own hands—and the whole story right along with it. He hadn't known this preacher, couldn't even remember the one before. In their eternal whining for money they were somehow all alike. When he was still a child they had regular collections to restore the organ and later the bells. This time it was to rid the carved confessionals of woodworms. "The parish urgently requests the help of its most distinguished son." Telegrams of this sort he normally just tore up—no, his wife tore them up for him. "Spare me the begging letters"—that was their agreement. But during this unhappy week she was at a spa, and he was exposed to direct contact with the mail. Rather quickly his spontaneous irritation had given way to curiosity, a vague curiosity flashing between blurred faces and trivia that stuck in his mind. And he had added one more concert after the twenty-second one. Even so, an unpleasant aftertaste remained. In the long run he didn't even collect enough money for the repairs to his fiddle. Ridiculous, the whole thing was ridiculous. They hadn't even reserved a room for him at the inn. He had to sleep in the parsonage—in which he had never set foot before—cheated of his memories: the little scuffles as well as the massacres, the crude thefts, the even cruder early flirtations in the bar. None of his secret observations, those earthy high points of his childhood, could come alive behind these grated windows. It was a starless night. He was unused to the outside stillness, in which his internal battle-cry was all the more clearly audible. Except for the preacher, no one had wasted a word about his playing. Not one of these philistines had bestirred himself, for the sake of the music, to a courteous modicum of exaltation. Not even for the music. It was entirely possible that they had slept during the concert, so as to be able afterward to wallow in their beer-bar as usual, but with all the more gusto. As soon as they sat down they would dive in, routinely heaping up before him all the vulgarities that he detested, before they pressed on to their real theme. If he ought to have been that theme, he was not, and his paranoia continued its celebration without them. Hesitantly at first, with scattered remarks impenetrable to him, they had probed their terrain, getting him in their sights from the corners of their eyes or with jerky head-movements. Then, becoming bolder, taking him in as one of their own, interrupting him without restraint and falling all over him. They were especially unrestrained about the fact—a fact that surprised even him—that Sissi, of all people, had married a pilot. Sissi, who had been born during the flood of 1954 in a pig-trough in the middle of the main square. Sissi—whom no village man had even looked at—Sissi had made mouths water and eyes pop. It was to be noted how people wanted to obtain a comprehension of this novelty by talking it to death and how they tried to switch their thirty-seven-year-old thought patterns, wavering as they did so between incredulity and a belief in miracles. Showing their colors, no one had deigned to attend the church wedding, while to the end Sissi hid her face behind her veil . . .

In any event he had imagined that his homecoming would be different than it was. Much different.

II

He still hadn't got a nibble from a fish, but that was of no consequence to him. He was every bit as delighted by the very notion of deceiving the preacher as he was by the possibility of popping into the latter's frying pan a tainted fish that would leave its traces in the house for a week. His boat rocked gently every time one of the tugboats chugged by. Behind him the willows bent to soak up the wet. The Danube was doing its best to claim them. Of the village he could see no more than the decaying castle, a thoroughly satisfying view: the unstable plaster pulling away from the tiles, the widening gaps between the shingles, the beams rotting away. It was going to rain soon—the gnats were already getting damned aggressive. In spite of this, there wouldn't be any more floods, however much he wanted to see the submergence of that stupid pig-trough, which, as the only one in the village, had endowed Sissi with a unique fate. Everyone else had followed the prophecies of the elders and obeyed the laws governing the herd behavior of a flock of sheep—including him, indeed especially him. The midwife had recognized his musicality at his first outcry. Even his violin was not a matter of choice on his part but was owing to the circumstance that the village had only one violin teacher, and he thought it would be more bearable to study with this teacher than to take organ lessons from the preacher. He had fulfilled their need, had bestowed on the village a musician, and in gratitude "Sissi and the Pilot" resounded in his ears without pause! They didn't have a clue as to his digital virtuosity or his perfect musical ear, nor were they aware that he was acclaimed even in Vienna. Still, his after-concert emotions were growing steadily more vapid. The initial burst of adrenalin barely kept dribbling, having long since been replaced by routine and boredom. The stomach cramps that he felt when he pondered the reality that in the end he was no different from other men were already inclining toward convulsions of a more severe sort. When he would have completely vanished, while branches were snapping behind him, he got the idea it was time to step aside. This time no one would find him, this time he would prove himself as a master of death.

III

He had not expected her, certainly not in her bridal gown, her veil over her face. He extended his arm to her, but she gathered up her silk and lace, slipped her pumps off, and jumped into the boat. They sat across from one another in silence. He looked at the gnats that descended on her and again flew away, until they wove him into the spell of their movement, and it was just he and the gnats. Meanwhile she was talking, but more and more involved in spinning a false story, she was failing to connect with him. Angrily she stood up, unconcerned about rocking the boat, and shouted, "Listen, there is no pilot at all! There isn't even a husband. My husband, what a joke! My Polish locksmith gave me sixty thousand schillings to marry him, and he definitely wants to stay here, just as you definitely wanted to leave. But now you have returned, and I have stolen your ridiculous little show! For that I would have given not just my hand but my very life."

IV

He didn't kill her. It would have been so simple to use his hands, which held the fiddle, which were strong and persistent, to push her head underwater. Sissi didn't know how to swim; the laughter had driven her from the shore. This time *she* had laughed at his startled expression—didn't he even know that he was sitting in *her* boat and that, besides, a fish had bitten? A conversation could hardly have begun more inauspiciously. Master and servant, everything set from the very start. And even if she did flatter him about how well he had played yesterday, how the music had intoxicated her, most of all she would have then liked to have come here with him as she had formerly done; she had instantly known where she would find him. He persisted in silence, would maintain his silence until he was finally alone again. While he was letting her talk about her good luck in having fooled the whole village, he suddenly conceived the idea of killing her and he was quickly wedded to this idea. One plan after another occupied his brain. Only the ending, the cliché climax, remained constant: how the villagers found her bloated body in the water. The instant he saw her, her figure was transformed, hanks of hair were hanging in her face, her wide-open eyes were frozen in terror, her discolored face was bluish. The one thing he couldn't decide on was the color of her lips. At one moment they seemed almost black, at the next moment whitish—but her triumphant smile did not change. Her arms, with which she was now violently gesticulating, hung limp from her body. Her bridal gown had decomposed into a sticky net, in which dying animals supposed they had found their ultimate refuge. And only her slender legs—at least one must have been severed by a tugboat passing too close to shore. Children at play would find it later, and the horror would not be forgotten. Then she had left, she had simply got up and taken the fish with her. The hook was lying near him—but anyway he remained silent, as if he had taken a vow of silence.

V

The preacher's rolling voice woke him before he heard the bells, which continued pealing after it had finally become quiet again in the house. No breakfast had been prepared for him. He found milk in the refrigerator and he made some tea before he joined the pilgrims' procession to the church. He was in a bad mood, having been obliged to leave the house without his morning coffee. He intended to depart afterward—the way things were, he had no idea what he was doing here. The people ahead of him suddenly stopped, then took a step; again the abrupt stop; a step, then stop, repeated continually until the procession stood at the entrance to the cemetery. The old woman beside him collapsed, the people ahead had already started intoning, "Blessed be thou, Mary." The man who had caught the old woman was crying as he incessantly murmured, "Our beautiful cemetery!" A loud voice arose from somewhere in the crowd:

"You know our cemetery, our well-tended little cemetery by the village church. Our women would polish the tombstones every week!"

And just as if they had been waiting for this invocation, everybody replied in chorus—even those behind him who still couldn't see anything:

> Yes, Lord, we would polish them weekly
> And the candles at the graves were lit each day!
> Yes, Lord, we lit the candles each day.
> Fresh flowers were always on the graves!
> Yes, Lord, fresh flowers were always on the graves.

No one would have dared utter a loud word in this final resting place. Even the children were walking with bowed heads and at most just barely whispering!

> Yes, Lord, that's how it was.
> Each person said his prayer before he left!
> Yes, Lord, let us pray.
> None of us has desecrated the cemetery!
> Lord, deliver us from all evil!

Many who still weren't sure what had happened fell to their knees, and those about them did likewise. Even he could not resist the impulse to bend his knees—just as he already had been unable to resist the antiphonal song.

The preacher said later that this desecration must have been the work of beasts. It was impossible, according to him, for people to have dug up so many dead in one night and still have had time to smash skulls and hack the wooden crosses to pieces. With the greatest gusto, though, he described what had happened to the fresh corpses and what the despoilers of the corpses would now die of. The most exquisite diseases seemed to be circulating in the village. He felt ill while the preacher was devouring his bacon-bit dumplings, dripping with grease. "They have consumed all the brains, that much is clear. They must be fairly superstitious, my son, what do you think?"

He ran out, retrieved his already packed suitcase as well as his fiddle, and was on the verge of disappearing without saying goodbye. But the preacher blocked his path and accompanied him to the grave of his parents, of his grandparents. All that was left of them was smashed skulls. The remaining bones glowed palely along with the others, railroaders' bones united with the necessary infrastructure, also bequeathed. His only dream: to get to the railroad. Only him they had banished. There was nothing left to ravage. Even so, he gave a few kicks to the bone fragments, trying to distribute them in the nearest graves. Generally he missed.

Translated by Richard H. Lawson

NOON SONG

KURT A. SCHANTL

FROM the travel letters of Giacomo Loredan along with their continuation by Sior Giovanni Capustrano from Padua (1561-1634).

... No, don't make any reply; you will also no longer have any opportunity to do so. But I beg you nevertheless to pause for a short time in your daily work and read what I would like to report to you from the edge of the world, read and then go back to your daily work again as if nothing had happened, forget it, don't even make an attempt to have your answer delivered to me; for bear in mind that as soon as you have received my news, I will no longer be reachable, not for you and also not for the others who believe to be in the center, in the middle of what you call your world. At this time, you see, I will have already set out on my long trip beyond the edge, through a hole in the borders which you have constantly tried to extend further, and within which you believe that you have established yourself so splendidly.

Keep on building, call forth all your artistry, lay keels for new ships with the greatest accuracy, knowing well that you are depending entirely on the internal logic of your knowledge, on the great interplay, the concert of physical and mathematical arts, if your efforts are going to be rewarded with success. Yet, after you have already agreed on a single great score, then certainly nothing more stands in the way of further progress, yes, I already see ships with a still lighter, quicker design traveling on previously established routes, calculated precisely by means of ocean charts, whose measurements are so exact that it will be possible to determine the position of a cork floating on the open sea. Even more it will be possible to measure the speed and direction of the winds and the ocean currents so that you can use them as the basis of your navigation and thus be able to indicate far in advance the day and hour of the arrival of your galleys in this and every harbor.

Tell me, can one conceive of anything more uplifting than an event that happens the way one has predicted it?

Could there be any stronger confirmation of the correctness of your view of the world?

You will be able to predict its performance, you can with the help of a compass, maps, sundial, and sextant steer from here to there on your meadow which you call "ocean," and—which you believe to understand completely—you have after all measured the position of the islands, the configuration of the shorelines, and have designated the points of the compass. Proudly you can announce: there is nothing in your map that remains unknown! And in the event that there might still be something, it is banished to the other side of these coasts: TERRA INCOGNITA— may whatever useless and godforbidden things that could exist there play as they will, for not without reason have our cartographers populated the white, desolated surfaces beyond the explored coasts with chimera—

And here for the time being I will conclude the last of my letters to you; yet it will be continued, to be sure not by me who will no longer have the opportunity to do so, but at my request Sior Giovanni Capustrano from Padua—who is well known to you—will take care of further correspondence.

Hic sunt sirenes was written in elegant antiqua diagonally over the surface that extended beyond the mountains of the cape. Hic sunt sirenes; yet he disregarded this warning. He neither let himself be bound to the mast, nor did he stuff his ears with wax, but instead during the first hour after midnight, he secretly left the galley which lay at anchor off the shore of the cape but within calling distance.

During that very night he climbed the foothills, scarcely resting in the protection of crevices and caves, and at sunrise he stepped out above the open panorama that was not exactly as drawn on the map but spread out below him, furrowed by gentle valleys.

Little satyr-like wild goats jumped about, grazed in the first light of day, in the brightness which, colored blue and sulfur yellow, overcame the shadows, until finally everything became light, everything turned into sky, and this broad, scarred highland gave way to brown grass and olive trees in the distance that looked like moving gray clouds. He stepped out, he bent down under the *surging* sky which struck him from the East, like a giant wave. The earth, small, the furrows, the valleys; everything was sky, high and pale, and the goats appeared as wandering dots along the narrow lines under it. And he himself was small, small to the point of disappearing, lost between heaven and earth. And only when he saw how the ocean far down below flashing emerald green and blue, with foaming waves that crashed loudly at the foot of the mountain and he could not discover the galley anywhere did this feeling of being abandoned leave him.

At noon the sea lost its expansive breadth, the borders between heaven and ocean blurred into a dull haze; no bird, no call, no running, only the chirping of the grasshoppers in the air, long, persisting, and shrill, and he walked, he walked slowly down the slope, shadowless, crushing under his steps the rust-brown blades of grass. He walked, the light and the earth became one for him, he walked toward the morning, into the darkness full of light, where under tired foliage the goats dozed. He walked and the chirping became song and the way his goal. He was moved by the stones and trees and by the rustling of the breeze in the branches. He stretched out in the sparse shade and listened to the song, and it seemed to him as if he were dreaming, on the other side of time, about the even beat of the rowing, of the distant bustling of the cities, of errors in writings, of parallel straight lines which meet in infinity, of angles and measurements, of distances and stretches, of nets of words in which he bounced and twisted, but everything puppetlike, ridiculously tiny and insignificant and at the same time so distant.

Only once, when one of the goats woke up with a start, and bleating and as if drunk jumped out into the light, a long, shrill, penetrating cry sounded: he felt a chill, and startled he believed he saw a figure with the legs of a ram who angrily chased across the floor of the valley; but it was only a single cloud whose shadow passed over the tops of the trees, the grass, the barren cliffs—for a moment—and then everything was quiet again.

Translated by Donald G. Daviau

THE DESPAIRING

ROBERT SCHINDEL

February 26, 1986

A bus, and inside it forty Jews in that gray filter of history. The last attempt to climb out: I cannot find the people at the north side of the Prater Star, I'm ready to drive back home, but at the last moment there's no way of ignoring Paul with his Pullman attendant's cap. Godforreal, we are taking off for Theresienstadt in Osijek, Slovenia, its ABC version.

Our eyes are not pointed in that direction, we are driving into the future which because of a certain past makes for such a grainy, badly lighted and tortured present. It is beautiful to drive like that into the Styrian idyll.

Next to me sits Lea, a forty-year-old woman who has had radical operations performed on her insides. She finds out that I am an editor. "That grunge fashion in literature, that's awful." She wants to make puppet theater as opera or opera as puppet theater, no matter. Her husband is from the Ukraine. "I never talk except in proverbs." But then they quarrel loudly, and with yearning that is directed intensely toward the inside. It's impossible that the sun even dares set when they are around.

At one point there is a major uproar because Lea over-paid for her passport photos. Now she stands there, because all that she gets back from ABC is fifty Schillinge; and now she believes that everyone believes that she is greedy for money. Her tears course down her cheeks all the way to Yugoslavia.

Esther Lichtblau is also coming with us. She is going to try to find a place among us extras for her pain, she the documentary maker from Vienna and Czernovitz, she wants to intensify and simultaneously put an end to her melancholy by means of moving images. Her camera woman, Nana, but we'll get to that later on, a florescence within the florescence.

Sany, the daughter of the literature-muscle-man Georges Weiss, a tomboy who has been equivocally socialized, today he tries to be helpful, is smooth, very ambitious, forthcoming.

In back there sits the Thurn and Taxis couple, two sisters between seventy one and nearly eighty, quietly-modest, very ascetic. Two Christian women among the cackling children of Israel, mute.

Somewhere after Varazdin the bus slips off the road. We arrive late.

How should I note it down, I just can't. To note it as # 41 about the forty, that is like writing from the hip, out of my throat, to hell with it.

Hannah and Mordecai, the Israeli couple, this ritual of forcing everything down, she is very pretty, he sings very very beautifully; I believe that all hysterics can sing so that your ears will fall in love with them.

The only one who knows what a concentration camp is, for he spent time in several of them, and he boasts despairingly of this singular feat, which helps harmonize his current brokenness.

However, Herr Recht, who only spent time in a camp between the Dniester and the Bug, does not not want to play a Jewish extra, but, well finally, an SS-man.

There are the unobtrusive ones, who will yet obtrude. The obtrusive ones will douche their dream-screams where the present is forced in behind the past-mask, will shower it off as organic sweat, but will remain obtrusive because their having died has become so vital.

"I just knew it, the Jews are not a family, it's stupid how that hurts," said Esther Lichtblau, and not only she.

These forty heads of Jews minus Thurn and Taxis rolled in their bus-container through the southeastern winter down to Osijek at the Drau in order to provide the ABC Television Company with close-up extras for their series "War and Remembrance." Here they adapted Theresienstadt, here they can be glad because we can imitate those who have been destroyed, how lucky we are, we're only extras in a film, in a game, where millions will be able to see on the T.V. screen that we're alive, how lucky we are. We are playing and truly, that is all that those who despair need to do.

Today we get our costumes. I too am dressed up. The costume

caretaker, a nice Yugoslav, undressed me, dresses me up.

"Vienna is a pretty city," a Zagreb costume man says to me while provisionally fastening the yellow star of David on my coat. "I studied there. How do you feel, oh excuse me, I mean does the costume fit, excuse me. I am from Zagreb—Agram," he says.

"Zagreb, yes, I see," I reply. It is true that Osijek has something of Trieste, despite snow and the river Drau.

Since I am now wearing the old clothes, the star, the hat, and no longer look like a thousand other Jews, but like ten thousand Jewish lambs, I do not have an unbeautiful feeling of play. Of course I am locked in these clothes and I think it is as though I stood at the Nollendorf Platz in Berlin next to the whores: before 1945, fifty some years ago I would stand there differently in Berlin with a star, with the hat, and fifty years, that isn't even a burp in the unity of time of our remembering. But now I walk jauntily past the whores, past the cops, and go into café Einstein, and if Paul is nuts about a girl from the Alps, the German population wonders about it only in secret.

Since I am perfect in Jewish lambs-clothes, I am allowed to transform myself back into the one I am today—a lightning-like liberation by the Americans, of whom the one whose extra I am playing probably kept dreaming during the long frost and hunger-boil realities; I am perfect because born after the fact, that is I can play.

Must we be the despairing? Where my sense of humor is struggling with my vanity for a suitable feeling for life beyond depressionburg in the general melancholy?

"Only when man plays is he totally human," one of those inwardly lit-up classics from Swabia said.

I begin to feel dreadful eating with the only one who has been to a concentration camp, and with the three others. Why are they so horrible to the waiter, so easily offended, so hypersensitive, so upbraiding, so impolite, and I don't even want to mention their pettiness?

"A waiter from Slovenia will never have any luck with such a chosen people," says Paul in the tone of an aside.

Tomorrow we're going to have to breakfast in concentration camp garb, to each his own.

February 27, 1986

While walking down to breakfast I first reflect, and don't know why, whether I should only drape the coat over my arm or put it on at once. I always used to put on my own coat at once, so I put this one on, too. While walking downstairs I catch my right arm covering up the left side of my chest, the chamber maid is coming my way. Surprised at myself I put it back where it belongs and set the yellow star above my heart free again. Downstairs at breakfast the children of Israel are sitting dressed in concentration camp uniforms.

Juppi, now we're driving to Theresienstadt at the river Drau, "makes no difference to me," says the only one who was in a camp, but Renee, whose daughter make no "macabre" comments about playing her mother as an extra, breaks out in tears, excuses herself and dries her tears, apologizes for herself and her tears, and still crying she goes apologizing to the toilet.

"It's because I saw the children playing there outside in the snow, Jewish ones from Sarajevo, and they are playing in the snow, and that was too much."

Eighty or more Jews from Sarajevo are here, look like everyone from Bosnia, at least from a Viennese perspective they do. An old man, who had been in the forced labor camps, greets Paul with the words: "You with your crown of thorns also look very original."

My own Jews from Vienna and the Ukraine, each with a face of his own that looks the way little Max and Hollywood imagine a central-European Jew to look like, come up to me since I've put on the uniform of the lamb and they assure me a hundred times over, between breakfast and lunch in the waiting room: "You're for real. A real one."

Finally Gerhard Frumm reassures me about the Jewish face, for he says: "There is no such thing as a Jewish face. That's an obstinate rumor, that's all."

In the waiting room, Sany rushes me to the next sobbing woman. Larissa is sobbing and is biting her lips and Oleg, her husband, sits next to her, doesn't move, looks off somewhere or somewhere where I cannot look. The two of them came from the Soviet Union eight years ago and to Israel. Larissa, however, couldn't take it there. "The climate," she says, and presumably really means the climate. So they got back as far as Vienna with Israeli passports, and not a soul is helping them, they have no work, lose their apartment, but the daughter is still a pianist, the son a violinist stayed in the Soviet Union, the little daughter has music everywhere, but they won't admit her to the conservatory.

"And there comes," Larissa tells me in German-Russian-Yiddish, "a Jewish Viennese woman—that one there—and asks me what the hell I'm doing there, why don't I go back to Israel or to Russia, at any event: off and away, awek."

"I've had enough," the Viennese Jewess had said. "I have this and this, and I also have that, and what do you have?" And a second one had said: "What good Jews there were are dead, those that are left are like you."

And Nana comes with the camera, Esther sits down with them, the whole thing is filmed for the film within the film, whatever they say in the waiting room; and how, Oleg is talking too now, they complain: "It's only possible to live among the goyim. Dying we'll have to do among Jews. I want to work, not matter what," Oleg gesticulates. "The Cultural Community wanted to give us a hundred Schillinge, we refused. Work yes, but don't doff your hat and please, thank you. Went to see the Rebbe for some light work for the daughter, she's a pianist like that, perhaps with the children working something like that. 'She should go clean,' answered the Rebbe."

I feel sore at heart, so that I am even taken aback because Esther whispers to me, I should lead them back to the previous topic.

You and your film, I think, feeling chilled and having no answers that help. But Esther of course is right: as long as it's on film it might help and whom does it hurt to step on the toes of the Cultural Community because of these Russians.

Willi Klang is a retired surgeon, but he keeps operating punctually until his seventieth birthday. He tells—I address him because of the conflict: "But didn't one of the Russians say that they didn't gas enough of those Viennese Jews?"

"Who knows," I say. "No way of inventing something that is going to make us smarter."

"At any event"—and now he puts on his Yves Montand face—"at Yom Kippur we open all the doors wide open for the needy. That one time, so that no one stands outside."

"Don't they stand around the corner?"

"What do you want, the Jews are no more than human beings either, thank God. And the Russian one didn't get the chance to learn, to think."

And Willi Klang sits down on a chair and recounts: "A few years ago someone calls me for a circumcision. 'Come around half past seven in the morning,' I tell him, "cause I got to get to the hospital afterwards. Well, by the time I'm done it's half past nine, and I drive to the hospital.

At ten he calls me. 'So what gives,' he screams through the telephone, 'we're all here, and why are you somewhere else?' A back and forth, fine, I drive back, do the circumcision, dress it, two hours later, what should I tell you, the grandmother opens the dressing to look whether it was done right. Don't misunderstand me, they just didn't learn to think."

Now we're walking to the set for our first take. What a crowd, SS drives past, we take off our hats. For our second take we go to the school, in the film it is the Jewish Community Center of Theresienstadt. There we are supposed to do blah-blah, until Klang—now he has his speaking role—shouts 'Attention,' because the commander is coming down the steps with another SS guy. We run off every which way but then have to go rigid and take off our hats. One of the eight assistant directors corrects the way two Osijek extras doff their caps, because they took off their hats and held it in their hands the open side face up.

I doff my hat twice in two scenes, looking at the ground, I now understand why Herr Recht wanted to play an SS-man.

ABC has distributed dolls, that is corpses, in the alleys, they look as unauthentic as real starved corpses do, so that it becomes a little uncanny before you get used to it. The sun is shining, the SS-guys and the Jews—some of them holding hands and supporting each other—go off to some bars.

Forty-five years ago, the current extras did not flip out. Will they be able to do the same thing now?

After lunch the singing is rehearsed with Mordecai and those from Sarajevo. Nothing works at first. If you can get them to sing at all, they prefer to sing songs that they know. But this creates a nice mood, Esther caught it on her film. I feel that I'm at a Zionist youth camp, still I become spry myself. Then they dance, as they're supposed to, arhythmically all of them, no beginning no end, somehow for laughs. The subsequent rehearsal of the singing—two bitter songs—thus has acquired substance.

The third take, a kaddish for typhus victims. All of us stand around wooden coffins that look as if they were ordered at a big wholesaler like Ikea, but Mordecai intones the mourning for the dead so beautifully that, if need be, you could start crying about how alive death is. Branko Lustig, the first assistant director, spotted me—that's how it always goes with me—at once, and placed me into a certain foreground, the same with Paul, so that the world won't forget what a Jewish face looks like. And

Gerhard Frumm, for whom all talk about a Jewish face is nonsense, is placed immediately to Mordecai's left; those who've seen it won't forget it for some time. My toes have become small reservoirs of cold, but still, it wasn't a bad day, and it's over at five.

As I was writing just now, Nana came in my room. We are talking about the day that was, and possibly this florescing is still going on in the florescing. On the other hand, I already said it, once again I prove to be a noticeable person; humor and vanity may be competing for an interpretation of what sense they make. But here is not the time and place to seek their disappearance.

Evidently a bunch of people in complete despair have been set loose in Osijek at the Drau; truly, they must be actors.

But Esther is making a film about her forgetting and her remembering and has ABC's permission to film, so that she can crawl into the extras' heart, into our heart who have our hearts variously armored, armor that is made of fear, Esther approaches me again, besides, besides.

But when Mordecai handed out Kleenex at the kaddish, so that the women—who else—would also cry a little during the filming, I thought: this must be a joke. Of course there was no Kleenex in Theresienstadt, you had to cry onto pure textile when the scene was filmed.

The day was good, all of them had something to do with each other, and so it was o.k. when I took off the lamb's uniform and went into a real shower.

February 28, 1986

Today they picked me twice and took the sharpest profile shot of me, and that is how the respective takes began. Someone has fallen in love with my nose which is somehow modeled after the Jewish noses that used to be caricatured in the Stuermer, so that—like a gong—my nose announces the desired mood for whatever scene of Jewish misery is to follow, a scene behind which—we will see it in a moment—the real life of Theresienstadt manifests itself; and to accomplish that, the camera dollies a few yards up—there is a deathly crash in the snow where, of 800 extras, some, then progressively more and more fall down, of course for the film.

During the first take I sit on the sofa with Hannah, and behind me lies our sick child and is fed by Hannah. In front of me sits Harry, our son, born in 1940 in Hungary, not that I need to explain anything really, and is playing something melancholy on a wind instrument; I have to listen to him, with an inward-turned face, and nose. Not exactly a brilliant achievement with ice-cold feet. Whatever Yankee isn't moved by that can't be moved, I can't help it either, but presumably some of them are going to bawl before they switch over to watch baseball. Up to forty people are crammed into the tubular one-room apartment, first of all the camera pans past me and Harry, then it absolves the whole row of miserable Jewish life; the take is supposed to be modeled on a painting that anyone who wants can see in the Jewish Museum in Tel Aviv.

All I have to wear are gloves and sometimes they even line them with lambskin. I freeze in the morning—everybody is freezing; and especially I freeze in the afternoon during the big death lineup. So far I haven't got used to ice-cold toes, but it's possible, standing in snow up to your ankles. But looka there, Branko Lustig picks me out of the lineup and seats me up front at a table where our Jewish painters are sitting and two other guys, from Sarajevo; the Jewish council in the snow. The Jewish police then come running, one at a time, and they report something—presumably, how many fell over, and we, the commission, write all that down on paper; except that I don't get any paper, I just sit there, on my armchair in the snow, and watch with a sunken face how the big line-up moves past, and next to it SS and German shepherds and eight hundred people.

It is so cold sitting there with your shoes in the snow—all of that once more forty-five years ago—but with naked feet or wooden clog or rags and not just for ninety minutes, but for an entire day, a night and one more day. It hits me that the anti-Semites should be the extras. Let them stand there not an hour and a half; but, say, sit and stand for three hours in the snow like that at minus twenty-two centigrade. On the other hand, if we freeze, our kind still won't warm up, not then and today the tea won't do it either.

When I don't have to stand at attention, I catch myself staring at the fur-lined boots of director Dan Curtiz; that is when I don't have to show my profile. He's made something of himself this Daniel Kohn from Budapest. It's all right with me, but I wouldn't have anything against his hurrying up.

During the next take I drop way down: I am supposed to disappear behind the broad back of a Slovenian farmer, for either I'm part of the Jewish council outside at the table or I am standing in line for inspection. The ABC cheapskates didn't want to give us a break during the next scene, we who had stood outside all this time, we just weren't supposed to be visible, that was all. Another extra who isn't supposed to be seen but who isn't allowed to warm up. So we hid, and it takes and it takes until the take starts. I did a good job of hiding myself behind the broad back of my frontman, and what if that guy doesn't fall over, and there I stand—stubbornly—in front of me masses of dead, the camera is up there, but you don't see my profile.

Then we go back to the waiting room and Esther Lichtblau films me through Nana's eyes, and I am talking just bullshit as I come into her camera, but Esther likes for me to deliver myself of nonsense, I am not only spontaneous but even authentic.

The tickets of life, how differently they are doled out if you are cold; unreality becomes so distinct and close that you believe it, even accept it as a kind of reality, which accompanies us from then until today.

And so it happens that Doctor Klang, who is practically ignorant of prayer, revealed an inner quality of Jewish prayer inside the tube of Daniel Kohn's Theresienstadt. As the camera panned past him and as the mike happened to catch his rhythmic prayer murmuring, though no one was supposed to understand the words, he prayed murmuring in words full of clarity and truth: "Sh'ma Israel, cold is me footsie, Sh'ma, footsies so cold, oy me ma footsies Israel. Sh'ma Israel, in the footsies is me so coldy, adonai."

There, I think when my feet finally warm up and the head remains wonderfully cool, it can happen, that there comes not the Messiah but a beautiful feeling.

Translated by Michael Roloff

Touché

Evelyn Schlag

WHEN I was sixteen, the most disreputable student of our school began to take an interest in me. That immediately gave me status with my classmates, who had been all set to write me off as a nerd, as hopelessly intelligent and, because of my diabetes, as just plain unfit. Not just any student from one of the other schools, whose reputation, after all, would depend on hearsay. Not some milkshop innocent, nor some bland face from the other section of the class. I was lucky, for I did not have to garner all those little experiences one by one. In one stroke I had overtaken them all, except, of course, for the two crafty girls from out of town.

At the swimming pool one summer a boy had softly run a finger along my spine. We were lying side by side on the sun terrace, our sweaty burning faces turned towards each other; out of the slits of the eyes our awkward glances were probing, jabbing, skidding off, penetrating deeply. Then his hand lifted, as if suspended by the elbow, and his forefinger tripped along my vertrebrae. Before I could draw even with him, touch his arm or his cheek, a shout from the street clattered to the hot concrete floor of the terrace. "My father," the boy said, and right there everything belonged to another time, the next month perhaps, or the next year. We were separated, he had to follow the summons, he could promise nothing. I stayed, prone on my towel, pretending to be dead, so as not to get him into trouble. He packed up his things, murmured something, a good-bye, I saw how our afternoon together was pressed thin between his lips. Then he was gone. This finger exploring my spine was my first encounter with love and desire, with sexuality, with desperation and the question, why don't you stay?

My dreams were much too big, as I lay on that terrace at the pool, at home on my bed, on the plush sofa in the living room. I propped up my legs against the wall, looked at my knees, stretched one, then the other leg, compared myself with mannequins reclining in armchairs, draping their legs over the armrest, or kicking up high in the air with one leg. In their miniskirts they straddled across wooded paths, and wore heavy knitted sweaters. In flimsy black and white checkered op-art dresses they leaned against the faded red wall of an Italian Carabinieri post and angled their legs. They never had flat feet, nor did they ever have to wear inserts. Their breasts were small in a way that only heightened their appeal. I never could figure out how they managed to do that.

For my dance course, which began in October, my mother had sewed a dress with a straight collar, long sleeves and an edge-stitched front placket that had two or three buttons. It was of thin woolen material, a paisley print with a pattern of green, blue and yellow amoeba. A girl from the next class, which was also Georg's class, sometimes came to the dance lessons, even though she already knew all the dances from the previous year. For me she was the rival incarnate. The way she raised her right hand when she began to dance, horizontally extending her fingers, every single lacquered fingernail latching into the hand of the boy who had the good fortune of dancing with her: that I would never be able to do. All the while she opened and closed her pink painted lips as if she were saying perfumed words. Her eyelashes never stuck together from the mascara. She had short, blond hair, which she backcombed and teased so perfectly that it seemed the only hair style possible in the whole wide world. I wore my brunette hair long, down to the shoulders, parted on the side. With a barrette I kept the hair out of my face. If this were the girl's hair style and I in turn had her short, blond hair, I would have been convinced that only long, brown hair was glamorous and smart.

Georg was a good dancer. I didn't yet know that men of a certain stature, not too tall, have a rhythmic body awareness. I saw how he guided the incomparable Helga by the hips through the ballroom of the Café Traxler—no, not guided: how they sent each other across the dance floor with invisible, electric impulses, the harmonized steps taming their energy. There seemed to be no planning of step sequences, they invented each dance and through its performance gave it validity. Helga tapped with her fingers, which were entwined with Georg's fingers, and Georg immediately converted the impulse into a sweeping turn, and another one, and yet another one. His face abruptly appeared after each turn, a proud face that crowned an inventive body, a face in which the dark eyes sometimes winked quaintly, a face with the stock smile of an operetta tenor. But it did not matter. If the self-assured and stylish Helga accepted that, it must be the thing to do. Her dress was similar to mine in cut; on her, of course, it looked quite different. The paisley print in various shades of yellow. There I was, with my parted hair and aquamarine dress, standing with other girls. I can very clearly remember Helga's hands, but not my own. At some point Georg came up to me and asked me to dance. His face, which I knew as one knows the face of a celebrity, demanded to be taken seriously. My girl friends melted away, shed their names. I didn't have as much as a word for them. I saw his looping gaze taking in my throat, my breasts, my shoulders, I saw how he lifted his comforting eyebrows, how piece by piece he took possession of me. On his temple he had a scar which was partly covered by one of his dark, almost black locks. He wore a dark jacket and black trousers with creases across the groin, a man's trousers. He corrected my grip in his left hand, put his other hand under my arm on my back and kept time with his head. I kept on tripping along with his confident, large steps, I didn't know what I should be concentrating on, on his insisting thighs that drove me backwards, on his hand just under the clasp of my bra which pushed me into the other direction, on his gray-stippled chin, on the corners of his mouth, on the upper lip, which I kept fixed in my view, so that I would not have to look into his eyes, even though to do just that tempted me the most. Everything about him was earnest. When he smiled or set his temperament free with a quiet little laugh, one could sense the grown-up in him, something that no longer belonged to the boys that were awkwardly stalking about this ballroom. When he had moved on to secondary school, he had repeated a grade, and later yet another one. He was three years older than I, his whole body moved with a quiet competence, with professionalism. His glances did not just happen; he knew how to look at a girl. I felt vulnerable to his ways, but I did not struggle against it. When he casually brushed his thigh against my pubic bone, my astonishment at once merged with the sense of self-assurance with which he continued to dance, as if nothing had happened. I waited for him to touch me again, and with the return of a certain melody in the dance music I felt him once again bring me close. With raised chin and his head slightly turned to the side he mimed the flight of the melody, smiled sensuously with lips firmly pressed together, like a connoisseur, like someone who knows all the arias of an opera by heart, like a dancer who commands not only his own limbs, but also those of his partner.

For a few steps, for the duration of a few beats of the music we soared along the dance floor, the soles of my black shoes sliding, gliding, performing a fitting counterpoint.

We had the same way home. His parents lived only two blocks from our house. He pointed out their windows, his room with the piano did not face the street. He did not care for pop music. His favorite composer was Liszt. I tried to remember whether we had anything by Liszt at our place. In one hand I held the plastic bag with my dance shoes, Georg clasped my other wrist between thumb and forefinger, as if to take the measure of my delicate frame. Then he held his clenched fist against mine, turned it left and right and struck a few chords into the air.

"Why don't you come in, I'll play something for you," he said. I did not see how that was possible. I was only allowed to go out for brief periods.

"As long as my father does not find out," I said. Just a little I was beginning to detach myself from his regimented world. His strict rules were always with us in our house, even though for a year now he came home only on weekends. My brother, my mother and I lived together with his commandments in our large house, and on weekends we all felt how these commandments were recharged, made ready to exercise their power for yet another week.

"What could he possibly do to you?" asked Georg. "Surely he doesn't beat you."

"No," I said. "Never that." It was hard to explain.

At recess next day a classmate came in from the hallway and said: "For you." I was to go outside. Georg was there, one hand hooked into his trouser pocket, his leg nodded, well? I stood with him at the window with my back turned to the bustle of the hallway. I did not know which teacher had supervisory duty. Girls were not supposed to be standing around with boys. My back winced with apprehension. Georg could not care less, he leaned with an elbow on the window sill and half-looked into the hallway. I was afraid that others could hear what he had to say. I would have wanted him to discreetly place each word into the palm of my hand, and then I would have hidden everything in my briefcase. But I was also impressed that he was not at all afraid, that he was above it all. Georg's performance was borderline in Latin and in English. His favorite class was history. I ate my cheese roll and took care not to have any crumbs get stuck between my teeth. Around me students moved about in twos and threes, down the hallway the caretaker was dispensing milk, chocolate drinks, candy bars, rolls with sausage or cheese. Our school was old and still had oiled floorboards, the radiators were black monsters on which one could sit as long as there were no teachers around. Georg leaned with his backside against the radiator under the window. If only he would be a little less conspicuous, but I did not know how to tell him without the risk of having him lose interest in me. After recess we had Latin. Besides German and English, it was my favorite class. I had wanted to review the irregular verbs that were going to be on the test this day. I loved my Latin teacher, she was reserved, she was single, and she maintained order in my head. Everything in this language had a logic, but one that was quite different from the abstruse logic that the math teacher used for his subject. In Latin even the exceptions made sense.

After the next dance lesson Georg took me to a path along the edge of the woods. It was late afternoon and nearly dark. At first there were streetlights, since many of the patients of the convalescent home started their walk into town along this way. Where the street narrowed, became steeper and led up to the woods, there were no more lamps. We held hands and wasted no time. At the intersection where we could have gone down to the street where I lived, we stopped. "Just for a couple of minutes," said Georg. We continued along the rising way. I could see the lights of our house, the room in which my mother was sitting and sewing and looking at the clock. Georg made us stop. He held me by both arms. His pallid face with the dark hair shimmered in front of me. I ran my fingers over his winter coat, a lined coat of dark blue material, which he also wore when I later photographed him. In the picture Georg stood in the snow, looking glum, pale, unshaven, with dark eyes turned back to me. He looked like Maximilian Schell in the film adaptation of Kafka's *The Castle*. When I started to read Kafka a little later on, I pasted this picture into the paperback. Now our coats kept guard around us, only our faces, our hands could come close. He grasped me with two fingers at each cheek, sparked his will into my head, and I climbed softly into his practiced kiss. I felt I was being initiated into a secret place, his mouth, secret though for everyone to see. Here he drew me into a new life. Here I stopped being a schoolgirl.

The next day a neighbor saw me walking home as far as the corner of our street, and not alone. By afternoon my mother knew about it. Now she too dreaded my father's learning about his daughter hanging out, as it was called. And not just hanging out, but seeing a scammer who was three years older and who had repeated two grades, a loser, dangerous and experienced. My mother did have to admit that he was rather good-looking. Of course he was not allowed into our house. And I was not permitted to visit him. But then I took up going to the optional French lessons in the afternoons, and on Sundays I regularly attended Catholic Mass again. My father was Protestant. Proudly he would tell how his father on his death-bed had refused to defect, refusing the Extreme Unction offered by a Roman Catholic priest. We, that is my mother, my brother and I, were the Catholic parasites. Every once in a while he threatened he would no longer pay the outrageous church taxes. I could imagine the disgrace of being excluded from Catholic religious instruction at school. "I will cancel your membership, I will cancel the membership of all of you," he shouted. Sundays, when I went to Mass, I took special care to avoid him before leaving the house. Instead of going to Mass, Georg and I turned into a narrow street which led to the back entrance of a house in which only an old couple lived. With a large key Georg unlocked the gate, I waited next to him, with shoulders stiff as if paralyzed, and then blindly followed him across the small yard. At any moment I expected one of the windows to be flung open and my father to throw a bolt of lightning between Georg and me. Screaming, thunder, crashing. I followed my heartbeat, which seemed to hurry ahead of me in the dark hallway. Then to a double door, which it took forever to open. We did not speak a word. Finally, the anxiety that someone might be in the room, which I then entered with a large stride, taking both steps at once.

    As soon as Georg had locked the double door behind us, we had vanished from the world. We were still in this town, of course, but the town could no longer see us. Without sitting down, without ever touching anything, having a glass of water or throwing a paper tissue into a waste basket, without taking off my coat, I crossed this room and vanished yet another time. A door led to a windowless alcove, in which there was just enough room for a mattress and a chair. A pillow, a blanket. My coat over the chair, Georg's coat on top. We took off our boots, nothing else. There was nothing else one could do in the chamber but to lie on the mattress. It was that simple. There was a dim light, which Georg immediately turned off. In the dark he dispatched his hands to gently straighten out my long hair. He unclasped the barette and promised not to lose it. He pulled my blouse out of the skirt. Whatever my mother sewed for me, whatever buttons, zippers or snap-fasteners, it went through Georg's hands. He did not undress me. He pushed up my pullover, blouse and chemise and seemed to be looking at my breasts in the dark. He then also pushed up the thin nylon bra; a ring of clothing warming my neck, I lay with crossed arms, and felt Georg's thumbs on my nipples, while his fingers gathered as much flesh from all sides as possible. When Georg unfastened my bra, it shriveled up on my chest to a ludicrous bundle. This rampart separated me from the action on the other side of it. Georg pressed the base of his palm on my left breast, groped with the middle finger to the other nipple, while using his free hand to extend his territory on me. My ribs were exposed, as was my navel depression. He pushed the edge of his hand under the waistband of my skirt, let the fingers follow, withdrew, advanced under the waistband of the pantyhose, seemed to know, surfaced again quickly and opened the fasteners of the skirt with one hand, deftly like a seamstress or a war invalid or a pianist. I listened to all the sounds, the unclinking of a snap-fastener, the soft chirping of a zipper, to Georg's breathing, to the empty room beyond, I was frightened to death that someone was trying to push a key into the lock. I smelled the musty cold smell peculiar to this chamber, in which we now perspired and shivered. Around my belly a cool plateau spread, at its edges searing mountains rose up. It was night, no stars, no moon, only a deep whispering voice and something in me that answered with a small, saucy fear. My voice often slid down my throat, and the farther Georg's hands stroked over his territory, the less I could hear myself. I was ashamed, when in the cold my nipples became erect between Georg's fingers. I understood so little. I sensed that he had intended all along to arouse this response in me. He pressed the top of his old-fashioned ring, as large as a finger nail, on the nipples. The ring already was at body temperature.

In this darkness Georg worked on my senses. Under his agile hands, blood pooled, hair parted, and skin became taught. When my body moistened, when I smelled different, when Georg began to wipe his fingers in his handkerchief, I felt ashamed again. I thought of his mother, who would be washing these handkerchiefs. He always used linen handkerchiefs. In the hallway at school I felt uneasy and broke into a silly grin whenever he blew his nose and then with a quick movement stuffed the handkerchief back into his trouser pocket. All winter long Georg was preoccupied with the task of putting me in touch with my body. It fully claimed my attention as well. Except for his mouth, which I could kiss, I was not in the least interested in his body. His hands, yes, his face, but to my relief everything else was covered. My body grew under his gaze, I left my childhood behind. His own childhood was remote, but it seemed that even then he had mostly been playing the piano. For him, playing piano had nothing to do with the kind of lessons on an instrument that my girl friends disliked so much. No one ever had to make him do Czerny études. He just laughed and with his laughter deflated all pomposity and pretense.

Even now my father did not suspect anything. Toward the end of winter my parents met him on the street. My father reported that he had seen the lawyer's son, a gloomy sort of person with a black scarf. The scarf that I had knitted for him.

We called my father our Sword of Damocles. Georg knew all about weapons. I shrank from the scar on his temple and admired it all the same. Dueling was his way of dealing with what was so difficult for me: conquering fear. Whenever he said, "I'm going to be dueling this weekend," I knew that a masquerade was in store. He would put on a velvet jacket and high boots, step with a heavy broad gait into a vaulted room, into another century; he would put on padding and protective gear, the kind of wire mask used by welders. But his cheeks, his chin, his temples, his brow, his head would still be exposed to the thrusting, slashing and striking. Depending on the skills of the attending doctor, the dueling cut would heal and then appear as a smooth red scar hardly to be noticed, or as a nasty trench casting its macabre spell. The flesh of the cheek stitched together. Before anyone else could tell me anything about dueling fraternities, about corporations and rituals, Georg had already defused all their calumnies. "No," I said later as a student in Vienna, "they don't shake pepper into their raw wounds. No, they are not keen on getting as many dueling scars as possible, on the contrary."

Georg taught me how to read the faces of the fraternity brothers whom I occasionally got to meet. That a certain scar across the chin was the work of a left-hander. How the fifth parrying position was executed. How a scar in the corner of the mouth could forever disfigure a smile. "You can trust anyone with a dueling scar, he is one of us." When Georg returned from his gloomy weekend bouts and had nothing more than a scar hidden in his hair, I breathed a sigh of relief and thankfully embroidered a design on his punctured fraternity colors. I held his blue velvet cap in my left hand, turned it around on my fist, fingered the ornaments on it, stroked the silken threads of the embroidery. Colorful scars for comparing and showing off. Those who did not have a girl friend invented a lover and asked their mother or sister to do the embroidery for them. I pressed my nose against the soft velvet, which yielded smoothly. My first experience of the intimate smell of men is linked with the sweat of the fraternity house and with pipe tobacco. There was a lot of talk of Germany, which I, never having taken a course in history, thought to be about as exciting as the words breast or vagina. I turned into a German girl in Austria.

Translated by G.G. Gardner

A LIFE

WOLFGANG SCHÖNER

AND her gait has a a bit of a stagger, not abrupt like those drunkards, those others. But it's there, also because she lurches from side to side with her bundle, and with the one above that. And her feet move in between, as if she had a center of gravity. But what remains behind wasn't any center, and whatever comes will never be one.
That's where the picture was. So lovely. A girl before a mirror ran her hand through her long hair as if lost in it. And behind the mirror a window, with sky and clouds so delicate and white. She looked at the picture as if it were of herself. And before the mirror her own hair, still in braids back then, out of its confines, and with her hand run through it. "Don't you always be looking at yourself in the mirror! Don't be so vain! An' if you look at y'self so often in the mirror you'll get a nasty ugly face in punishment and your hair'll fall out!"
The classes, then, a dreary path through the years. The others all around, noise and clattering feet, a pushing and shoving; what do they want anyway? That leaped out at you over and over as if it meant something.—One she liked; clever and lazy, probably a little fat too, and with a thick mouth that was always a little crooked, as if mocking. When he saw that she liked him he was the meanest of them all. Once he pulled so on the braids she still wore, pulled her down to her knees in front of him. Then she saw his eyes, they were quite distant . . . masked . . . and as if intoxicated with pleasure. Before she could scream though, she knew for a moment that this pleasure was hers.
With girlfriends, it looked sometimes as if it might work out well. And yet something was beneath it all like shallow groundwater, and in the end the same thing always came back against her: a hardening, half irritated, half indifferent.
Thus crept time. She felt imprisoned, the exit unattainable far ahead, at the end of the classes. As if she had to endure something

unconquerable until then. Or persevere; actually both of them were not what she wanted to call it. She found no words for it.—Once during class she learned something that was as if it came from within herself. "And the people of Israel journeyed through the desert." For centuries they wandered and around them was nothing. She thought at length about this. At night she sometimes started up out of a tortuous anguish, as if the emptiness were pushing from both sides against her, like a wall as high as a house.

Below the flat gray. Dirty, dusty; it expands, endlessly long. It is like a viscous flow, all of its own, from morning until dark. The paths, so many and as if free-standing, where to; there is something like a hope that the choice could be made and something up there in the day will change if the choice is the right one. Time, though, levels the paths, imperceptibly, irrevocably; then it has become immaterial and only ever the same again. For that which spreads itself out beyond like a net has long since drawn in on itself; in it a forward momentum that is stuck in the congealed day.

The years when she did water colors, work on the side; different things, mainly temporary. Her paintings were delicate and watery, flowers, much sky, trees; usually there were clouds in them. People were less successful. She looked at many books back then. In one she found a picture, an old one; she looked at it and felt as if a knife were cutting slowly through her body. It was of a man on the ground, clasped by shielded arms, his right hand in a chain, at his breast a battle ax that held him in check. His right leg was lifted high, his foot clenched in pain, his mouth opened in a scream; the dagger piercing one of his eyes. In the back, at the entrance to the tent, the woman wide-eyed with lust, her face gleaming as if insane with triumph, about her wrist a rope of pearls, in her fingers the shears; out of the other hand the shorn hair wafted like the smoke of a torch.

A love affair persisted; probably his laugh had pleased her the most, flowing so broadly and assuredly and sometimes gurgling like a stream. He was portly and strong, did what he did unhurriedly. There were those afternoons, when he lay in bed, the beer beside him that she didn't like but drank with him, and they drifted through the hours as if in a cloud-like, thick fog; time ceased to exist, surrounded them soft and dense, what was outside paled; and at the bottom of this sinking she found herself floating and yet as if drenched by a clinging weight, calm and tortured, lost in something incomprehensible to her and yet flooded with a deep pleasure, at once comforting and disgusting.—After such days she rushed back, filled with intensity, to her paintings. One she worked on at length; it was of an oddly stiff dancing couple: he stood there strong and burly and almost carried her, her head was high over his, thrown back, the arms flung out, her loose hair flowed far down her back. Overhead, the full moon, passing clouds. She didn't show it to him then, he found it, looked at it briefly, said "How romantic!" with a mocking look about his mouth.—It seemed as if something slid across the floor, unseen and yet noticeable and ever quicker. Finally she reproached him for his slowness, for he never took care of anything; yet as she spoke and thought she had cleared her path, thought she had a kind of headstart so she could give matters a twist she liked, she was abruptly and brutally brought to a halt by a swift, unexpected hatefulness, as quick and sudden as if it had been right in front of her for a long time like an invisible wall. "Do you think you're better than the others, huh, with your scribbling and your plaits done up in a bun? A crazy woman y'are, nothin' more!"

His voice sounded almost no louder than ever but it roared inside her. A few days later he was gone.

She tore up the page with the dancer. A feeling like sand, a bilious feeling, like bitter ash, twisted her lips upward, she stood and walked about her room, her fists at her side. What was in turmoil inside her was demolished at once as if by powerful gigantic knives. It rose and rose and burned, a smoldering corrosion; but before she screamed and rage tried to break out like a flame, a deadening blow occurred within her, a tearing nausea penetrated the very bones of her hands, she ran—the shears—and while it crashed over her like a black wave heavy as a stone, she slashed, slashed at her hair until it lay about her on the floor. She felt as if the metal gave off a screeching sound every time she cut.

Her gaze lowered. Things rushing past on the sides, confusion, shadows crossing each other. Nothing. And behind it and higher up, stiff, pared down to indifference; too often all that, too often. It has become like a greasy curtain, high as a house and immovably heavy.—Once, but then suddenly the burden tugs so much, bends over to the side; as she is bent down by it, then it draws back slowly, and it unmasks itself for her gaze that settles on something, and slips toward each other, as if it were rearranging itself. A wooden frame and the corner of a large pane, behind it things, papers in piles, folders, pens, writing utensils. It makes up a face. A sparse mustache where one always expects to see crumbs and some kind of dampness; cheeks with tiny blue-red veins that look burst; small oily eyes. Then a cuff, out of which extends a red stubby finger. "That's where it goes, how often have I told you that already!" Pokes in a cubicle. That there, that over there, so you can find everything right away. It was immaterial to her.—And hunched beneath the weak light bulb was the bare dome with the sticky hairs surrounding it, in the evening in the back room, when he wrote his bills. Every time she looked down at the spotted skull that nodded and twitched and at the plaid cuffs. Then she left.—And suddenly the screams, half screeching, half whimpering, and the fumbling red finger above the cubicle—a fountain pen—she didn't comprehend—"Thief!"—the voice breaks. On the tilting floor the things slide away sideways, accelerated and silently, ever hated and tiresome, demanded from the outside, a distorted pile of junk, that collides down below at a distance from which nothing more penetrates. Within her she feels the nausea like a gray dry foam. Then she leaves. Behind her the door shuts.

The time passed; like a slow sinking. She hadn't painted for a long time now. Something was always pressing in from somewhere, the rent, always in arrears; it still caused a sharp painful jolt occasionally. But it passed. In the stairwell always the same faces, dreary and distant and yet somehow lurking. Petit bourgeois and Philistines all of them. She had one friend, she was different. "Don't give a damn." She had been in prison once, for personal property stuff, recently yet again.—Life went on. Over all the unevenness and sharpness, the flowing of the days lay like a cover that held everything together and that she could nestle into even between the irregularities and edges. Once she took a two-week trip to her cousin in the country; during that time she gave her apartment to a recently jobless friend who had a cat and a child and didn't know where to turn. When she returned she found herself evicted. The screaming of the child, locked up alone days at a time, had alerted the neighbors. The manager's inspection of the apartment revealed conditions that violated the lease, for instance the extreme soiling of the apartment by child and animal. They acted quickly, probably also considering the chronically late rent. To cover what was owed, everything that wasn't already part of the sparse furnishings of the apartment was simply confiscated; nothing more than a suitcase of clothing was left to the former owner. When she, luggage in hand, walked down the stairwell, a few tenants stood at an open apartment door. They directed their gaze at her, dispassionately, stiff and icy, silent. A seething cloud wrenched her head to the side. With her hand on the rail she came around the landing and onto the steps. "Slut," said a woman's voice behind her. A few weeks later she met the friend on the street. "Whadd'ya doin' here?" Could she help her out with a little something? She needed food and maybe money for lodging in a cheap hotel . . . "Ain't got nothing. And anyway, who'd give me anything?" She turned around and disappeared.

She still stood there as if listening into a sharp and unfathomably wrenched open void. And then something began to spin at racing speed within her, it rose like the sound of a siren and threw everything that had filled up this inner space all these last years flat up against the wall. Her legs began to move, she no longer saw where. A petrified, hammering scream pierced her head. She made it to a public park; she sat there on a bench, sat and pressed her forehead into her hands. A pain so choking and fiery wended its way through her body, and with it rose up images from days that were past and forgotten; there was one, too, a girl . . . sky . . . clouds; and above it all the torment descended so searing and so agonizing, that it seemed to her as if her body were torn into bloody strands.—She sat until it was dark. When she got up, everything in her was as empty and as charred as soot. Slowly she went her way.

After this day she no longer cut her hair.

The street. No longer encoffined in those dens full of ridiculous junk. No more obligation, no captivity. All the rat race around her—what is the point, anyway? Lost and mistaken. Only cowardice. But to be beyond all of that—and to have nothing any longer.—But they run, these words, fragments, a babble.—And through the years it closed like a dome, stone on stone, twisted out of voices and noise, a gigantic frozen scraping, that encompassed her ear. But she no longer noticed it.

There was the direness, the cold, lying on hard ground; an arising, with pain and difficulty, into an empty day. The dirt; and a meal that she got from somewhere, with those like her; yet she was disgusted by that word. She always arrived in order to be the last one.

In the beginning there was still an urge within her, that she could get herself going again somehow. But then ceased to exist. How? she sometimes wondered.

Through the streets she walked as if held captive. She could look at no one, because all of them looked at her with gazes that simultaneously consumed and stung. In the presence of each eye that looked at her, her own shrank back as if in the presence of nettles, and at the same time rage rose up in her. Who did they think they were!—

Slowly a tough dense cover lowered itself over all of the confusion around her that enclosed it and joined it into one single endless body, chaotic and nameless, present and vacuous. Whatever it was, it didn't affect her. For not much separated her from the path that she had taken day after day, at least not very much, yet on the whole so immeasurably much, that everything else was as if smoothed out and distant. She looked at nothing; she heard nothing, she knew that it—everything—was cut off; it was no longer important. The path that she walked, that enclosed her like a gutter, remained, without hope, without escape; it was jammed in at her sides as high as a wall and the years in which nothing exists any more, in which nothing more happens, were stony, immovable, implacable.

The hall. She walks it; finally, there .... On both sides, the burden, the pain rises and looms in her body as in caves.—The street empty, late, the perforated metal of a trash can, the light of the street lights orphaned and shrill, shadows on the walls like soot. She stops there and stands still. Her heart murky and candent, a fragile and brittle feeling; and suddenly from beneath it springs sadness, unspeakably, in dense, heaving blackness, fills up everything, encloses everything, a never-exhausted current, and takes her up in it. About her hand a breeze, soft, unnoticeable. And she did weep much and did strew ashes on her head, as was fitting. She rested on her knees, her fingers traced over the ground, over and over the tears erased in the dust.—The needs of the body, food, filth, the daily implacable urge, as it pushes and urges and grows; the disgust every time she had to go get food. To have to be a captive of this shame and dependent on those who have, but she had nothing. And they were the same ones who were implacably against her and everything that destroyed her, hard as stone. The rage tore at her. For what grows is weak so they kill it. But to freeze, stone! And all of them acting so free and so fine and condescending: to do it to them, so it would choke them!—The streets again, drawn together, the narrowness as braced in chasms at both sides, against the emptiness all around, that presses in like mountains. In between the hall that she walks; the end of it blinded. And the Israelites passed through the desert, so it rose up in her. For decades, and round about them was nothing. But the others.—How are you? Like a splinter it leaps at her ear. Ridiculous, spat out, forgotten; what right should someone like that have to a word like that? Within her is life, there on the edge. That is where it grows, too. The tunnel remained for her like she remained for it, they are one, only the one, and there the growing too and that it remains for her, and she for it. There it lay, what she had to name, almost close enough to touch, and she found it: that everything had been laid aside.

"Well, will'ya look at her!" "What a pig." "Must be a zillion fleas and lice on her." "They can't even live there." It pierced her from close up, sharply the terror raced into her heart and the fear. A hunted look—in front of her a semi-circle of youths—one held an open bottle of beer—impudent and grinning the face of a girl—so she turns at once and begins to run. Behind her the sound of a few steps—"Run, you old bag, run!"—Laughter—soon it is quiet.

Blackness spins before her eyes. She sits hunched forward; what was that? What struck her? Like board by board from a wall, it tears off plank by plank. It was she herself! And filth?—She stands up, walks along, doesn't see where. But it seemed to her as if her head was being pulled ever more tightly together from all of that; as if the bones were growing inward; and then there was only room for one single thing.—In the gloom she stayed where she was, on a bench, her gaze hung in the darkness as if in a broadly stretched void. The night passed. As it got lighter and the colors returned, she listened around her into a soundless, high-domed stillness.

In the streets of Vienna you sometimes saw one of those people who are called transients, one who was more noticeable than the others of her kind. As is common with these people, she carried her meager possessions with her always, in two fairly large and probably also heavy bags, one in each hand. She was clothed in an old brown coat that she obviously didn't take off even in the hot season of the year. The odd and actually terrifying thing about her was her head, to be exact her hair; for it began to harden above the skull, not all too far from the hairline, until it grew together at the back of the head into what appeared to be a rock-hard, closed crust; there it disappeared into a large voluminous cloth that hung over her shoulders and enclosed it. In striking, even painful contrast to this disfiguration—to look at it without a rising feeling of nausea was certainly impossible—was the face, especially the eyes, marked by a heavy oppression and at the same time worn. This person almost always looked down at the ground, too, never around her, and it seems that she never asked anyone for money or the like (which would have been successful on only the very rarest of occasions, given the impression she would doubtlessly have made upon anyone else. It usually would have ended unsatisfactorily, maybe even dangerously).

A life nonetheless—how does it happen, how does it end? One knew about the essence at the outset; but not that it counted and how. A person notices its existence in the midst of all the strangeness, and as far as outsiders make up that strangeness, the person is broken by both. Being lost was a constant, everything became lost that was capable of being lost; the transformation of one's own lies into truth undermines the remaining truths. But blame is not becoming whatever had been your nemesis; to remain that which was destroyed by the nemesis. Accompanying everything was the conceivability of reality, the outside element of that which is within: here, the contempt for one was merely another hatred of the other, and itself for the I that they never were.—and that could have been. In its place, a void: beneath the threshold of one's own life must happen what happened to her; it ends up as mere material that would have belonged to the soul that it finally suffocates. So the tangible is reduced to the failing illusion—that such an illusion could be powerful is impossible to imagine after the tangible wins out—and what remains possible after the remains bears the name of refuse. There might have been some meaning, at most something comprehendable here; even perdition's ability to comply does not save it. The rift goes even deeper; no sinner can go the whole way if that person waits for nothing but the end. The fact that such a thing counts for anything was the final deception; the final task though, was just that: waiting for the end.

It was a long and rather straight street that she walked, and it led gradually uphill though a part of town where she had seldom been. Initially, trees stood on both sides of the lane of traffic, as yet barren of leaves in this early season of the year; the row of trees ended. The rows of houses to the left and right were evenly spaced, secretive. Here the style of building seemed to be less oppressive and massive than in the lower parts of the city. As if a light wind slid past the facades. Abruptly the street descended; along the sidewalk a waist-high wall, bars through which bare twigs stretched themselves. Then she stood before a narrow gate between two tall cement pillars; it was open, she went through it.

Stairs led sideways from a narrow platform and turned to reach the floor of a park set out here in a hollow, unexpected compared with the surrounding terrain. Next to the stairs rose a perpendicular cement wall up to the street, elsewhere were steep slopes. Yet the park was quite small. A narrow strip of lawn, still empty and barren, a tiny playground with a sandbox, benches all around, behind it the branches of bushes. There were trees, too, high firs, beneath them ran a path that she followed. After a few steps she reached the bank of a small pond which was here in the center of the park. Close to the water stood a peculiar tree. The trunk, which had up to then been straight and upright, began to bend at barely the height of a person, to knot up; the branches that grew out of it emphasized this contortion more, so that—twining about each other in this tiny space as if cramped—they made up a snarl resembling serpents' bodies or intestines. Out of them sprouted innumerable thin twigs that reached downward, tight and spindly along the confusion of branches.—She looked and looked; and turned, and went on. In the pond, on an island no longer than two paces and not any further than that from the bank too, the trunk of a once powerful tree rose whose crown was totally destroyed, probably by a lightning strike; only one single branch, heavy and brittle, stretched itself far to the side from where the ruptured trunk had split. Beneath it stood the cattails of the past year, bleached and yellowish-gray, bent like broken ribs. The path turned again, led over a small bridge, under which the pond's overflow was situated—a weak odor, like suffocating putrefaction—and rose on the other side up the hill. Here it was partially forested, dense in places, firs and the soft branches of the yews; the ever steeper and higher slopes down to the pond covered with deciduous trees, through, around and beyond whose now bare branches tall houses became visible. Windows, bright against the sky, clouds. Down below the water shimmered upward with a deep black shade of blue. There was still no green, no blades of grass; the ground between the trees naked and barren. A bird ran off the path toward her, leaped up the hill, looked out of its round yellow eye at her. It was there, too, nearly at the end of the path, a small area enclosed by a wall, where the old leaves collected, moldy and gray. A few steps before it she collapsed, dead.

Translated by M. Veteto-Conrad

INNOCENT DREAM OF AN INNOCENT MAN

JULIAN SCHUTTING

WHETHER he had been concerned about it his whole life long or not, one day he, being awakened by such a loud ringing of bells as never before, would oversleep saying early mass for the faithful, or whether it was merely this night's conviction—like the one that a good Christian should let the advantage of dying in one's sleep pass by unutilized out of respect for the crucifixion—that wanted to carry him off into an ever deepening sleep—

almost forty years after being rescued from a Nazi death cell by American soldiers and several days before his slow death, the aged, clerical gentleman dreams a dream dreamed by no one before him, about his apparently old-fashioned fear of death that was reawakened by his soon-to-be-realized death, something that would make one laugh unabashedly, had someone like Buñuel conceived of it while half asleep:

it was the morning of the execution, but he had overslept; hastily, as if his guardian angel had opened the cell door for him and indicated to him it was high time to flee to his own Egypt, he gets dressed, jumps in a taxi, wet with perspiration because of pangs of conscience about the sleep of the just and of the disciples on Mount Olive who had fallen asleep out of desperation, implores the chauffeur to drive faster, prays for clear passage in front of each train crossing gate that is lowered, as if he were en route in order to bring the sacrament of extreme unction to a dying person burdened with mortal sins, so that—it's almost six o'clock—he only wouldn't miss his execution,

and so, instead of letting happen what has overtaken everyone else, he pursues that which not only evades no one but also happens to everyone, as if God-knows-what would elude him, if he were not to enter right away

Innocent Dream of an Innocent Man 239

into the realm of irrevocable non-being, led astray perhaps by the uniqueness, and therefore also by the impossibility for repetition of this one occurrence,

from the nightmarish race between temporality and him who has time, with powerful beating of the heart, presumably only waking up at the moment in which he is out of breath, and with his last ounce of strength falls at precisely the right moment into the bullets of the firing squad—

Dream image, which also causes compassion to laugh, that one wants to reject a fortuitous fate out of a strict sense of duty, and driven by the most evil times to ridiculous pangs of conscience, undertakes everything possible at his disposal in order to thwart his rescue by fraternizing in his dream with the rider over Lake Constance, who (—instead of just being relieved, that that which could have happened to him, didn't happen and that everything had run its course with God's help—) was so startled at discovering he had not drowned that consequently he actually begins to suffocate immediately on land, as if he were experiencing during his present drowning having drowned far out there, assuming that he, in order at least to do something after the fact, to take his own fate into his own hands, does not rush back to the lake and hack open the ice that had remained whole beneath the wary hooves of his horse,

Dream, which makes it conceivable that the fear of death had so confused one of the ones who was driven by the hundreds to the one door, that he pushed in the wrong direction with a dream reversal of the meaning of flight, pushing forward with the call of one of the keepers or beaters: "back to your place, everyone will get his chance, we won't send anyone away!" for the length of one free moment's breath made believe he was not in vain one of the last to be standing in line for the means of survival, bread or a ship's ticket,

Dream of an innocent man, who perhaps less for reasons of not wanting to miss the one-time chance of soon being with Him in heaven, than of the fear of death driving him to death in the face of the multiple deaths prescribed for him in the case of unpunctuality.

Translated by Paul F. Dvorak

Arrival under Dramatic Clouds

Wolfgang Siegmund

From: Wolfgang Siegmund. Vom Glück, ein einfacher Mann zu sein!

It was as though a picture from a storybook had come to life. Snow clouds over the train station, round and puffed up like so many balloons, almost near enough to touch.

They seemed to be in a race with my train. Out of boredom, since nothing else was going on. And everywhere an alien world:

That man in a blue uniform, the conductor, with the red whistle in his mouth, a short wait for me to leave the train. He whistles. And silently the clouds start to move, tumbling faster and faster across the shoreline of the sky. The train, far behind at first, then chugging loudly in pursuit.

Clouds of snow and passenger cars, faithful images of childhood, they both knew where they were going, for a long time I watched them fade into the distance . . . .

The tiny figure on the platform, that was me, shivering, wearing a coat, that was me. And then some confusion: was I really arriving, or was I already waiting for the next train?

Suddenly the horizon was bathed in a severe monastic light. And I knew I was staying.

I often wonder what it was: this light, was it the Light?

The cold rays warmed me, were familiar, wouldn't let go of me. I turned in a circle, I inhaled the landscape in heavy, deep breaths. I thought of images that I hadn't seen for years, things incompatible with my city life.

I thought about small forgotten chapels perched on the sides of little mountains, those orphaned shelters for a girl named Mary. I thought about rays of sun slanting across the plaster. I wafted around in the light and in the mountains. And then my gaze returned to this platform, where I was alone with my two suitcases.

Here, too, was this peacefulness. Here, too.

I put my hands around my neck, as though they were my turned-up collar. White clouds rolled from my mouth. Breath rising higher and higher, until it blended with the ordinary fog.

I was alone, and not only with my thoughts.

And I already caught scent of the sea. Felt its presence, its breadth. Everything here stood at its service, every wall, every house, every billboard. Everything was serf or slave to the boundless body of water a couple of streets away.

Here at the station not a sign of it was to be seen.

Should I say I had lost track of myself at that moment, I had successfully escaped myself, I was no longer back there, at home?

There it was, this old desire to belong to myself and myself alone. And the equally strong longing for the opposite: to belong to no one, not even to myself. To be free, as real men say. In the whole cruel world. But how could these desires be reconciled, how?

Your indecision now pulls a part of you to the left. To the right with what remains . . . . Watch out! Your indecision combines the opposites and plunges down at you like an ax. It shatters your invisible house, your invisible love, everything you believed in. And all that in a single day. Watch out!

I often had conversations like this with myself. I called them "pocket conversations," to fend off loneliness.

And I still remember vividly how these thoughts were accompanied by a ponderous silence, something out of a painting, moving over the summer roofs. One that arises when glacier white blends with brick red.

A distance then lay between me and myself and I felt afraid. And nevertheless I relished it.

Now it is time to fight against the silence, since it will conquer you if you don't. A game, as though no one were familiar with the road ahead of you. Right now. No one is there waiting for you. What were you thinking? No one standing on platform 3, face hidden by flowers, waiting to reveal a beaming smile, because you are you, simply because you are you, because you have come, for a day or two . . . .

"Don't you have anything for me?" the woman in the waiting room asked. And I was looking into eyes that were older than life, at a mouth that had long since touched every forbidden thing, at some point or other.

"No ring, no gold piece your mother gave you, not even a nice word for me?"

I was looking at a shivering figure: hands buried in the warm ribs of the waiting-room radiator, while the rest of the woman was lying on the bench. Under ragged clothes signs of life.

This woman, a whiff of total loss, her breath heavy with the drinks that a man bought for her, so that afterwards she would be even more homeless than on this lost night with someone or other.

"What are you looking for here, are you looking for the big wide world?"

"Yes," I said, "the big wide world."

"In that case you picked the wrong time of the year. Buy me a drink and then go back home. The big wide world has departed, my dear. I am all that's here, the most beautiful woman in the station cafe. In the winter it's a damned good hiding place, no one will find you here. . . ."

Embarrassed, I stood there between my suitcases, embarrassed I ran my hand over my slicked-down hair. I was so proper, so terribly urbane, I was everything this woman wasn't.

"Well, what are you doing here, cat got your tongue? Hasn't the little man ever been out there in life before, hasn't he ever taken his lumps?"

No, I thought to myself, he has never been there, in the Land of the Lost Women. He is familiar with this land only from the mumbling of hardened men whose stories in trashy magazines tell about what they heard, a long time ago, from women like her.

"Buy me a drink over there in the cafe. Then tell me your story, if you have a story to tell. But what am I talking about, a stray like you doesn't even have a shadow to call its own . . . ," was what that woman said, wearing everything she owned and looking exactly like I felt.

There in front of me, in countless fragments, as though she were my shattered mirror image. An X-ray picture of the real me. I had, to be sure, done a better job of camouflaging my exterior.

Time passed, silence.

I was standing in front of the large red letters of the timetable, stuck on a large poster behind glass. Three times a day there was a way back to my city from here. I was happy about that, I—coward!—was also happy about that.

The snow I had brought in was now lying on the floor in black mushy puddles. Dirty footprints on tiles that had been shiny.

I don't know how it happened, but soon I found myself sitting with her in the cafe.

A dark room, a bar, some kind of pinball machine, empty tables. Everything you need to make a hell.

After the first drink, or the second or the third, she started to laugh, a laugh like it was squeezed out of a festering wound.

No, that was put a bit too dramatically.

A long time ago, before the abuse that now slanted like shadows across her cheeks, back then, to whom did this face belong? I asked myself, awkwardly sitting across from her, my hands hidden under the table, drenched in sweat as they were.

I must confess: never in my life had I exchanged even a single word with a woman like that. I thought they lived in places people like me don't look at, near public facilities we wouldn't use.

Was she still young, or old as death? Used up, or still unborn? Her face told a story I hadn't heard before.

"Say something," she said, "I'll give you five minutes for each drink. Your eyes are asking how do I make my living? By sitting there and listening to idiots talk.

"A couple of kisses, a little cuddling, then off to the park, that's how you figure me. That's exactly how you are looking at me.

"Call me a listening-whore, call me whatever you want to, I won't be ashamed. Anyhow, when a man starts to talk, it's like taking off his clothes, and then when I nod, it's like his last thrust in the moment of ecstasy. I'm not afraid of things people are afraid of, not anymore. I've tried them all, they all taste the same, start talking."

I thought of nothing but going back, but there was no way to go back, then I wanted to start talking, but nothing came out of my mouth.

Here, in this private confessional, here of all places, nothing came to mind. My tongue lay bloodless, limp, rolled up in my throat. The only thing that came into my mind was that I ought to go. But something in me couldn't.

"Isn't anything bothering you, not a single worry, nothing weighing

on your heart? Or have you bought me enough drinks?"
 I still remember. I stood up then. Threw a coin into the chrome-plated cage with the perpetually cheery exotic voices, pressed the white knobs with edges blackened by the sweat of so many fingers, and said in a surprisingly loud voice:
 "I have never lived . . . ."
 "They all say that, that's nothing new on this earth, can you prove it?"
 It was meant as a joke when I told her yes, I can, I have incontrovertible evidence.
 I opened my long, gray philosopher's coat, then the middle button of my exotically flavored jacket, and finally I showed her my lily-white chest.
 "That's me," I said, without knowing what this evidence was supposed to prove. Of course that was me, who else could it have been.
 "But I don't see a thing," she said, "just a glimmer on the lining of your jacket, not another thing. It's empty in there, just a glimmer on the cloth, my poor little man with no chest!"
 It was all a joke to me, just a joke, I kept going:
 What could a man do about it, who might be able to help him out?
 "Try a doctor. But even he won't be able to do anything."
 Poor thing, I thought to myself, so consumed by alcohol. And she said:
 "Poor little stray, of course he would thump your chest, your doctor, and say, go home, you are too healthy for me. But it wouldn't help you."
 "You mean, I would get up and leave and at that instant . . . ."
 ". . . your chest is gone again, vanished, disappeared."
 "Then my chest would be gone again?"
 She nodded.
 "So: I dress, therefore I am?"
 "That's the way it is. First you have to experience your own chest, live out the abuse—live through your body, that's all I can tell you."

 And then she opened her parka, all those layers of clothing, tore at the buttons as though they were nothing but bourgeois ballast.
 A bit of light blue knitted vest flashed by, a bit of an old checkered men's shirt. Finally she grabbed at the cloth and parted it, like you would shove aside a dirty curtain for the first summer day outside.
 I was expecting reddish white skin, roughened by the daily routine

of drinking. But the surface she revealed shimmered tan and smooth. I was prepared for a bra that had been through the wringer. But the one revealed to me was decorated with thorny little roses, and mother-of-pearl beads sparkled delicately across the cups.

"As you see, my breasts have been played out for a long time. But that does mean that they once lived."

And I stared like a calf at the beautiful refutation of that assertion.

Then she stood up and asked for money, for the gadget on the wall, that Irish game with three darts and a disk.

She grinned as she left me alone at the table, and I grinned back, as though someone had pulled me down just in time from the pole with the high-voltage wires. That's how confused I was. Which no one noticed.

Not even the bartender, who was silently paging through a greasy tabloid, through stories about even greasier movie stars or about how Roy B. really died. A bartender in a world of his own, in front of his bottles hanging, necks down.

Something in me started to ask questions, something in me suddenly woke up. How did she know what I was in no position to know?

Had I gradually turned into something, imperceptibly, over the years, that I didn't want to be: a cripple, shamelessly out of touch with reality, cowering basely in the face of real freedom? An anti-bourgeois Babbitt with twenty-twenty hindsight? A run-of-the-mill old-fashioned intellectual out of the nineteenth century?

No! I was the exact opposite! I was a cultured, attractive man in the prime of life, full of earthy vigor, at the height of his prowess! A person whose affirmation of life was purely theoretical.

But what was I doing here? With two suitcases and a passport? I enjoyed life so much that when I slept no thoughts hovered over me. No question about that!

And yet, when I now cast a side glance at myself, someone else was sitting there.

Wasn't everything that I thought I had experienced, beauty, sin, ineffable grandeur, wasn't everything tightly bound and sewn between two covers? Whatever: has my well-versed life so far consisted of nothing but paper?

Or did this lost soul have only this single set phrase? One she kept downing like schnapps, knowing that she could unerringly score a bull's-eye on any man, be he beggar, monk, or Don Juan?

Permanently injure him? Whenever she wanted to, this secretive street teacher.

Perhaps she didn't even mean me. Meant another man, who turned her into what she is now. A bag lady. Somehow I felt sorry for her.

I decided not to think about her anymore. But it was this decision that enabled her voice to bore deeply, without resistance, into my skin where it was thinnest.

"So, is hot and heavy lovemaking something you've only read about in books, or have you also run across it in magazines?

"You owe the little woman an answer, my dear...."

And every time she drew back her arm, the red dart between her fingers, a new question flew at me. Was I the target....

"What do you know about the jungle out there? Is it just something out of the beautiful print on your India paper?

"Well, what do you say?—Oh ho, I get a free game. You know, you really ought to let yourself play free, too, little man...."

She said "little," although I was at least a head taller than she was. What in the world did she want to know?

Once when I did make love, passionate love (that is, from a safe distance), I carelessly left the doors to my heart—my maximum-security cell block—unlocked for half the night. Once—that was enough. Could anyone ask for more? Not these days.

Granted, more than for love I was lusting after a spine—the spine of a book, the printing on the binding, the leather corset that kept words of endearment firmly in place.

Only when the pages lay spread open under me was everything as it should be.

But that's how everyone is! Everyone I knew. My answer, given without moving my lips. And the woman? After each bull's-eye she gyrated her pelvis like a sputnik whirling around an all-too-familiar world.

Granted, for me the world was not as round as a pea, as is generally accepted.

My world raged, cried, and laughed in a nut-colored home. In a frame

Arrival under Dramatic Clouds 247

made of dusty book cases. But that doesn't immediately render a part of a man invisible. Or does it?

I looked at my arms. Scorn rose up in me; the scars of my work were readily visible: my right arm was bent from carrying heavy literary magazines. The left one out of joint from plunging into boundless ideas. A double case of tennis arm caused by perpetually returning existential doubts—that's the diagnosis my doctor would have offered, if I had asked him for one.

I found myself smirking, this cynicism was just what I needed . . . . Or was it—hadn't I always been too smug about my unhappiness?

Until I had embarked upon this flight I had even been aware of taking a bit of pleasure in writing about the depravity of the world. In registering my protest, from a shadowy beer garden, in journals with modest circulations.

Now and then a brief commentary on this land's hostility toward foreigners, now and then a comic-strip balloon about fascism in a new dress . . . .

It all flowed so easily from the pen of the oh-so-vigilant intellectual, like an advertisement for a fire sale. Too easily, perhaps? But that's how we all were, all of the people I had known so superficially, back in the city I had left.

Like all of them, I, too, felt the suffering of the Turk and the Albanian only via the evening news. And no one from my circle came from Anywhereelse. It was true: back then we all had the same caustic white face of the white man. The same honey-yellow glasses, with sprinklings of Cuban tones, in front of our eyes, all longing for the same thing: a two-day revolution. No effort, no pain. Preferably without moving from our cozy fireplace . . . .

"Years ago you boys were wearing pants made from the canvas of a covered wagon. And each of you owned at least a second major key of the harmonica in your olive-green peace bag. Am I right or am I right?

"Today, on the other hand, just look at yourself. Today you are all the same . . . ."

And I did look at myself:

Black pants of pure rayon, black shoes with thick soles, safari tested, from an exclusive shop, no ant has ever crawled over that spit-polish shine. And then this smile of the "night out with the girls" variety.

Yes, the bag lady was right.

"You all wanted to become Andalusians, didn't you, unapproachable and proud, men who sound like guitar solos in the distance. But then why did it all sound like the miserable echo of a frog concert in the morning dew? Did your strings all break?"

The stranger spoke to me without turning around. It often seemed that she had been waiting for me here for years, with a Spitfire in her mouth.

And now she was firing into my innermost being with perfect accuracy, destroying my shallow defenses. What had I done to deserve that?

She made a mess of my first day in America. She spat on the very spot, the very part of me that was already awash. And instead of leaving, which anyone in my place would have done, no question of that, I sat on my chair like I was chained to it and thought about the past, fool that I am.

Yes, the past.

From an out-of-the-way cafe to even more remote parks. Pumped full of projects that no one was prepared to pay for, that no one really believed in, our group least of all.

The past, nothing but idle strolling with a pinch of neoexistentialism and our military crew cuts. And then at parties, which didn't end until the prettiest girl had fallen off the potty seat. No, dancing wasn't our thing, the whole body was good for only one thing: reflection.

We gave such vulgar conviviality a wide berth. Instead we hopped into huge community kitchens like so many kiwis, in order to stutter something to lonely hennaed women about the soaring potential of words.

Or about imminent take-off.

A pack of lies, but how nice it was, the best time of my life.

Yes, we cackled all night long like a garrison of drunken roosters and clenched our fists or pounded with open hands in puddles of Chianti. Oh well.

We were high on dreams, we called ourselves "the conscience of the city," without striking a blow we let our fighting years ebb away.

"And then? Why don't you say something? What happened then? Think back, you have time, no one looses his chest without a reason, you don't get rid of the hairy background for your necktie all that easily. Want me to help you?

"All of a sudden, in the middle of your carefree years, something happened, what happened? Do you remember? Don't be afraid my little man? Me, you'll tell me everything. Surely the little man isn't ashamed in front of a bag lady. After all, she doesn't understand a word he's saying.

"But I do see that he's tired. Up until now you haven't understood a single minute of your life. Oh ho. There's another free game."

And again the machine rang, howled, and rattled, to the accompaniment of tawdry lights swirling around the target. I paid and left.

Translated by Jerry Glenn and Jennifer Kelley

It's a Cliché, Isn't It?

Erich Wolfgang Skwara

THE sun is still high on the horizon but it's the end of the day. A day in June. The end of all things as far as their relationship is concerned, he knows it; yet, after their last togetherness, less than an hour ago, he knows nothing at all. If five minutes are enough for you, he had warned her—at the same time—using hundreds of pretexts to keep them from going to his room—for so long until he had nearly felt saved. Time seemed to be doing him the favor of passing more rapidly than usual; but then the five minutes were fine with both of them. There was no denying their lust for each other, or its relief, this calm for the briefest moment, this resting in themselves and in each other, and thus in the world.

What's the matter with his principles? He hasn't any, that much is obvious; and she knows just a touch too precisely what it is that she is after, namely, that one thing. And he might feel flattered that he is adequate to her purposes. Perhaps it really does flatter him. Later, at night, she will be expecting his call, that's what they agreed upon. But he won't call, he's got that left in him. Then, in four weeks, on his next business trip to London, he won't go on with this affair whose monthly rhythm is beginning to smack of bourgeois mediocrity. He will do his all to avoid announcing his arrival from now on. And of course he will stay at a different hotel. In one where he has never been before. He will have London all to himself again. It's over. He's had it. From now on he will slink like a criminal through the largest European metropolis, he can see it coming. He will feel endangered, caught in the act. How liberated he is indeed! He with his boasts of being a man of the world will scurry through London watching anxiously, a hundred lies, he calls them excuses, at the tip of his tongue. Because, of course, even in the city of ten million, you inevitably run smack into the one person whom you wish to elude. What, you didn't get my letter, I just got here, I was just about to call . . . Stuff like that he will blurt out and blush. The compounding of his own filth. Does he need any of it? He started it, he broke it off. Big deal.

At this moment, she, the singer awaiting her breakthrough, is singing her number from "Suor Angelica" at an old folks' concert in an embarrassing hall in Pimlico. It makes no difference to him how well or badly she sings, he lacks all interest in her artistry. An hour ago she flitted from his bed; her stage fright, which had rattled her throughout the day, seemed to have evaporated. Whoever can forget all about their performance over a moment of lust is not an artist, he had thought. But he said nothing. Caught up in his own distraction, he had tossed her a negligent kiss, from bed to door.

The end of all things: a sudden burst of love overwhelmed him for his far-away wife, for his smart children, his private life, and the solitary peace of his travels. Why did he deceive people, why himself? Why did he go on becoming the victim of lust? Not even intelligence protects you, he thinks angrily. Now he feels calmer, he is sitting at Manzi's, no trip to London without a trip to Manzi's, he delights in his crab cocktail and the Scottish salmon, as well as a bottle of Sancerre. He takes none of his women to Manzi's.

All the time he has known the singer, he has only made love to her in hotel rooms. Using the cleverest of ruses, he has managed to avoid ever going to her home. She joins HIM. She is supposed to come to HIM. Nor does he want to see her child, this leftover from her failed marriage, this allegedly darling girl. But today it happened: his singer dragged him to her little suburban house. She played the tapes for him, the takes for her first album, if he is to believe her. How could he say no to that? He couldn't.

Then, as soon as he found himself in her cramped living room, he knew that it was over. Puff went the magic dragon. Pathetic but true, he concludes now. This living room forever devalues the body of the person who is at home there. She played the tape, anxiously and full of expectation, no one but he has heard these takes; excepting the technicians, of course. She sat down on his lap and wrapped herself around him. I have to be very close to you, now more than ever. And he found her weight a drag, scarcely noticed her singing. There were so many singers in the world, each of them with their own dreams. At the end he fed her a few compliments which she drank greedily from his lips. Her tongue was firm and strong, perhaps all singers kiss like that.

She wanted to show him her bedroom, but he vetoed the sightseeing tour. She didn't appear to notice his cooling toward her. I always dreamed of having you in my bed, she babbled on, and he knew with even greater finality that it was over. Over? There hadn't been anything. He was thinking devotedly of Victoria, his wife, on whom he ought not to cheat. Not today. Whom he cheated on all the time, yet never in spirit, and that was the end of this. You can always turn a new leaf.

I want to sleep with you, the singer demanded. She was demanding a right.

And now he realized that he had cherished her body only so long as he could transport it like stolen sweets off to the Gloucester, the Royal Gardens, the Athenaeum, or the Park Lane. To climb into bed with her in her house would mean to be in a kind of union, would be a sharing; and that went too far, that he did not want. He understood that only too well. And she, too, perhaps understood it a little.

Shouldn't we have something to eat? Do you know any restaurants? Something pleasant, nearby? You show me the way.

She knew no nearby restaurants. They went to a pub by the not far-away river, into an ugly house, and the walk there—between weed-overgrown backyards and brown rowhouses, through nettles and dog droppings at which, each time, he held his breath—disgusted him. Small children were playing in the garden of the pub, and they too annoyed him, and his singer soon sat there overwhelmed by helplessness from such rejection. He did not play hypocrite about liking anything, he did not want to be that polite. She had hoped the early summer river-scape would delight him, now she could no longer reach him. He suddenly longed for the upscale addresses of his business luncheons, and over a glass of cider and a roastbeef sandwich, both of which he left mostly untouched, he showered her with the names of marvelous restaurants. Because they were sitting bucolically by the Thames, he sang the praises of Le Vieux Gallion and Martin Pêcheur at the Parisian Seine. The singer had no idea what he was talking about, he had been aiming exactly for that.

The pubs closed at three P.M. He cursed these British idiocies which, however, did not keep them from having to depart the premises. Taking detours, they found their way back to the miserable house. Underway, he tried calling Victoria from every telephone booth they passed. He wanted to tell his wife how much he loved her. That she of course would not be at home in the middle of an afternoon was not immediately obvious to him, not in the least. He regarded it as a punishment administered by the gods; the punishment for his infidelity. And the singer stood outside, in front of the booth, still hoping to get him into bed. But luckily, her babbling included the one word that would save him: Richmond Park. That was supposed to be not far away at all, and a wonderful place.

He wanted to go there now. Off we are to Richmond Park! At once—he would brook no contradiction—why weren't they there already? Bristling, she drove him there. He sat in her small red Citroen, on a passenger seat on the left, because this was a French automobile built for the English, and he felt confused but also calm. Thus they crisscrossed the park in all directions. Everywhere groups of stags and does lay about under the trees. But nowhere were there stags and does together, mingling. There was no chaos as in the little Citroen where he and she sat next to each other, much too close. He happened, inadvertently, to place his hand on her left thigh, he felt her twitch and despised it. Yet noticed his own growing excitement. The twain inside him, the divided ludicrousness of the man. The woman's ludicrousness was of no concern to him. The park was a lifesaver, you drove and drove endlessly. He just happened to roll up his jacket sleeve, pretending to stretch himself while casting a shy glance at his Omega. But the woman saw through him. The car has a clock, she said, pointing at the dashboard.

Soon it was five P.M. Her concert started at seven, there were two hours left to kill. She'd have to get going, yes, the time was getting near. As though it were really a matter of being faithful, of being faithful to his wife, to any woman. All men are pigs, and women take it or even like it. Of course, just lamely stating it is not enough. They left the park. There was a white villa for sale in one of the expensive quarters—the tempting innocence of its facade, who wouldn't want to own such a prize? But then someone like him could never hope to afford a dream. Every stoplight filled him, who wanted to stretch time, with joy. The heavy lurching rush hour traffic oozed the way he wanted it; every lost minute was like a gift. He accepted his transformation without astonishment. A fortuitous blessing.

All blessings are unearned. At the hotel, which they reached far too quickly, he asked the singer to join him for afternoon tea in the lobby. Anything to avoid going up to his room with her seemed justified. Nonetheless, her evening gown, which she had always with her in the car, was draped over her arm. She would have to change upstairs. Later, there was still time. First they would have tea. She drank like someone dying of thirst, one cup after another, the waiter had to bring a second pot. He, on the other hand, devoured everything edible that high tea had to offer. Sandwiches, scones, fat raisin cakes with raspberry jam and clotted cream. Until suddenly she was pressed for time. He had to take the elevator upstairs with her, he did not like the idea of her being alone in his room. His suitcase was lying open, half unpacked next to the bed. He had spent dozens of nights with her, and now he mistrusted her. Or did he mistrust himself? They took the elevator.

Why are there so many women in the world who are satisfied with less than little, with traveling salesmen who are solid married citizens at home; with men who, for a few kind words, basically only want one thing: to save the price of a whore. These poor, needy women! As magnificent as they appear, as calculating as they may be, as equal or superior, they are at the mercy of that one thing, of the lie, if it must be of the degradation—just to feel complete for those few instants, and to be that much more destroyed within moments afterwards. His own lust consisted of a clinical listening for a woman's sighs; and only at the pinnacle, whose ascent he was able to direct far too rarely, he found his confirmation. Who is using whom, who needs whom?

They were both standing in the room. She only wanted to change her dress, but pushed up against him, wanted to be kissed, and he heard himself asking what he had never wanted to ask her all day long—whether five minutes would do. They claw-clasped each other, it was beautiful, it was inescapable. The agonizing day had been for nothing: the pub at the Thames, for nothing Richmond Park, these hours of avoiding being close to her. They would have done better to crawl into the wide bed early in the morning. Now all they had left were seconds. Exhausted, gasping she dove into her crumpled evening dress, it's only an old folks' recital, never mind, any rag will do. Hurry, hurry, her movements became frenzied, Pimlico was far away, I'm due on stage in thirty minutes!

He is sitting at Manzi's and is filing his small relapse into infidelity under the rubric of forgivable sins. An accident. Faithfulness lies ahead of him, as certainly as his well-oiled marriage. Next time he will call a whore if it must be. At the next table, he discovers her only now, sits an enchanting woman. Unfortunately she is not alone, there's a guy sitting next to her, but isn't it normal for a man to desire his neighbor's wife? If the beauty should look at him, he will begin the flirt. Her companion turns his back to him, which is perfect. Above all, before leaving town tomorrow, he must make sure to buy his wife a gift, and before going to sleep tonight he will write her a letter, a love letter, and he will make a good-night call as well. Why, after all, is there the telephone, why the mails, and why do you have eyes if not to discover beautiful women who sit next to you? Why are you successful and in the prime of life if not to demand and receive the best?

With a fright he notices that it is getting dark. He tries to fight it, evening after evening. He orders another Sancerre and feels stuck. Oh how he would like to speak to a human being now, he ought to know more people, too bad, he can't imagine whom he might call in London at this hour, asking them to come and join him. He looks at his beautiful neighbor. She notices him and smiles. It is an unmistakable smile, she finds her companion boring. How well he understands, and everyone knows it too, the frustration, the inadequacy, a stale taste, the shivering before the onset of night.

Translated by Michael Roloff

SCARLET FLIGHT

WILFRIED STEINER

ON his way to the university, bellmer decided he should visit his therapist that afternoon. by now this thought no longer filled him with shame: only back when in a trusting moment he had told professor berthold of his recurring feelings of emptiness, and his superior had turned into a fatherly friend from one second to the next, with good advice and the gentle hint about the advantages of psychotherapy, had bellmer shown his true colors. professor berthold's glance had struck him like the cane of a governess. he had felt like a little boy who had been caught masturbating and now had to suffer all the consequences, from the onset of locomotor ataxia to its painful cure. in the end the graduate student had gratefully accepted the tip from his future examiner. after the previous chaotic night the prospect of therapeutic elucidation comforted bellmer as much as the firm curve of the steering wheel in his hand.

at the institute summer calm had descended. only a few students still had exams to take; he himself and a few colleagues were preparing for the coming semester or were working on papers. whatever else slinked up and down the corridors was just the shades of vacation dreams, sad souls with sea faces and palm-green eyes, sunset makeup on their watery cheeks.

the air in his office was stifling; on the floor lay piles of papers and books, the typewriter was hot from the summer sun. bellmer opened the window and immersed himself in the subject matter for his winter seminar. a humming sound startled him. a fly was buzzing around his head, then a second one, a small swarm, a black cloud. tiny proboscis sipped sweat from his pores, nibbled on the skin of his forehead, drank thirstily from his armpits. bellmer swatted about, staggered to the bookshelf, grabbed with the instinct of a logician the master's thesis of

Scarlet Flight 257

a student he couldn't stand, and went for the brood like the brave little tailor of old. after a few minutes the battle was over. the swarm buzzed away through the open window in search of more peaceful places to feed. stuck on the cover of the master's thesis were fourteen blots of blood and tissue, squashed bodies, casualties of the battle. "a whole pile of little corpses," thought bellmer and was taken aback by his own thought. just then the white skull of a bull poked its way through the crack in the door and grinned at him. bellmer stashed the besmirched thesis in a drawer, wiped the remnants of his dreams from his eyes and said hello to professor berthold.

    in the lands of the snow beasts the north star burns brighter. it is the iron navel of the heavens, through it the gold chimneys lead into the other world. whoever eats the mushroom, climbs through the navel into fourteen heavens, through the shadow it casts on the earth into the realm of the dead. a reindeer as exchange for the mushroom that gives you wings. snow flies on the red dome. drink the urine that comes from your body, the flight does not stick to your organs, it comes from you and returns to you. drink the urine, the reindeer are growing scarce.
    the snow fox is in your cabin, its blue tongue licks your cheek. its tongue licks your neck, it is the tongue of the winged tiger. its tongue licks everywhere, it is ayami, your spirit protector with the red and white face. she wants you. she comes from the great mother of the animals, she has a mission. it was she who came as an eagle, plunging her claws into your loins. she showed you the power of the mushroom, the dream of the fourteen heavens, the bath in the waters of hell. her rough tongue breaks open your skin, it turns red and white like her face. she is the daughter of the mushroom god, she has chosen you. the scarlet wings that she has woven are fixed to your shoulders. tonight she visits you, dribbles snowspittle in your ears. the night is high and white.
    ayami is here. she wants you. come now.
    in the heat of the snow the bodies swirl. metallic, awesome, violet the first of the heavens flickers. its light is magnetic, charged with the current of earth. ayami is above you, she gnaws the sharp crystals out of your thighs, she extends her white and red neck, her soft throat toward the blades of the cold night. nothing cuts into her flesh.
    for a long time you didn't know how firm the flesh of spirits is.

ayami showed you that the mouth of the great goddess stops at nothing.
you know that the red lips and the white teeth are the secret of flight. for the stone of the earth's weight has jaws like a bear, only ayami's lips present it the snow fish that it chokes on.
in the heat of the snow your spirit protector digs her fingers into your armpits till you black out. the northern lights shoot their daggers past you. in the heat of the snow ayami sucks on the red and white mushroom of your middle.
this is the night of the flight. green and awesome violet the heavens whir. spirals flame upwards, the staircases on the horizon invite you to climb. but ayami has another message. your skin shines like white blubber, your lips are feverish. the golden channel to the navel of the fourteen heavens rusts over, collapses. on the roof of your yurt the stars race by. one heaven is enough.

"relax," said the therapist. he always said "relax," even if bellmer had arrived at the session feeling carefree and easy. it was more of a ritual statement than a serious request. while bellmer was taking off his shoes—the fluffy rug was supposed to be in direct contact with the blood vessels in the soles of his feet, and besides, the therapist loved cleanliness—he decided not to mention the actual occurrences of the previous day. he wanted to concentrate fully on the dream. the therapist listened in silence to the sequence of nocturnal scenes, only occasionally expressing his attentiveness and his keen interest with a grunt and an understanding nod.
the therapist liked to smoke a pipe, but during the sessions any distraction was prohibited. now and again, bellmer reached for the chest pocket containing his pack of cigarettes, as he always did, and as always, caught sight of the patiently warning glance from the full moon face of the man sitting across from him, and his arm sank back down.
bellmer was finished. "very interesting," said the therapist. he scratched his calf, a proven method of unobtrusively looking at his watch.
"then let's get to the bottom of this."
bellmer was anxious to find out which role he would have to play this time. "imagine that you yourself are the head of this bull," said the therapist. "what would you say to this exceptionally large fly." bellmer had to move to another chair, straight across from where he had been. he was now the bull, and the empty chair was bellmer. "relax," said the

therapist. "what's coming to you." lots of things were coming to bellmer, but nothing appropriate to this session. "what are you feeling at this moment." "sort of warm," said bellmer. that was his favorite sentence when he couldn't think of anything else.
after several minutes the client took heart.
"quit buzzing around my head like that," he said to the fly, or rather, to himself, or rather to the empty chair. the therapist listened attentively. for a moment it was as if he felt he himself was being addressed, but the analysis commenced immediately. "typical father imago, no question." bellmer was reminded of earler analyses and frowned. "how are you doing now," said the therapist. "don't hold back." bellmer fidgeted on his chair. "which images are coming to you." the client's fingernails went toward his teeth. "think of your father!"
bellmer looked at the moon face, then closed his eyes.
"guillotine," he said.
the therapist didn't know whether to react with confusion or satisfaction. he decided on a convincing "well, then." just as one of bellmer's fingers was within reach of the tip of a cigarette, the therapist looked at his watch, without scratching, right out in the open, the hour was over. "I would like us to summarize what we have accomplished today." the client was obstinate today. "my father is a warm guillotine," he recited. the therapist said nothing.
while he was putting on his shoes, bellmer thought somehow simultaneously of the monthly check made out to the order of the treating professional, of a guillotine blade bearing the sharp profile of his father, and of his own constantly soiled carpet.
"it's good that he doesn't know about the mushrooms," he said out loud to himself, crushed out the cigarette that he had finished smoking during the dismissal ceremony on the wooden door of the therapist's house, and got into his car.
the speakers gushed out a sumptuous torrent. snowy paths appeared, hills of white chocolate, marzipan meadows in bright march green, oleander blossoms beneath a heavy sky, cake yellow stubble fields, the dark nougat of the leaves in autumn trees. bellmer reached for vivaldi whenever he had told somebody off. the wind cooled his glowing cheeks. the open car window was a sign of his good mood. normally he avoided the draft, the harbinger of nagging colds, trusted only closed rooms.

. . .

Translated by Heidi L. Hutchinson

What? How Long Has It Been?

Gerald Szyszkowitz

STASZYNSKI is filming in a major department store. In the city center. In the fine jewelry department. The same scene over and over, because Lisa never gets her lines just the way he wants them. He demonstrates the intonation of the sentence to her before each take, and she still does it differently every time; the mood is tense, and sure, go on, if he's not satisfied, she says, he can gladly go out and find himself a new leading lady.

The glass display cases, mirrors, and jewelry brightly reflect the dazzling floodlights. Lisa hates this merciless glare! And the made-up, larger-than-life photo faces of the international supermodels on the walls! And the tormented face of her director! She hates him. And he hates her.

Suddenly in the background next to the sound engineer he sees a face that reminds him of a woman he loved a long time ago. Her name doesn't come to mind. Martine, perhaps, Fort-de-France, but it is not Martine. The woman perplexes him. He has lost interest in Lisa's scene and calls out, "That's a take! Thanks! Set change!"

Richard says hello to the Creole woman.

"I am Marie-José," she says, "Martine's daughter."

Ah, now he remembers! Yes, of course! He knew this woman when she was just a girl. The two of them spent every evening on the cliffs with the other young people, until one time, at moonrise, he did not return to Martine, but, recklessly and in a fit of passion, stayed behind on the beach with this girl, a few days before he flew off to the States without her, carefree, vigorous and full of confidence in a new life ahead.

But just a few weeks after his arrival in Washington, D.C., where he had the pleasure of teaching by day at Catholic University and washing dishes by night, he found his yearning for this girl growing stronger and stronger. Although he seemed to have his whole life ahead of him, he

What? How Long Has It Been? 261

had a feeling that his most important encounter was already in his past and that the memory of this young woman would never leave him. And he began to yearn not only for her, but also for the blue morning haze over the harbor of Fort-de-France, the laughter of the seagulls at sunrise and the sweet smell at Maurice's after his first morning glass of rum; in short, he hated Washington and yearned for the smells of the Caribbean, let himself go, missed his kitchen duty and his lectures, made no effort to get his feet back on the ground, left career-obsessed America behind and went in quest of adventures in East Asia, about which he faithfully reported back to his Creole girl. But in spite of his frequent letters, she reached a point where she didn't want to wait for him any longer, and so she got into bed with another man.

And nevertheless, here she is, now. Why?

"Marie-José, yes, of course! Forgive me, but it has been forty years!"

Is she fifty? More? He is reminded of old photos from the colonies, of the dreamy, slightly blurry faces of beautiful black women from before the first World War. Her handshake seems almost awkward, but has something both sweet and provocative about it. Richard can't help smiling. "Are you here by chance?"

"No, I'm not here by chance."

"And why did you come?"

Marie-José presses his hand to her lips. Lightly, easily and calmly, as if this hand were her only safe anchor in the storms of life. "You were the love of my life, Richard. Now that I have my life to look back on, I know that. Even though we never slept together. That's why I came."

Richard is confounded. For years he had suppressed the memory of his time on the island, but with the face of Marie-José, with her luminous dark eyes and her slightly protruding white teeth, the forgotten images of the island reemerge, and Richard smells the sugar cane fields that they had lain in, tastes the aroma of fried fish, hears the steel bands and, because his sound engineer is unabashedly staring at this woman, is jealous just like back then, impetuous and tender, ready to chase off the sound engineer and take this woman in his arms!

"But back then I wasn't your choice!"

"I know. Georges was. But Georges is dead. And so my next thought was of you. You're right, in the end we weren't lovers, but in the beginning we were. And for years after you left I thought of no one but you! With each of your letters my yearning for you grew! Every day I ran to the post office, to see if maybe a letter from you had come, and when there was one, I was happy for a week! Even when all you were writing about was your adventures with other women."

"None serious! None of those were serious!"

"Now you say that. After it's all over. But back then I was sick with jealousy!"

Richard shakes his head slowly. "And so you got yourself another man."

"You stayed away too long, Richard," she says and grabs his hand so impulsively that she has to reach for it twice. Seemingly carefree, as if no one could see them, the two walk hand in hand between the glittering jewelry counters to the escalator and ride up a floor. Richard looks at Marie-José from the side. She seems so innocent. She lays her dark-skinned hand with its colorful rings gently on the escalator rail and casts her eyes downward. It's hard not to notice how her breast is heaving beneath her bright yellow silk blouse. Slowly Marie-José lifts her eyes. "You have hardened," she says, "and yet remained a child."

Richard shrugs his shoulders. "Now tell me . . . You've come here on my account?"

"Does that frighten you? I have been a veterinarian in Paris for thirty years. At the race track. Next to the airport. It's less than two hours away and . . . I still love you." She looks at him, searchingly.

He runs his hands over his eyes. "If you really still remember those days with a vestige of love, Marie-José, then please don't play games with me. It was over between us. You went out and got yourself someone else, and I avoided you for decades."

"To the ends of the earth. Yes. Surprising amount of stubbornness for what you would have me believe was a small, long forgotten feeling."

Richard attempts to hide his insecurity behind an angry outburst. "It was over between us! Over!"

"It wasn't over. It hadn't even begun. I was always told I could only sleep with the man I was going to marry, and you were white! We weren't as multi-cultural as we are today! In Fort-de-France. Back then. That was the problem. You didn't dare marry me, and you didn't want to seduce me either. You were too respectable for that. But the world is different now. Now I could live with you. Anywhere. I'm telling you this without meaning to scare you, but I have reread all of your letters and I won't love anyone else in this lifetime, no matter what happens. Only you."

Full of mistrust, Richard tries to discover, in the eyes, the tone of voice, and in the dark face of this woman, the lie or at least the reason for this exaggeration. Finding no clues, he says with reproach and sadness, "You are mocking me."

Marie-José nods. As if to confirm his distrust.

"And again you don't believe I love you? Just like back then? When I wrote you ninety-nine times I love you, I love you, I love you! But you just wiped away all of my pleas! I can prove it to you! On the evening after he died I took all of your letters out of the strongbox and read them word for word. Crying. I cried for him and I cried for you. Are you interested in them? I have them along. In my suitcase. Your fifty-seven letters from Washington, San Francisco, Tokyo, Hong Kong, Manila, Rangoon . . . I even kept the envelopes. Except I gave the stamps to the mailman. He really wanted them."

"You kept all my letters?"

"You didn't keep mine?"

Richard shakes his head. "My mother was over eighty when she died, and the Salvation Army picked up all of her stuff. They must have been there."

Marie-José is neither disconcerted nor insulted. "I don't need my letters. I have yours. That's enough. I love them more today than back then. Because by these letters I know, forty years later, how great our yearning was! And that nothing was over!"

Richard tries to sidestep. "No fairy tales! You got yourself another man—just anyone who happened to be there, who grabbed you in passing—and after that, I never heard from you once in all those forty years! What kind of love is that supposed to be?"

The two of them have arrived in the ladies' wear department. On the mezzanine. The film crew is far away; Marie-José takes hold of Richard's arms and wraps them around her body. "Hold me tight. Please. Yes. Like that. I'm here, Richard. Here with you." Marie-José enjoys this embrace so much that it makes her dizzy. And for an instant she believes she sees a growing tenderness in his eyes. She asks cautiously, "Why did you leave me so head over heels back then?"

Richard tries to find his way in her face, a face that has changed over the years and yet has stayed the same; the silky black turned-up eyelashes and the seductive, half-closed Caribbean eyes seem so familiar to him, and he kisses her lips, as if these lips were still the lips of the girl that he, himself still a child, had loved for years and for thousands of miles like no one since. He thinks these things as he feels the woman's body against his, until Marie-José opens her eyes and asks him, "Why, Richard—I haven't understood to this day—didn't you stay with me?"

He hesitates and then lies, helplessly, because he no longer can think of a reason that makes sense. He takes a deep breath and says, "I wanted to see more of the world . . . And I had a girl friend in Vienna. She was waiting for me. Yes, you may laugh, but there is such a thing. Commitment. I couldn't do that to her."

"But you wrote me letters! Not her! For three years!"

"Yes! But it didn't do me much good! With you!"

Marie-José casts her eyes downward. "What became of her?"

Richard lies again. "After you wrote me that you were getting married, I got married, too."

"Her? This girl friend in Vienna? Well? And now? What about now?"

Richard feels short of breath. "Now?" His heart has begun to beat erratically, having trouble dealing with his emerging affection for this slender lover of his early years.

"I still can't do it to her now."

Marie-José lifts her head. "What can't you do to her?"

"Leave her for you. That's what you are asking me, isn't it?"

Marie-José strokes Richard's cheek, to comfort him over the fact that he didn't have the strength to accept her back then and that he obviously can't do it now either. Although he would like to. She waits a few seconds and says, "All I asked you was what's going on with you? . . . Have there been many women? Like me?"

"Huh?"

"On the side?"

Richard shakes his head. What can he say to her? Doesn't everything just lead to misunderstandings?

"Did you know, Richard, that I've been a grandmother for half a year now? A dull, respectable, middle-class grandmother? Makes you think. About what's still important. And I don't know much about you, but I do know one thing: no one has ever again written me letters like yours." Hesitantly Marie-José kisses Richard on the cheek, this grown-up child, then suddenly they turn to one another, embrace and kiss, as if they were saying good-bye forever, ride down the escalator without a word, and walk hand in hand out of the department store.

It doesn't look like he'll be returning soon, says the filming director and calls a sudden end to the session. Everyone nods in agreement, except for Lisa, who says sarcastically that a friend of hers had a child with a man from Ghana. That didn't work out either.

Translated by Heidi L. Hutchinson

ROAD WAR

SYLVIA TREUDL

from: *Sporenstiefel halbgar. Liebesgeschichten*
(Wiener Frauenverlag, 1990)

STANDING in her boots holds her erect, as if a plumbline were firmly aligned below, toward an invisible center. To be strong. Maybe armored. At least to give that impression. In leather. To feel the material at every step as a permeable covering that nestles and tightens and softly crackles. The heavy jacket on her naked shoulders like the comforting embrace of a friendly bear, maybe of an older brother. The old yearning for protection and comfort that always has to be held in check.

Clara smiles.

Slips on her cardinal-red gloves. Gathers her hair together with two strokes at the neck. Sensing the leather on her skin even more keenly, enjoying the tension that arises in doing so.

It is a beautiful morning in late July. It, too, has just made it through a night of full moon. Her smile disappears. She shakes her head. Something else now.

She approaches her motorcycle as one would a horse in the box. On the left side and from behind. Slides the palm of her hand over the nice curve of the tank. Good morning, motor.

Only then inserts the key in the ignition and fires it up.

The sleepy droning quickly gives way to an even hum of the motor. The morning seems to comply. 650 cc, all in black, ready to go.

She maneuvers the five hundred fifty pounds, parked on the downgrade, out of the space between a fragrant linden tree and a garden fence. That's why she chose the place: awkward but picturesque. The others stand prosaically on the asphalt behind the country inn. Six nice

Japanese motorcycles strung together in a row. Number seven is the only nonconformist.

She can permit herself that. After all, she is the only one in this group who has given up sitting behind somebody else. Who prefers to be responsible for her own extravagances and her own driving.

Besides, she does not feel as if she owed this group anything special. She had acted on a whim in accepting the invitation of the others to join them, to come along; or so she maintains anyway, in the direction of the mirror. And had often asked herself, during the past few days, whether it was the right thing to do. Each time and at the same point, she had ended up feeling insightfully angry at herself. She had to admit that she was exhausted after fifteen days of being alone on the road, which she in part worked off as punishment. When she met the others at this gas station and was invited to join them, she had convincingly feigned prolonged indecision. Alma, who did not seem particularly enthusiastic, had abruptly and silently gotten on the motorcycle by her driver without casting a glance at Clara. "... *and I am the dark spirit who despairingly pleads at the window each night—and then, for fear of closeness, quivers away again in the thin air....*"

Clara understands; about Alma's role, her own, about group dynamics, and territorial fights. A fair amount of defiance had probably also influenced her decision. If the other person wants a fight, she can have it.

Mounting, helmet on, letting the motor idle half a minute more, taking a deep breath, almost no butterflies in her stomach anymore. Now she would only have to prevent the extraneous Rimbaud line from echoing in her mind. Must finally get a different radio station in her headset, since *Orpheus and Eurydice* is starting to become unbearable. *Que faro senz' Euridice* . . . he should have thought about that earlier.

Actually, Clara grumbles, as she carefully gets the odometer going, that story is even more scandalous than *Romeo and Juliet*, and much more probable than *Philemon and Baucis*.

She casts a final scrutinizing glance at the instruments and then engages the clutch. It is still early, but already surprisingly warm. Black leather and black lacquer beam hot waves at each other. Impatience wings her thighs and her wrists.

Gliding out of the spot, a shot of oil, then gas, more gas, breaking out of the static state.

Is it that? Is it *that*? That *too*.

Absolute happiness eclipses everything else in this moment of departure. Summer fields, meadows, a blue silk sail high above her and a good feeling for the bike beneath her.

Getting into full swing. Good morning, life.

A few tears, like condensation, under the half-open windshield. It's from the road wind, only the wind.

Cutting into curves, revving the motor up to full speed; transferring to the other tender inclination. Waves of fields and clusters of trees, a narrow ribbon of tar with a pungent smell to it, having already absorbed too much sun; softening, serving as a base for the wide-gripping tires. She touches the tank, which feels very warm, as if she were placing her hand on a lover's chest. Happiness. Not: straddled on a motorcycle and doing rounds in the area, but rather: swaying in unity, gliding. Happiness.

Going farther. Farther. Farther away. A long way.

Without baggage or ballast.

That it would never be night again!

Behind a curve taken inattentively, a field of sunflowers spreads a yellow-golden bowl out under her front wheel. She laughs. Good morning, Mister van Gogh. Today any cliché is allowed.

Decoratively placing her black against the yellow, she stops at the edge of the field. She regrets not having the right "hardcore" cigarettes à la freedom on two wheels, and lights up one of a lite brand.

Jeans over naked skin, over completely naked skin, suddenly appear between the hefty stalks of the high yellow-crowned flowers. Before she allows her gaze to reach the face of the figure, it disappears, leaving only the hot air trembling above the cracked ground among the thick-standing plants. She blinks at the annoyance. Leans on her motorcycle and feels rather weak. She had not seen anyone yet today, not even an industrious farmer on a tractor. The morning belongs to her alone. That's better than breakfast.

Get on again now and trust the road. Drive and stop only for gas. No food and no sleep. Drive until invisible. *Ghostrider*. Disappear. Without purse or papers or explanatory notes. Simply disappear.

Typical escapism, Karl would say. He would again use it as an occasion to quote something from Lenin, whether appropriate or not. Precisely because the occasions had become rare, someone like Clara, in his eyes, should not allow herself the luxury of decadent thoughts.

She smiles. Again. Actually, with interruptions, ever since waking up. Smiles. That will change. For now, she is still smiling.

She gets on. Turns. Turns around. Drives back.

When she joins the group, which occupies the breakfast room in the inn, the day is already partly spent.

"*This is the last day of our acquaintance*. . . ." She stops smiling since she does not need a mask anymore.

Sits down and orders coffee. Just coffee.

"You were already out and about?"

He tosses her the question seemingly inconsequentially. No one, besides the two of them, knows that she could not have had any more than two hours of sleep. Clara looks directly into his eyes; she will not have much more of an opportunity to do so. Rolls of baggage and saddle bags are piled together in a corner, ready for the trip.

Alma catches on quickly. She is sitting next to him. Where else, since she of course sleeps next to him too. Embittered, she reaches for a breakfast roll.

He returns Clara's gaze. No, he will not lower his eyes. That, however, does not mean that he is prepared to look at things all too carefully either.

"Yes, I took a spin in the morning sun," she responds in a serious voice, looking deeply into her cup so as not to grin at him broadly.

Now it was the sun.

The night before it had been another heavenly body, terrifying in its perfection. It was duplicated in the lake, as if its twin brother had crashed and fallen into the night-black water. A stage set, the epitome of sentimentality, but neither of them had laughed.

They had not asked each other either about the alleged reasons that led them individually to the lake. Shortly after midnight. Each for himself or herself. Alone.

Pure coincidence. Co-incidence. It's so hard to sleep when the moon is full.

No excuses, no embarrassed apologies. And no more cautiousness either.

As if they wanted to take revenge on each other for the two weeks full of civilities and this road-buddy play-acting. That's enough. No more words. They had talked to each other enough.

It's only words.

He gives her the choice of a place to make love. Of course she chooses the boat dock. They do not delay and they are not in a hurry.

They do what they have been wanting to do, for days. Do it well. On the warm wooden planks that have been storing up the sunshine for weeks. In the water, with seaweed and wet hair around their necks and shoulders, everything silvery from the moonlight. The talk, the silence, the love are framed by a slowly exhausting night. The moon brother retreats to unknown depths of the lake; the fingers of dawn appear over the crowns of the trees on the shore.

They part under the chestnut tree in front of the inn. Silently and without further plans. Still composed and already prepared for the despair that will catch up with them, soon.

None of the others gives any indication of discovery; but Alma knows about the night.

That is clear from the way she gets up from the table, demonstratively leaving the two of them alone with the chitchat of the others. It demands immediate clarification and correction of error.

The group slowly dissolves into individuals. With melancholy regrets they load up their motorcycles for the last time, check the tension of the chains, put on oil, and lovingly occupy themselves with the metal. "*This is the last day....*"

Two weeks on the road, with the odor of gas on their hands, the sweat of leather, and a pleasant tiredness in the evenings. There is still a lot of summer and landscape in front of the windshield as they prepare for departure. Trying to be carefree, they refuse to think about their first day back at work, the haze of the city, and autumn.

They leave right after breakfast, wanting to use the last day as well as at all possible. A roaring, chrome-flashing squadron flows into the seething July morning, headed for the daily routine. The relaxed mood, to which they all believe to have a chartered claim after two weeks of vacation, is something they cannot quite manage to maintain at the noon break. A nameless tension presses down more heavily than the heat. Irritation, barely curbed, occupies them as they search in vain for a friendly closure behind the cool drinks. Clara and the waterman stay apart, yet they continually catch each other's gaze. They are as inconspicuous as a red gas can in a barn. No one objects to quickly resuming the trip. It is almost with relief that the three people in leather say goodbye. They will be the first to leave the group a few miles farther along toward evening.

Clara, absent-mindedly packing up her bike, catches bits of a faint but vigorous argument. It is beyond earshot, yet with her well-conditioned sense, she can hear it.

Alma and her motorcycle man. That was to be expected. Clara had actually been expecting some kind of outburst all week.

After years of experience in dealing with such situations, Clara understands exactly. She knows too that Alma will lose now, for the moment, since she is making mistakes in the staging. Wrong setting and her timing is much too short.

Clara smiles in a friendly way at her roll of baggage. Alma, pale from anger, just manages to catch the passenger seat of the Suzuki that is getting ready to leave the group. "Zero points in this round," Clara thinks maliciously. "Another reason why I prefer to travel alone: the departures are stronger."

The group then definitively hurries to get back on the road. The four who take the highway exit shortly thereafter are sent off with waves and beeps. No one feels the need to take off her or his helmet again.

The deserted moonman moves his heavy cycle directly behind Clara's tail. Arranges it so she has him in her rearview mirror. She smiles and feels herself split into halves, cleanly filleted lengthwise. A wild, wicked euphoria rivets her right hand firmly to the gas control. Her left side, where the heart is allegedly located, is already misery personified.

But as long as she is still on the road, she is invincible. The hard part will come upon arrival.

They stop again, act as if a bit of the pressure were gone. They want nothing so much as finally to get away from one another. To save whatever can still be salvaged from the day, from the botched conclusion of a vacation. It will be precious little. Other members of the group take their leave, avowing nonetheless that it had been nice.

Reduced to only three motorcycles, they take the on-ramp to the freeway.

The sun sticks to the rearview mirror like a red ball. It has its fun in a skirmish with the chrome.

Two rest-stops later, Clara and the booted tomcat are alone.

Both had intensely simulated a friendly farewell to the last couple who guaranteed them security from each other.

Clara closes her eyes for a moment, shifts down, and revs up the engine as if the devil were after her. As she looks in the rearview mirror, she almost believes that to be so.

They romp in a wild chase, fleeing determinedly, like lemmings. Finally they settle down again to a more civilized pace.

Clara is glad that the anatomy of a motorcycle obligatorily prescribes two handles that one can hold onto.

The freeway miles seem to pull like an assembly-line belt beneath her. She has lost the nice rhythm with her bike.

She turns halfway around to give him a brief signal to pass.

He comes up close, bringing his cycle next to hers, and then drives along next to her. She is glad for her sunglasses. Glad also that an approaching car forces him to vacate the passing lane and go ahead.

Now she has him in front of her. She relishes the chance to imagine that everything had been real. As if they were traveling together, sharing a common goal, maybe a future.

Misery personified takes over her right fillet-half too.

She knows that he has her in his rearview mirror, knows that he knows that she knows that . . . the story about the mirror in the mirror in the mirror, like on the Quaker oats box that she had loved as a child.

She gives him a signal to speed up.

As he shifts into his highest gear, she turns onto the long curve of an exit to someplace she has never heard of before. Freeways are one-ways.

Translated by Beth Bjorklund

How a Doll's Skin Grows Tough

Elisabeth Wäger

THAT God created the dark, so that it may be night, and all loneliness may be this black thing you can touch. Your fingers, it felt as if they were glued to the cold. Down below, something bursts in, like the end of life. The days are never tomorrow, but they are behind her, stealthily approaching, grasping for her, pursuing her to the end-point, by the river, where it is quiet and where her breath suddenly stops in the night. And whenever she says: now it is over, it is really over, completely black.

Lord, she says, that is how it is with all creatures. I am what I am. Those, she said, are the words I have to speak. As far as the darkness, where the river lies, where somehow my path will continue. She says that hope—the darkness—sometimes has a greenish cast to it. For the duration of a glimmer it seems as if her heart could take hope, green hope, when it was spring, in May, when she was wearing a veil over her wavy hair and she was smiling, so properly and pertly; and his head was a little above hers, so that they fit inside the gilt frame. Her skin would have felt as soft as tissue paper—her skin was flawless. For years she smiled at herself wryly, let herself be escorted down from the wall, a decorative shadow—for she had never actually looked like that. If she opened a newspaper and thought she had looked like *these* women, who were beautiful . . . No, the photographer was responsible for the whole thing. She had never looked like a madonna.

They would look at each other for a long time, the one who was smiling at her and the one who, unsmiling, was looking at her counterpart. They would look at each other in silence, feeling they had nothing to say to each other and no basis for being compared. How, she wondered, can the other one just keep smiling like that, how can her smile be so cold and frozen? And how can she keep smiling at me as though there had never been anything between us?

It seems as if everything had gone downhill, starting on a single day.

People like us never prosper. For people like us things always go downhill—or somehow we muddle on, one day just like another. One day like another of being conditioned in a cage with someone wielding a whip. Sometimes the whip hits you, sometimes not—at which you think you are lucky. She also smiled wryly from the picture of her first communion-day, this girl enjoying her big day. Her dress was borrowed and a little too short. Her not-new shoes had been polished over with white paste—it was hardly noticeable. But the shoes are there in her memory, painted white down over the soles—used shoes, that was immediately apparent. And what was immaculate (like her skin at that time)—what was immaculate had been borrowed and had to be returned the next day, a Monday, in as immaculate condition as it had been on the day before her red-letter day.

They were big days, she says: big days. Just to look like a guardian angel once. Or like the little bride of our dear Saviour. But she did not look like a little queen—for sure she did not look like that. "Stand straight and look right at me," said the photographer, his head inclined slightly toward his right shoulder. "Keep your candle straight, hold it straight, not crooked." And in the picture it looked like someone had pressed her head to her shoulder. And somehow she was smiling up from below—she somehow always smiled up from below like that. To the right was a table with a bouquet; a curtain was draped behind her. It was scarlet, like the red inside the church. And now, so they said, she was a different person, the Saviour was in her body; and she had escaped from one more day.

Those celebrations weren't my days, she reflects. Her grandmother said: "I'll get along all right. As long as I live, I'll get along." A grandmother dies one day or another, and then it's all over. Then I'm alone. Her grandmother was sleeping at her side, she was still there. And the little girl looked at the ceiling and reflected that she would get along all right if Grandmother was no longer alive; she could do everything just like her grandmother. Things would also continue like this for her when she was alone. She had her grandmother, who was getting older and older, and herself, who was growing bigger and bigger—as her grandmother often anxiously determined. Her grandmother, who was getting tinier and tinier and who someday will be lying tiny as could be in her bed, so small that one will be able to lift her and take her to the graveyard in a tiny coffin. Grandmother is getting so tiny, reflected the girl, that I can carry her, that she won't be any problem for me to carry.

How a Doll's Skin Grows Tough 275

Because she never makes problems, and that's more proper—much more proper—that being big or growing big, or even still growing in later years.

One morning Grandmother had a small hump on her back. As if it had grown overnight. And from this day on, Grandmother was even smaller, even tinier, and the girl thought that Grandmother would die soon. She noticed how Grandmother's jersey was twisted, how her apron string no longer stayed in place on her shoulder, how her grandmother was not standing straight at all—but just the way she, the girl, was standing in the picture. She noticed that it hurt Grandmother to look backward, that she almost never looked backward anymore, and did not look over her right shoulder at all. Because the hump was there, and her grandmother was now stooped, was more and more given to looking downward, to the ground. If it goes on like this, the girl reflected, the hump will soon be bigger than Grandmother; and she wondered how she would do the carrying then, how she would manage it.

One day or one night Grandmother had perhaps made a decision not to look backward anymore. One day or one night she had perhaps decided to abandon once and for all everything that lay behind her, never to turn around again, never again to look at what lay behind her. She had then wished the hump on herself as a sign of her decision. She had then decided that everything was moving forward and toward the ground, that what was behind her was over and done with, and that for her the time had come to see what was lying ahead of her. No longer did Grandmother talk about the past, no longer did she tell about what had happened to her in her youth. Grandmother did not speak of the future either. She spoke to herself, conversed with herself, and only rarely could her granddaughter understand any part of what she way saying.

Grandmother addressed herself, conversed amicably with herself, told herself things, called herself Liz in a nice, friendly way and answered herself in a nice, friendly way. She said to herself, "You have done very well, Liz." It is no longer true, she told her granddaughter, that someone could simply tell me: do this, do that, and make it quick! Today, she said, things are different; no one speaks to Liz like that anymore—not like that. One Saturday she said to her granddaughter: "And now wash my back." The girl soaped the washcloth and washed Grandmother's back and her hump, and saw her skin stretched over her bones, and the girl thought, now my grandmother is dying for sure, and she cried to herself and wished that this was not her grandmother, that this was a different back, not the one she was someday going to have to carry. "Don't be silly," her grandmother told her. "What is there to be crying about?" That's the way people are, Liz. That's how they are. The girl wiped the tears from her face, helped Grandmother into her chemise, staring at her thin arms, her emaciated body, her skinny breasts.

"That's just the way it is now," the grandmother said, smiling at her granddaughter. "That's the way it is, now that Liz finally has a hump."

The room and the kitchen, they were something solid. They could be counted on to be there when she came home. And if the stairs were those of other people—as she and her grandmother expressed it—and even if the rooms were those of other people, still they felt like a coat, like a woolen shawl.

When she emptied the garbage on the compost pile for her grandmother and went down the stairs, when she heard voices at doors she walked by, she felt a cold wind envelop her body, while inside she felt very hot, and her heart was pounding. When she got back upstairs and her grandmother asked, "Why did you run like that again?" This feeling when she was indoors, standing in the kitchen, putting the bucket under the sink . . . Here I am. And although she was now indoors and quite alone, she felt this pounding inside her. Nowhere else did she have this feeling, only here. Here she was not alien, here it was warm, while outside it was cold: in school, in church, on the street.

When her grandmother, telling about the past when she was not so tiny, talked about the war, when she told of hunger, of cold, of want, and of a dead father, and wanted the girl to visualize the war on her own, wholly on her own—it seemed then as if everything were side by side: the communion picture, the street on which she ran home, the stairs, the compost pile, this heat, and her pounding heart, this chill that extended right up to her door, the voices behind the doors, and the darkness that extended as far as the lamp above the table.

Now, though—now Grandmother's war was over, now Grandmother's words had changed, now her ideas were expressed in different words. When they had gone to bed, put out the light, and were lying in their beds, the girl prayed. She was on close terms with the Lord God, and she asked of Him that everything might stay as it had been, she and her grandmother and the rooms of other people. And her grandmother spoke tenderly to herself: "Nighty-night, Liz."

Who could ever send a person out into the cold, coatless and without a shawl?

Come, hold onto me tight, she says to her son. We have come quite a long way, she says. We must run far from here, we must escape from the wind. As if it wanted to take something from us, although, she says, we really have nothing. Grandmother's grave has been forfeited. When you stop making payments, a grave is relinquished. She's likely far away, she says to Peter. Who? Someone you never knew and never could have known, she says. Not your fault. Just the way it was, it was just that everything happened the way it had to happen. For a long time now I haven't had that warm feeling in my heart when I put the bucket under the sink. It's not like it used to be, when everyday in those rooms everything belonged to each other. Now when I empty the garbage bucket, I just go and come back. Between going and coming back, nothing happens.

It's empty now, even if you take steps, forward or backward. It's been a long time now since this old feeling vanished. And with Peter it's a duty, an attachment, and then comes the guilt for the sense of duty and the love that is there—but in which nothing can happen except the birth and then the days without interruption. Now, since Peter, it's already been ten years, since the others, twenty years . . . And her feeling of joy that her sorrows are abating, that her birth pangs are past, that you feel so good—as if you didn't exist: without pain, without hurt.

That's the way it always was when something was wrong with her, when something was so awry that she was aware of her body. Then it seemed as if she had suddenly come to herself again, and she was terrified by that, and the others looked after her. They noticed that something was wrong with her, with that body of hers, that she was longing for something without giving anything in return.

Peter, he remained to her. They tugged at his head, tugged much too long at his head, pressing on his brain, she believes, and the effect of that stayed with him. She thought they had simply pressed something into his brain, had pressed too hard on one place so that he might come out, might enter the world. And that at that time they had pressed something back on him with lasting effect, something that he could have had an urgent use for, then later something that he could have used for himself. Now she had approached the pressed-in place. She would have to fill up the place. For Peter she would have to be the thing that was no longer there.

So it was that Peter had remained to her like a part of her. At first she reflected: that's just like my luck. But then she thought it was quite clear that that too had to befall her. Because she thought that that couldn't be all there was, at age forty that couldn't be all there was. Something unforeseen would still have to happen. Happiness? Yes, maybe even happiness. And then it seemed as if Peter had grown attached to her. Day after day the child grew attached to her. At first to her hands, then he grew dear to her heart. In that way she would preserve her own sense of purpose and her feeling. Peter and she were standing by themselves on one side. The others were standing over there, across the river, over the wall, behind the wall, far away. And it was not just a dream. The others had grown up, had grown away from her, a long time ago. She had Peter in her heart, and so it remained.

Grandmother, tiny and hunchbacked as she was, together with Peter swelled up in her heart, and they pressed—both pressed on her until tears came to her eyes. It was perfectly natural that Peter now ran beside her, that she held him fast by the hand so he wouldn't run off, that he understood nothing, understood nothing of all that had happened and could happen. But without asking questions, he was with her, like everything that had befallen her without inquiring of her, he was with her. And when she said, "I'll clean up the blood," he looked at her with his warm brown eyes, and she thought a shooting star had fallen into the water, very briefly and brightly, and she thought she could wish for something for herself. For Peter and herself.

Peace for the lost country. Peace for the lost and promised land, her promised land, the horizon far, far from her, often bathed in rich red sunlight, she said, and often in black shadows, like life. When she was little and stared respectfully on hearing the word "life" from Grandmother's lips or in school or on the radio . . . She assumed then that her life was just beginning, that this wasn't her life yet, but that it would finally have to begin. Life in colors, bright colors.

Life—so she heard, so she assumed—was still something unfathomable, but later something comprehensible, overnight it became comprehensible and understandable. Life would be something like her mother's coming back, her mother whom she could hardly remember, and there she was, and her grandmother was crying, and they were visiting her mother in the hospital. And when her grandmother said that her mother was resting in peace, and because peace seemed to her to be something like life, something beautiful and worth striving for, something that would eventually begin for her, if she would just be patient and good—for that reason she did not want to disturb this peace, did not want to ask her grandmother what this peace was like, so that she wouldn't disturb whatever it was that allowed her mother to rest in peace. Then her grandmother added, "Mama is resting in the city."

The city was something that both attracted and repelled country people. She knew that people went to the city to look for something. For work, to seek their fortune. Well, peace too, like Mother. Her small photograph of Mother was like all photos: one element or another was familiar, something from far off, while the rest was indiscernible, imaginary. And later, after Grandmother's death, when she was placed with relatives, she sensed rejection when the conversation somehow got around to her mother. She didn't ask questions, she let her mother rest in peace and wished for her part to be left in peace by the others, without being maliciously sneered at.

In this stillness, she once said, one could get lost if one had nobody, if one had only memories that meant nothing to the others, memories that were too small to share with others, that several people couldn't share. One day a package came in the mail. A package with clothes, shoes, a coat, a vanity case with a little box that Grandmother quickly secreted in her skirt pocket.

When for fun she took the high-heeled shoes from the box and slipped them on and, as she said, gave Grandmother a show, Grandmother had to laugh. And, so the girl imagined, that was a long period of peace for her mother—peace as something cheerful, like the life that she was not yet acquainted with. And finally she had something to show to her friend Maria too. Namely, this box, with everything that was in it, which was her mother. It's been so many years, she said, I don't feel her anymore, I don't know anything anymore.

She thought it might be a nice day. She put the cake on the table, made coffee. Walter came home first. Walter was the first-born; he was the one with whom everything had been a surprise to her. That he should be there, like a child who should give new meaning to life, intervening in her life . . . With Walter she discovered, as with her grandmother's death, that she grieved deeply, that giving birth was torment, that grieving for death resembled that of giving birth. She learned that one thing and another are to be forgotten, that cares will take the place of sorrows, and that the days, which urge one on, anesthetize suffering and make you forget it.

Walter forged her and her husband together, forged her to her husband. A child, a family, a warm kitchen—she wanted these unconditionally. Walter solidified the security that she wanted. That made her strong. She had overcome her pain. She was finally in a circle that was bigger than the one she came from, that made her into a woman. It seemed as if with *this* life her life was now beginning, could do no other than begin. When she thought of herself she thought of her child. The child gave part of himself back to her and abolished her loneliness.

When she was alone and when she came to know her husband, she thought that now having someone, as she said, would make her loneliness vanish. True, she did not continue to be alone, but the hoped-for feeling that everything would be different at a husband's side, that everything would be greater, solider, and stronger—that feeling did not develop. Instead she often felt divided into pieces—in fact, torn apart. If she had once wanted to be something *through* him, she finally was left as just a piece *of* him.

Everything that had to do with the child was her province. She had assumed that the feeling of having a child in her body was transferable to every other personal province. But everything was the way it had been before. With the exception that for the others and for him she grew fatter. At one time her belly had briefly reminded her of Grandmother's hump, except, she had thought, that *she* was not carrying it, and this now meant life, or good hope, as the saying goes.

Translated by Richard H. Lawson

A Vigilant Eye and a Vigilant Ear

Wolfgang Wenger

JUST look at him: that face, those squinting eyes, the trembling eyelids, the quivering mouth. Look at him, but don't get any closer, don't touch him. Such a glassy stare; he fixes his eyes on an object, stares at it, and doesn't let it go. Look at his legs, they're cramping up; he stands there and is so tense, he does nothing but look. His pupils don't move; there's not the slightest movement of his eyeballs, only a constant twitching of his eyelids. His breath is shallow, he has a fast pulse; he'll get his injection right away; he knows it and is watching to see the picture again. A house in flames, a crying child, a fleeing woman. Or only the burning house. The idea of the woman and the child was concocted when he had been running for days. Does he know it? Look at the deposition; he said: I have killed.

    Whom have you killed?

    He said: the child.

    Which child?

    He said: the child that would have been possible, possible with this woman.

    Look, his legs are trembling, he's getting ready to run; he's probably already fleeing in his imagination. He set the fire with a lighter after he had poured gasoline from the attic to the cellar without missing a single spot. He had left all the doors open so that the fire could quickly spread through the whole building as soon as it was kindled at one place. There aren't any witnesses to this, only a lighter that had been thrown on the lawn. He must have set fire to his house at the doorsill and then fled, just as he reported in the deposition. If his statements are to be trusted, he took the freight road through the forest until he came to the river; then he continued along its bank as far as the mountains. There a hiker found him lying on the ground in utter exhaustion. He said he had been on the road for days, keeping a running pace and taking only a few breaks. Look, here's his testimony: It was cold in the night; I lay down under a rocky ledge just for a short time, maybe for a quarter of an hour. I had to go on, away from here, away from all these stories, this house.

What stories?

You don't know? Lübeck's shattered bells? The burning opera house on *Unter den Linden*? Every picture is a curse, every thought of it one more reason to do it.

To do what?

To try it on my own house.

Look, he's lowered his head; he notices that we're observing him. Now he's holding his hand in front of his face. Look at that high forehead, the soft facial features, an intelligent, sensitive man. He was a chemist, the head of one of the research divisions of a pharmaceutical firm. His house was just recently built. He wanted to live in the country a half-hour by car from the city. He had never married and never had any children. His girlfriend doesn't live with him. When the police told her that he had set his house on fire and was now here in protective custody, she didn't believe it at first. She described him as a level-headed man. She didn't think he seemed capable of doing anything rash. However, he had a tendency to view certain things in an exaggerated way. Look here, it's in the deposition:

Did his inclination to exaggerate have something compulsive about it, a kind of quirk perhaps?

A quirk, well, that's possibly the wrong word; it's rather anxiety, you see. Again and again he would look at illustrated books of the Second World War, of wars generally. He said, what function of the brain can it be that permits you to be acquainted with the possibility of war and to live with it, or if you're not acquainted with it, must you first learn to encounter it, must you attempt to do it on your own? I asked him, attempt what? He said, the joy of destruction. He had these photographs hanging in his house, the shattered bells of Lübeck and the burning opera on *Unter den Linden*. He sometimes stood for hours in front of them, and then he said, he only needed to want it, it was now time.

However, he had never been irresponsible, the woman said. She had been struck by no rash behavior on his part. He planned everything very carefully. Look, he's smiling at us. He still hardly speaks, but he smiles when someone waves to him, brings him his meals or his injection. To be sure he gets dressed, he certainly takes care of his hygiene, all bodily functions are normal except for his pulse, the much too rapid breathing and the staring pupils, as if he were still running, as if he were moving with enormous exertion toward some goal. Look, he's waving to you, he seems to like you. Everyone described him as an amiable person—understanding, not at all belligerent, but nonetheless with a great ability to get things done. It was easy for him to establish his career. He always treated subordinates tactfully. In spite of, or precisely because of, his accommodating manner, his authority was respected. Besides that, he was an expert in his field. Look, his eyes are taking on that glassy stare again. He's probably imagining that he's running again. He'll be calmed down when it's time. He's still insisting that he has killed a child, a potential child. An *idée fixe*, certainly, but not without a reason. Fear of a possible war, the murder of a potential child. A life in phantasy. But then this deed? What did he want to destroy with his house? Read the report his girlfriend gave:

When he was drunk, he often said he wanted to forget. Forget what, I asked him. But he didn't answer, he only looked around in the room and lit a cigarette. You have it made here, I said to him. Then he smiled and drank a toast to me. His work seemed to have given him no problems. He liked to talk about the successes of his division. Sometimes he laughed then and said the periodic table, the ordinal numbers, how simple. Uranium 235. How simple it would be. Everything is a question of symmetry. Why not shove the axes a little? Produce irregularities? Anticipate the entropy? Do it in one single, quick act? However, he had no craze for destruction. He was attached to the things that he liked, especially his house. He once called it his second skin, but then he laughed and I didn't know if it was a malicious laugh or if he only wanted me to stay with him a little longer.

And the child? Did you want children?

This statement, to have killed a child, a potential child, I know. He didn't speak often about it and in no case as if he had the desire to have children. But sometimes on trips, when we drove through towns that he liked, he would say, this would be a good place for children. He didn't like it when children touched him, he even avoided their glances. But he liked to stroke my small nephew on the back of his head as if it were necessary to console him, and as if he were doing it in a vicarious way to all children.

And you? Was he fond of you?

I don't know. Sometimes it seemed to me as if it would be possible for him to leave me at any time, but he stayed with me just because something had once begun between the two of us.

Look, he's listening to us, he understands exactly what we're saying about him. Observe his forehead, he's frowning, he's showing the utmost skepticism, now the movement of his mouth, not sarcastic or scornful; he's probably indicating that we should try harder. Make more of an effort. Do you understand? He's requesting us to reconstruct his life, but no one may speak to him since he, as he himself has said, has ended the deposition. We can't expect any more answers. He would only stare at you, not angrily, but probably a little helplessly. His flight must have taken him past a housing development. A grocery store at the end of town reported a break-in on the morning after his disappearance. Only edible products were stolen. Smoked sausage, bread, but no money. It's obvious that it was he. To be sure he refuses to give any information about it. He certainly knows that that makes him suspect. That doesn't seem to bother him, however. His pride prohibits him from giving himself up. It's obvious that he was considering a longer route. It wasn't an unplanned, panic flight. They found him wearing newly bought tennis shoes like long-distance runners wear. He had a canteen with him. He had prepared himself for a marathon, as he said. At first without a destination, but he alleged it would have come to that, if he had only been en route long enough. He had failed, he maintained at the interrogation; he had simply remained lying on the ground after a fall. His girlfriend described him as an individual with enormous stamina. Whenever he was involved with scientific experiments, he hardly slept for weeks. He once said to her that with every project there was a point at which everything returned to itself; it was necessary to break off work just before that point. If he overlooked this and came to an end, that was to be sure no end, but merely exhaustion, it was best to be able to destroy the work, not because the result, insofar as it could be designated the result, was bad, but in order to extricate himself from the imprisonment into which he had worked himself. He was extremely conscientious. He carried out even routine tasks in the laboratory with great concentration. He is said to have often stated that he had to discern and eliminate all sources of error. He overlooked, however, the slovenliness of colleagues. Look, he's staring again. He's tormented. His hands are clenched fists. Look on page nine of the deposition; there he said:

There is this now famous aerial photo of the destroyed city of Dresden. You are acquainted with the bombardment of February 13-14,

1945. The skeleton of a city. Foundations, portions of walls, burned-out houses, on some of them the outer walls were still intact. Again and again I look at these photographs, my eyes glide into the city, I leave the photo behind me and feel the ground beneath me. Then someone crawls out of the air-raid shelter, runs around, throws hand kisses to the sky. Over there was Albert's store, wasn't it? And there Joemi's pub? They did a perfect job of that. Perfect. And the best? The statue of Luther in front of the *Frauenkirche* has fallen from its pedestal. Behind it there's rubble and the two remaining pieces of the church wall. One must film that and point it out later.

This page nine of the deposition concerns us most of all. There's no contesting the direct connection to his act. I'll tell you that this corresponds precisely to the pattern. And if I may divulge something to you, I don't think that he's crazy. Rather than that, I'm assuming that he's putting on an act for us. His statements are carefully conceived. He's consciously making himself the object of our investigations. Does he want us also to become a mystery to ourselves with our questions? Look, he's still twitching. That is of course no act. He keeps seeing his burning house over and over again. He had an enormous record collection. Almost everything by Bach. The best recordings. After work he liked to listen to music. He is said to have maintained that Bach is the most precise of musicians. Can you imagine a lover of music destroying his record collection? He had paintings, too. A lot of Japanese paintings. He liked what was unobtrusive, but it had to be precise. He told me he loved the meticulousness of the Japanese. He now sees all that being burned. Bach, the Japanese art. The thing with the child is to be sure the most difficult. Do you have an explanation? Let's think about it. He never bound himself seriously to a woman. He saw his girlfriend once a week. Every Saturday evening. He always kept the date; he never canceled it. He never came too late when they occasionally met in the city to go to a movie. His girlfriend said he was a great listener in a conversation. His answers were always to the point. As a man he likewise definitely had his good points. Look, here it is in the deposition.

You're not passing that on, I mean, you're using it only for scientific purposes. I tell you, he knew how to touch a woman. It was as if he were showing her her own body. I was always very proud of myself afterwards. I considered myself, how should I say it, it sounds banal and at the same time strange, in any case, afterwards I always thought myself extremely beautiful.

However, it seemed as if the woman were withholding something. There was something about this man that disturbed her, something that she didn't dare express, maybe not even to herself. She stated that he only reluctantly let himself be touched, but described him as a perfect lover. I don't know if we're getting any closer to the matter this way. He killed a potential child, staged a possible annihilation. There's a place in the deposition that sounds especially strange. He describes a photograph that was taken after the bombing of a German city. A woman is being dragged out of the air-raid shelter by a soldier and a civilian. He said, those senseless eyes of the woman which were looking somewhere, but not at the destroyed city. Eyes, as though she were seeing a film, as if the city were only a backdrop and the people actors, a little amateurish perhaps.

Let's try to imagine his running. An arsonist, his reputation, his career are lost. He's running without having a destination, but he planned this flight. He imagines how his record collection is burned up, and his Japanese paintings. He knows he'll be fired, his girlfriend will leave him. Is that right? Are we making a mistake? Is he leading us around by the nose? Look, he's smiling. He was listening to us. Does he find the way we're talking about him appealing? Look, now he's waving again. Don't go to him, don't talk to him. It's not that he would be violent, he would just fall back into that rigidity again. He knows how to exploit your helplessness. Look, he's turning away. A clever guy, he never tried to take advantage of a rival. He always showed his cards, so to speak. But it was in just such a way that he has concealed himself so perfectly. He made everyone feel that they knew him. But at the decisive moment he reacted in an unpredictable way. It doesn't matter to him if one looks him in the eyes. He agreed to the questioning for the deposition, gave clear answers. Why does he lie then? Do you understand that? Imagine how he poured the gasoline in the rooms. He certainly was smiling. He certainly did it with the greatest calm. And then, when he set the house afire, he was careful that he and his clothes that were saturated with the gasoline fumes didn't catch fire. Did he look around again? Did he make certain that the house was really burning? He took the freight road that starts behind his house, runs diagonally through the woods, and then up to the mountains. What thoughts were going through his head? Look, here in the deposition we let him free associate; he said:

Leaning on the window there on the eighth floor and looking down on the street. And looking over at the facade of the office building, and again down on the street. And suddenly the spark. Very quickly, very matter of course. A quiet explosion. Naturally in slow motion. Joy would be too weak a word.

We allowed him to free associate, but I say that he's lying. His earnestness betrays him. He's putting on an act for us. You don't believe that? Look, now he's twitching again. Observe his neck. Everything is tense. His chin is projected forward, his lips pressed together. As if he were suppressing a shout. Everyone described him as an even-tempered individual. No loud words, no outbursts of anger, but no weakling. What he said seemed to be certain. One could hardly resist his arguments. He always listened to his opponents. No emotions, then an appropriate answer. He said in the deposition that Johann Sebastian Bach composed his music with complete calm. His printed music corresponds to a meticulously followed plan. We asked him what color occurred to him in that connection. He said, steel blue, and he smiled. He betrays his feelings. That's my diagnosis. Look at him. Those eyes. The rigidity has gone. He looks forlornly at the window. Those eyes are so empty and tender. You're grinning? But look over there. His girlfriend described him as a taciturn man, above all he spoke very little on trips. But his attention was uninterrupted. It seemed to her as if his brain held everything that he saw and held it fast forever. Even years later he remembered every detail. A trembling of the eyelids, a quick look to the side, a door left open. See, he's smiling again. Are we making a mistake? Let's look at the deposition.

We asked him: what did you see while you were running? What images surfaced?

He said: desert dwellers are sitting around a fire in complete indifference. The meat that they're eating is dried up. They have been wandering for weeks without having found any water. Now they're settling down and eating. The water is getting scarce, but that doesn't seem to bother them. At the moment they are still able to drink.

See how carefully he listens to us. He is extremely alert. Scarcely a word escapes him. He observes us with the greatest attention. He doesn't disclose his conclusions. Let's continue with the deposition, he said:

The wasteland Dresden, the wasteland Leipzig, but Hiroshima, Nagasaki, perfect. And there is someone; he has survived and sees it and runs. He seeks water. The perfect desert dweller. A burning

thornbush is his house.
 Look, now he's looking at us. He's laughing. A clever fellow. And yet, his eyes. So empty. He has killed a potential child. He considers exactly what he says. He doesn't speak in images, he speaks to himself and wants us as listeners. Why does anyone set his house on fire? Why make up lies? A potential child? A chemist, lover of music, admirer of Japanese painting? My diagnosis: betrayal. His intent: to forget. Are we making a mistake? No word leads to another. No story can be told to its conclusion. A life with only beginnings. A puzzle in which the decisive parts are missing. And yet, look at him: how he's standing there, all eyes, all ears. What did he see on his flight? The shattered chimes of Lübeck? The burning opera on *Unter den Linden?* What did he hear? The cries of children in a hailstorm of bombs? The whimpering little boy in the arms of the woman who was struck by a bomb? A potential child? A potential history? Look, now he's smiling again. He seems to be content. Soon he'll get an injection. He causes no problems. His attendants describe him as a simple case. He eats what he is brought, isn't rebellious. Sometimes he even says "thank you" with a nod of his head when the dishes are taken away. The whole day long he merely stares in front of him. We've asked him what he's been thinking since he's been here. Look, here on page twelve of the deposition:
 It's become a wasteland, the city and the land all around it. Here and there someone's squatting and is looking at the ground.
 Nothing else? Always just this one picture?
 Sometimes the burning house, too. I see it and run. The fire spreads throughout my head, grasps thought after thought, destroys everything, erases everything, no memory anymore, a wasteland of thoughts, and then someone's running as if he had a mission, he's running with the greatest exertion, as if it depended upon his being the first one.
 Does he reach his goal?
 No, he gets tired, sits down. falls asleep. Then in the morning he doesn't know anymore why he began his flight. He opens his eyes and waits for someone to come and tell him.
 Look, he's hiding his face with his hands. His legs are trembling again. He's squatting. His upper body is bent forward. Now he's preparing for a sprint. He lets himself fall to the ground. Too tired. Imagine how he runs in the mountains. Perspiration on his forehead, now and then he stumbles, falls, gets up; it continues this way without interruption until he ultimately stays lying on the ground and gives up.

In his head cities are like wastelands. From what time period is he looking back? Has he run away into another historical time with every mile that took him away from his burning house? Into the time of the wasteland, if you will. Is he acquainted with it already, the indifference of its inhabitants? How they sit there and wait for an end that had already taken place a long time before? An end with which they've been acquainted since the days of their childhood? Potential children as potential wasteland dwellers? Look, I'm making suppositions and he's smiling. And look at his eyes, so empty, so exhausted. Look at him and form a judgment. Say it to him and he will look at you and smile. But then leave. Don't expect an answer.

Translated by Margaret T. Peischl

Authors about Themselves

C.W. Aigner

I don't see myself anywhere in contemporary Austrian literature. Furthermore, I've never pursued this issue and have no plans to. For five years I was local editor of the *Salzburger Tagblatt,* the newspaper that went under the name *Demokratisches Volksblatt* at the time Thomas Bernhard worked there, a few years after Bernhard left was renamed, and the same number of years after Aigner left ceased publication. No further parallels to or influences by other authors are known to me.

Translated by Heidi L. Hutchinson

Hans Jürgen August

In terms of content, my short stories dwell on the theme of interpersonal relationships and how they develop. From the simultaneous search for, and fear of proximity as well as the varied expectations of the participants, a texture of tension develops that also forms the narrative basis of "Europe in the Rain." A theme that has occupied me for years—and that probably can never be brought to a conclusion—is that having to do with narrative perspective and the question of what the narrator can know about a story. In "Europe in the Rain" the narrator is reduced to not much more than a movie camera. This device creates the very detailed and descriptive style of the story, which in turn intensifies the cool, emotionless ambiance of the story in which the story takes place. "Europe in the Rain" takes place sometime and somewhere in Europe; and it is no longer relevant—although it is revealed—that when I wrote it I had in mind the Rhône Valley in France. The title, incidentally, is taken from a picture called *Europe after the Rain II*

(1940-1942) by the surrealist Max Ernst.

Reading is bound up with literary reflection. For this reason the works of Franz Kafka have doubtless had an effect on my writing, as well as the works of the Argentine author, Jorge Luis Borges, and above all the works of Julio Cortázar, of the British writer, James Graham Ballard, of Italo Calvino from Italy, and of Americans such as Thomas Pynchon, Raymond Carver, Charles Baxter, or even—but to a lesser degree—John Updike and John Irving.

Translated by Richard H. Lawson

CHRISTIAN BAIER

Literature is perhaps the most inadequate form of the struggle for a dignified human existence, because book fairs in Frankfurt, cultural events in Klagenfurt have pushed literature—writing—into an exclusive ghetto, and the frightening thing about this is that a majority of the writers accept this social shadow existence, indeed, have to accept it because they are forced to live on the income from their work. Instead of being conscious of their social and political responsibility to turn art back into a fist, the literary world (especially in this Austria) squanders itself, is greedy for official recognition, for careers. Against this front of "those who think differently," the gentlemen who administer darkness so that it will remain dark in people's heads naturally have a very, very easy time.

When I began work on "Joseph" it was not yet clear to me where this book should, would, perhaps also had to lead me. Only gradually (and accompanied by many setbacks and long periods of interruption and of questions about whether a "literary treatment" of Goebbels' biography is even legitimate), did the parallels to the present, the collective level of the plot crystalize. And naturally I was also aware of how close I was to the material, how little I was concerned about distance. But it seemed to me that distance to the person of the protagonist as well as distance to the national-socialist idea was a mistake. For national socialism, indeed, totalitarian thinking results from a hermeticism growing out of character as well as out of ideology, from doctrinaire one-sidedness. I would like to compel the reader to identify with Goebbels (purely from lack of other alternatives), in order to discover where fascism actually begins, namely, not with clicheed phrases, empty pathos, militarism, and anti-Semitism (or more adequately expressed: xenophobia), but as a human being's attitude toward his surroundings. Many of Goebbels' behavior patterns are familiar to every person (naturally in countless shadings and nuances); who hasn't stood at the window out of scorned love and toyed with thoughts of death, who (out of a sense of homelessness in terms of character) hasn't at some point in his life sought stability and a way out of his own lack of ideological orientation (whether on the right or left, whether philosophical, esoteric, or religious)?

The paths to fascism are manifold, and I believe that everyone has at one time or another stood at the crossroads and has had to decide between ideology (as a superstructure of thinking) and the tight-rope act of intellectual freedom (and concrete irresponsibility).

Any other means of forcing the reader to identify with the protagonist did not seem effective to me, and if this book has any justification at all for its existence, it lies in this possibility of identification.

In contemporary literature I miss effectiveness. Permanent self-mirroring (artfully packed in a flood of words and stylized Stifterian descriptions, spiced with an intellectual garnish), arouses in me the suspicion that we are in a new period of decadence, that a new *fin de siècle* has begun, and where this autistic aesthetic leads ultimately is well known. I fear for literature because if it is lost, if it drifts into mirrored cabinets and spiritual labyrinths, then society has lost a corrective (even if a very modest one), then a spirit of opposition falls silent and Georg Büchner's prophecy comes true, namely, that we are after all only marionettes, manipulated through invisible strings by dark powers.

Translated by Donald G. Daviau

ILSE BREM

I like stories that are characterized by deeply probing insight, texts that get to the root of the events and the people. Stories that combine reality and fantasy are of particular interest to me. That is why Franz

Kafka and Gustav Meyrink are among my preferred prose authors, as well as Ingeborg Bachmann, Ilse Aichinger and Marlen Haushofer, whose stories reach out beyond the existing world and its order and are imbued with a utopian feeling of hope.

My story "The Boat" is a document of loneliness. Since a human being is closest to his true self when he is required to endure loneliness, he never comes closer to his origins than when he has become totally conscious of his loneliness.

Eros and Thanatos, affirmation and denial, alternate in my prose texts. The latency of dreams flows directly and with ambiguity into words and symbols, but the key to fulfillment in this life remains elusive. My texts reside in a realm between dream and reality, conscious and unconscious. The source of both word and image is the inexpressible, the incomprehensible. Yearning wishes to cross the borderline between the earthly empirical and the conceivable, but is cast back to the definable and comprehensible, knocking at a gate that remains locked.

Translated by Heidi L. Hutchinson

Heidrun Brunmair

The line that I try to follow moves in a zigzag pattern, changes without any effort on my part into serpentine shapes, then at times into a circle and begins to follow me. The most important points on this line—as far as I can determine and identify them—are relationships between people of both sexes, the resistance to the usual moral notions of our society and to the regimentation of individuals into conceptual pigeonholes, the dismantling of prejudices, and so on. If I have the choice between prosperity and an upright gait, I will choose in favor of my spine. Because of my steadily growing helplessness and feebleness in the face of unavoidable compromise, I have developed in the course of time an ironic, almost even cynical style, which frightens me and for almost a whole year has brought me to total silence. I have taken up a position of outsider with regard to present-day Austrian literature. Innumerable authors have influenced me (and my work). I can't enumerate them all but mention in random order: Adalbert Stifter (whom I have only recently learned to appreciate), Gustav Meyrink, Alfred Kubin, Saul Bellow, Italo

Calvino, Robert Neumann, Erich Fried, Ludwig Marcuse, Arthur Koestler, etc. For the work on my radio plays, such authors as Jan Rys, Ingeborg Bachman, and Günter Eich were very significant.

Translated by Renate Latimer

Stephan Eibel

of course I can say this man or that man or this woman or that woman is a model for me. but i don't say it because i don't perceive it that way. i don't experience my life through models.
in my head i clarify for myself....
in my head i encourage myself: somehow or other you will get out of this thought-imprisonment. from the thought-imprisonment of the secret police. and don't forget about the female secret police.
at 25 i thought to myself: writers, male and female, are the ones who understand freedom, who give freedom, who take freedom, who have a feeling for freedom.
today i know: it's just not that way!
most of them are just as much secret policemen and secret policewomen as most of the others who carry out professions in this country.
i can't even say that the street people or the vagrants are not secret police.
if a policeman is criticized in austria, you hear people say:
he's a human being too
if a politician is criticized in austria, you hear people say:
he's a human being too
somehow or other i caught on rather quickly (at about age 2), that police, politicians, managers are not ants.
even though the majority of these people here have lived in other countries, other countries are called foreign here, the "out-land."
austria isn't located on the ocean, where the land runs "out." many austrian men and women are at the ocean in the summer, when it is also very warm in austria, and say "out" to their children when they put sand in their mouths and when the children continue to try to put sand in their mouths they say "pfui" and mean "pfui, yuck." therefore the foreign "out-land" is emotionally the "pfui, yuck land" in austria.

i don't wish to live in a (father)land, but in a region!

Translated by Paul F. Dvorak

JANKO FERK

My development as a writer is a daily journey between ellipse and parabola. One doesn't need to have great exegetic skills to "straighten out" these mathematical concepts. The ellipse is meant to indicate the reduction of my poetic language, and the parabola the daily despair of the writer who is not quite sure whether or not he has already written his last sentence. Anxiety is not a problem for me, but there is nothing worse than the fear of not being able to write another word.

In my case the writing process always begins in my head. As soon as a "story" has taken on its own being—by that I mean the things that I have written—and the only thing left to do is to retell it, I write. Writing is retelling. About the most personal things imagined, of course. The most important thing involved in retelling a story—for me—is the first sentence. Once I have the beginning, what remains "merely" consists of time and work.

I hold Bernhard, Handke, and Jonke in high regard. I've read just about everything these authors have published, and absolutely everything by Handke, including his translations. If it wouldn't appear presumptuous, I could point out some of the connections. I value the master from Prague to such a degree that I can take the liberty of citing a couple of points. The simplest and most basic one is quite straightforward: Franz Kafka was bilingual and he was a lawyer. It was a fateful development not just for the literary half of my life but for my entire life that I came across *The Trial* at home when I was ten years old. I immediately put the book aside after reading the first sentence, but precisely this sentence has continued to haunt me to this day. It was at fifteen that I then read *The Trial* for the first time. And after that everything, several times. I don't want to say that I would not have become a writer or a lawyer without having done this reading; I would rather state it more directly—without Kafka it probably would not have been the case. In any event, that's what I would like to believe . . . In the end what gives me pleasure is finding the form and the possibility of connecting law and the philosophy of law to writing and to Kafka. I don't want to be concerned with anything that separates them.

The form I strive to achieve is that of the timeless present with an unusual precision; the story is therefore not irrelevant, it exists as fact.

As a bilingual writer from Carinthia, I'm a stranger from a different country everywhere I go. The difficulties begin with defining these terms. I can't be pigeon-holed into one category or the other—it's not that easy. I'm not a Carinthian writer, but if I were, then I'd be an Austrian writer. I'm also not a minority writer, because if so, then I'd be a member of an ethnic group and so forth. I truly dislike the Latin word *author*; I like the word *creative writer* better, but best of all just the designation *writer*.

For me personally there is no Carinthian literary scene, and I therefore can't identify with one. I see myself only in relationship to what I have written, which is not to say that I don't hold the writings of colleagues from Carinthia in high regard. There are many that I read and consider extraordinary.

The "stench" in its exaggerated and heightened form is the reality that I have to experience, the sur-irreality.

Translated by Paul F. Dvorak

MARIANNE GRUBER

Recently at a reception somebody asked me as I balanced sandwiches and a glass of wine: and who are you? The question was awkward because it demanded a self-portrayal, but it was not at all unfriendly. It was also not new. It was not in this century for the first time that we fell into the barbarity of seeing everything from the perspective of—πραξισ and ποιεσισ and thus immediately in terms of use, usability, and usefulness. Fortunately the man did not want an answer.

In the common sense approach to social conversation in the United States, the question would have meant how much did I earn from my profession. My income from writing is so ridiculously small that I would do best to remain silent. In good old Europe one used to want to know the other person's ideals; today people are only interested in ideologies. As far as ideologies are concerned, the fact that a stubborn anti-ideological stance represents an ideology of its own, prevents me from adopting any of them.

If one takes the demand for self-portrayal seriously, then the whole idea becomes really absurd. Nobody truly wants to know who another person actually is. Besides one scarcely knows oneself, so what is there to say? It's best not to talk about it. Perhaps one can go as far as discussing the reason for writing, what it means or could mean. Writing as a way of confirming the world and of self-assertion, as an extreme form of survival, of grasping the world, as counter-creation and revolt, sometimes out of sympathy for the children that we all once were and that are still being born in order first of all to learn loneliness in order to do something completely useless out of inclination and desire as an act of defiance in a world that subordinates everything to practicality and purpose.

Or one answers with a myth, mythologizes oneself. In literary-historical terms this means to produce a theory, a theory about one's own life. Now the original meaning of θηορειυ is to perceive. To perceive what one will perhaps see. That is most likely to happen by living and writing. In brief, there is a story due.

Ever since the appearance of my first book, I have made it a matter of principal to travel and give readings with Kalawapino. Born in Australia in 1980, Kalawapino belongs to the family of dwarf koala bears. Basically he is my ghostwriter, very serious, strict, and fervently devoted to my typewriter. It is everything to him. Me he tolerates as a means to an end. One of my "students" in the school for writing once commented that this little bear, my ghostwriter, was an aid to overcome my shyness. Possibly. It is true that there is a certain shyness in me. A psychoanalyst would most likely talk about regression. Children sometimes ask me whether Kalawapino can really talk and why only I understand him. But ultimately he is perhaps simply the symbol of the profound absurdity of all significance.

Translated by Donald G. Daviau

ERICH HACKL

"Not to accept the insults one has suffered and also others; to understand them as long as one has the strength to draw a breath and then not be alone. To find others who feel the same, read the right books and not give up, I call that happiness." I found that sentence in the novel *Schwestern* (1982, Sisters) by the Austrian writer Marie-Thérèse Kerschbaumer. It stands for what compels me to read and to write. I do not write "made up" stories. I look for actual situations; if they contain this outlook for happiness, I try to repeat what I have heard, together with the proven facts and the memory of my informants. This places me in a hopeless situation: the search for aesthetic plausibility in every story requires liberties I cannot take, because I do not want to change the "real course" of a story (insofar as it can be documented). So I am always writing at the brink of failure. Still I go on, since by telling stories I am clinging steadfastly to man's ability to communicate his experiences. This ability has been and is threatened by war and violence, but also by the smooth terror of the media industry. People are not talking; apparently they have lost their appetite for knowledge and feel no need to let others share their experiences. So I go on telling stories to break the silence, to prevent the forgetting and trashing of people's experience and the actual or ostensible destruction of communication through which experience is imparted.

Translated by Carvel de Bussy

WOLFGANG HERMANN

Darkness always prevails at the beginning. Contours emerge slowly, becoming more and more intelligible, but it's all a viscous mass and clarity is a long way off.

That first great book lights up the inner landscape like a steely bolt of lightning on a humid summer night. This first great book was *The Persians* by Aeschylus, a book that came into my hands at the age of eleven or twelve. Then on a rainy Sunday in Vorarlberg I read *King Lear*. I entered the first class of the Gymnasium and cried when these scarcely understood riches opened up to me. At thirteen I read Peter Handke's *Contented Misfortune* and decided one day to write myself. And I began to dabble with some first attempts at stories of the Wild West.

Later on I won new friends, chose *my* Indian tribe and am still accepting new brothers and sisters: Hölderlin, Novalis, Keller, Stifter, Hofmannsthal, and Proust—whom I worshipped for two years. Still later came Emmanuel Bove, André du Bouchet, Philippe Jacottet, René Char, and Marivaux followed by Silvio D'Arzo and all those who see the basis of all phenomena in the smallest and simplest things. Then came the tranquil ones, the powerful ones whose glance dispelled the surfaces: Saint-John Perse, Tsvetaeva, Celan, but also the great wanderers Seume, Robert Walser, and, once more, Hölderlin.

My place in Austrian literature? I do my work because nobody else does it.

Translated by Francis Michael Sharp

Margarethe Herzele

WRITING - because a person does not have the courage to speak! and
WRITING - instead of screaming, and, so as not to suffocate! At present, I would like to say:
WRITING - because it is enjoyable to find (invent) answers,
- to cover a page with signs
- to be able to dwell frequently on beloved beings (such as people/animals), landscapes/situations, emotions
- to invent fantastic figures or a (psychic) home, and,
- because it is gratifying to educate (moralize), to transmit experiences and facts, etc.
- thus a thousand reasons, and yet much more . . .

It is probably obvious! For even as a small child, to the consternation of my parents, I scribbled the nicest, whitest walls full. PICTURE WRITING prevailed until I learned the alphabet, and even later. Since the WRITTEN WORD is much more intimate and private, I carefully concealed it and often did not let it out of my head. Thus I remember, (already) as a school child, entire nights without sleeping a wink. I concocted interminable stories—as shelter and substitute for life. To that came the creative will to render, to express the experience of life; and, for lack of opportunity, it transformed itself into beloved dance.

A writing rage and courage awakened in me (in the early 70s) only after success in the visual arts and critical work in the area (newspaper reviews); and after being deeply affected by L. Durrell's *Alexandria Quartet* (the intersection of real and poetic life, a sparkling joy of life together with the deepest pessimism). Thus writing and painting ran parallel, besides household, employment, and the rearing of four children. Poems (picture titles and picture records) had originated already in the 60s, and graphic cycles had mutated to stories. But I had to take to the streetcar to work on the poetry, since there was neither space nor quiet at home....

How I would classify my writing? Besides Durrell, Márquez' *One Hundred Years of Solitude* inspired me; but I do not have any models. Here an idea, there a sentence or a formulation that I liked.... It interested me more to plumb the depths of psychic spaces. I found that, for example in Drach's *Marquis de Sade*—specifically in relation to my DRAWINGS. Shrill, unadorned, spontaneous transposition of simultaneously occurring emotions (60s and 70s). The drawings developed into poems, and the poems into stories. Finally, I am now attempting to bring it all together in a three-part novel.

I see my writing as a kind of ULTIMATE AIR-ARCHITECTURE, because the invisible, not entirely tangible things must carry the weight of the real. I would like to uncover the INTERSECTION of the real with the super-real aspect of life. The latter does not manifest itself because it is not allowed to; but it leads and directs even the most real and most banal aspects in unadmitted ways. I choose the designation "architecture" because I love architecture, and everything runs in a reasonably orderly, sound fashion, according to (its) inner laws. Thus "building" on poetic structures, I would like to make them open enough to affinities and brief resting places; or better yet, particular views and insights. That is actually our fine task, is it not?

Translated by Beth Bjorklund

PAULUS HOCHGATTERER

Although we scarcely have personal contact with each other, I consider myself part of the group of younger Austrian writers who devote themselves to traditional narratives, in accordance with the great masters of Austrian literature. The most prominent representatives of this group are probably Robert Schindel, Norbert Gstrein, Alois Hotschnig, and recently Robert Schneider as well. I feel less attached to the other half of recent Austrian literature, those writers oriented to a more linguistic-experimental pole, such as the Vienna Group. As far as I can tell (without having any distance to judge such things), I have been influenced by Adalbert Stifter (even though the reader might not recognize it at first glance), by Heimito von Doderer, Ingeborg Bachmann, Sigmund Freud (at least as much for his abilities as a writer as for his theory of psychoanalysis) and (according to my nature, I am tempted to say) by Thomas Bernhard.

Translated by Todd C. Hanlin

KONSTANTIN KAISER

The human being must still become something, has not come to himself by a long shot: that is my fundamental perspective. To take part in the battle for the emancipation of mankind with all my fears and preferences, off-beat cleverness, paradoxical inventions is the selfish motive of my literary attempts. I would simply like to be in the world, too.

Nevertheless I write whenever the experience of homelessness oppresses me anew. While the words still manage to describe this and that, the word itself appears to have become homeless. In my short prose pieces I try to become master over this oppression, by describing possible places or non-places where I believe that I perceive a coalescing of circumstances! Sometimes such occurrences result in a small space in which people can move: with a clumsy gesture, a quickly fading smile, a perhaps pedantic, agreeable, necessary communication.

In its problematic aspects all of that is quite Austrian, and yet I have never been particularly fond of Austrian literature, because I find in it much of the narrowness against which I struggle. There are exceptions: Karl Kraus, not as a Chamberlain and Weininger admirer, but as an indefatigable defender of his presence of mind, Paul Celan, Theodor Kramer, Berthold Viertel, and all of exile literature, even where it has failed. Otherwise the poems of Yannis Ritsos or Nazim Hikmet and the tales

of Lu Hsün move me more than the masterpieces of Austrian origin.
I leave contemporary literature out of consideration; most of the authors writing today are even more unhappy than I.

Translated by Donald G. Daviau

ULRIKE KLEPALSKI

The first true love of language: Karl Kraus. The tenor of my work: there is no taboo, it is diction that establishes the rules. "Literary Figures" whose biography and whose work have caused me to open a book and to listen to my surroundings, who could be called models are: Hölderlin, Nietzsche, Musil, Bachmann, Haushofer—there are many. There are several authors who annoy me and my language tasting, but I will not name them. Literary models, counterparts, parallels, lines, tendencies—there I find myself in general on a wobbly pedestal which is in constant motion. Fallada and Baudelaire accompanied me for almost two decades, so did Kafka and Kubin, and they still do. Rosei's experimental lyric impressed me; from him I learned to treat my own text critically.

Translated by Helga Schreckenberger and Jacqueline Vansant

WALTER KLIER

Up to now I have worked on the further development of a "classical" modernism, including the satirical illumination of its assumptions. In that respect I consider myself less related to my Austrian contemporaries than to a multitude of European and American authors.

In a positive sense, points of contact within Austrian literature might be works by Albert Drach, Hans Lebert, and Alfred Bittner, as well as a few early texts by Elfriede Jelinek.

The project *Luciana Glaser: Winterende* (1989-1990, with Stefanie Holzer) represented an ironic infiltration of widespread neo-romanticism (Norbert Gstrein, Robert Schneider, et al.).

Direct stimuli or models (which also always imply the possibility of ironic obeisance through reductive treatment) for *Aufrührer* were such texts as the novels of Claude Simon and *Tallhover* by Hans Joachim Schädlich, for "King Sepp," various texts by Robert Pinget, for *Katarina Mueller Biografie,* a film by Buñuel, the title of which I have forgotten, for *Kaufhaus Eden,* texts by Heiner Müller, for *Flaschenpost,* Kafka's *Briefe an Felice* and John Kennedy Toole's *Confederacy of Dunces.* However, these are possibly only apparent associations that are meaningless for the reader.

At present I am working on the question of the authorship of Shakespeare's works, an attempt to reconcile scholarly, essayistic, and belletristic forms.

Translated by Lowell A. Bangerter

ROBERT MENASSE

I was born in May 1955 in St. Achatz at-the-Forest. The extensive dying of the woods, the disastrous consequences of which became evident in St. Achatz as early as the mid-60s, literally broke my parents' hearts. Thus I was placed under the care of my uncle, who was considered an eccentric in St. Achatz, but a poet in the rest of Austria. To keep me quiet, because he did not wish to be disturbed while writing his poetry, my uncle encouraged me to write too. In order to keep me quiet for as long as possible, he would repeatedly give me the longest novels he could find in the rental library and recommend them to me as models, worthy of imitation. It was only later that it dawned on me that my uncle himself was in no way interested in these so-called models; for his own poetic creations he sought inspiration solely in brief examples of text, such as could be found in conventional histories of literature. Since then, all learned replies to the question of how literary traditions develop strike me as something very unworldly.

When I myself succeeded in creating some unrest with my writings, my uncle distanced himself from me. Since then, all answers to the question of how breaks in literary traditions and contexts come about also strike me as something very unworldly—in other words, estranged from the affairs of this world. Meanwhile, my uncle has received the Austrian State Prize for Literature. The only way I can explain to myself that I have not yet received this same prize is that the word of former prize winners carries much weight in the presentation of future prizes. Thus, a writer's origin, childhood, and youth may become his curse.

Translated by Eva Dukes

Barbara Neuwirth

To assign oneself a place in Austrian literature of the present and to find support is truly no easy task. In a certain sense I stand outside Austrian literature of the present with my writings: fantastic literature does, it is true, have wonderful roots in Austria, but it is neither modern nor is it especially recognized by critics as an independent challenge. I can therefore say little about current writers, male or female, to whom I feel close with my texts, although I can talk about writers who have attracted me because of a similarity (thematic or atmospheric) and from whose texts I have drawn pleasure and, perhaps, guidance: I'm speaking, of course, of the fantastic Austrians (and there are no women among them, as if fantastic literature and inspiration based on powerlessness and helplessness were masculine provinces): Paul Busson and Gustav Meyrink are highly imaginative beginnings, even if in their works the religious-esoteric element attains a status that it could never achieve in mine. Kubin, of course—I feel a deep understanding with Kubin. I love Perutz; above all his "Nachts unter der steinernen Brücke" (Nights beneath the Stone Bridge) has always touched me and created a bond with him. Then Kafka. It is, of course, presumptuous to associate myself with Kafka, but I have consciously to close myself off to his passion and abhorrence, his revulsion and his sadness, his searching and his loss, because it comes too close to me and I find reality so convincingly portrayed in his fantastic elements, which is not the case with Kubin. Finally, I'd mention Canetti. That's presumptuous too. But here too my heart beats faster; I sense a love for literature, I read those things that engage me. *Masse und Macht* (Crowds and Power). That's my favorite work by Canetti.

Peter Schattschenider and Marianne Gruber also write science fiction in Austria. But he is someone who, quite the educated natural scientist, devotes himself to technical developments, and Marianne Gruber is a master of science fiction with social issues. The old-fashioned fantastic, the stimulus to the imagination, is not a topic for either of them. But to me it is the most important thing, whereas the aspect that Marianne works out so well only occasionally takes on form in my work.

So I'm afraid that I haven't been very useful to you with this list of my favorite authors (even if they are to be found, in the main, in fantastic literature, and even if I'm excluding my other favorites, Paul Celan and Hertha Kräftner—and Rita Seliger, whom I'm trying to bring to the public's attention myself—because I don't feel an affinity to them as an author. I am, after all, not a lyric poet, and Kräftner's prose was much more visibly written into the here and now.

Translated by Michael T. O'Pecko

Martin Ohrt

Why write?

Writing as correction. Fabricating one's story in such a way as to be able to live with it.

Writing as playing with possibilities. With one's own inability and the weaknesses of others. With the consequences of disavowing paths already embarked upon.

Writing as confession. Holding on to moments in which I was closest to myself by being close to another.

Writing as addendum. Substitute for words, for hands that come up short in expressing the situation.

Writing as addiction. As a necessary means of survival in order to know the self in the presence of the self. Writing as revenge against the adversities of life.

Stance as Writer

Searching for ways beyond post-minimalism of shaping into new forms what has been said a hundred times, developing the language out of the creative context. Each story, each situation has its own language. Overall a striving toward conciseness, reduction to the essential.

Translated by Paul F. Dvorak

Kurt A. Schantl

Who Speaks in Me?

To answer this question, I am forced to make a confession. It is nothing other than the admission of a thief. Even if only of the literary kind. Yes, I am about to expose myself as a kind of "literary vampire": I admit that for years I have been transgressing against colleagues who have long been dead and thereby restoring them to life, so that they can sustain me in life. And so in the course of time I have developed into a bundle of literary dependencies.

And if you ask me today: "Who speaks in you?" I must answer that I don't know; for I have incorporated, appropriated too much in me. It is also no wonder: somewhere, I believe it was in Le Bon, I read that if I wanted to trace my predecessors back, let us say, merely to the year 1000, I would have approximately twenty million ancestors . . . And do you really think that there wouldn't be at least a single one among them who, assuming favorable circumstances, would bequeath his legacy to me? One who with what I have soaked up would be capable of producing a calcification, a sublimation, indeed, even a transmutation?

When viewed in this way, you will understand that I am nothing but a collection of sweepings, a compost pile of my reading. And what does it help to know that "the past conditions the present," as I have noted in Walter Benjamin's theory of the survival of literary works in his essay "The Task of the Translator."

For precisely that reason I agree with Umberto Eco's insight "that the past, after people recognize that it cannot be destroyed because its destruction leads to silence, must be considered in a new way: with irony, without innocence."

Translated by Donald G. Daviau

EVELYN SCHLAG

I am one of the authors who had their publishing debut in the eighties. The authors who had achieved prominence in the seventies—for example, Innerhofer, Wolfgruber, Rosei, Frischmuth—were important for me, since they demonstrated that contemporary Austrian literature had a place in the German reading culture. When I first began to write, I felt an affinity for Peter Handke in his prose, and for Friederike Mayröcker and Ilse Aichinger in their poetry. It is surely not a coincidence that all of these authors are Austrian.

In all of my writing, in my early texts as well as in my current work, I am concerned with extending the limits of my language, without however engaging in the kind of project that is typically associated with experimental literature. Approached with sensitivity, words and the structures of language yield their inherent expressive possibilities. A text is of particular interest to me, if its contents are articulated as never before. I find matters of ideology or theory to be of lesser importance. A central theme in my work has to do with relationships, with the encounters of men and women. What it is possible to know of each other is what I try to discover in my writing.

Translated by G.G. Gardner

WOLFGANG SCHÖNER

My position within contemporary Austrian literature is as unknown to me as the literature itself; my relationship to it can be compared to that of a penguin to the Sahara. It is likely that my association with that small number of authors in whose world and proximity I feel at home (though all of them are unfortunately already dead) thoroughly ruined me for contemporary opinions, ideologies, and trends. Yet I welcome with pleasure as Austrian co-inhabitants of my spiritual space Johann Nestroy, Ferdinand Raimund, also Heimito von Doderer (though the latter is frequently redeemed solely by the capacity of the magnificent formal principles of his works despite the content's duality, for example when he idolizes the more or less accomplished but in the end also wildly proliferate, extroverted personality that never poses a problem for itself—Mary K., Kakabsa, Chwostik. Or when he treats with contempt the ego which is barely on the way to finding itself—for instance in the case of Stangler or Schlaggenberg, who at the same time are Doderer himself; when, as a result, he uses up the fatological substance of figures for whom coarser stuff would have sufficed, and in diametrically opposed fashion sets up a process of becoming human that is above all his own. This is most noticeable in his diaries; one can say of them that he worked doggedly during his entire life on the elimination of this in himself, what he created was not only based upon it, but also would have ended up being what he was). Furthermore, I wish to mention Georg Trakl from whose lapidary poetry the same notes resound as in the music of Hugo Wolf, and finally Karl Kraus, the proximity to whose works and person allowed me to experience my distance to the surrounding authorial centuries not as a deficiency but rather as liberation and thus to see it as the precondition to this happiness.

Translated by M. Veteto Conrad

Wolfgang Siegmund

I am a simple neo-existentialist: I am what I write out of myself. I want the truth, the whole truth, and nothing but lies.
I believe in justice in the distant future.

In the process of this search, the 'Adriatic feeling for life' keeps me afloat, a feeling that tells of laughter following catastrophe, and what then follows: the fabulous sense of desperation in the face of success . . .

I have no models, positive or negative, Austrian literature is foreign to me; I am a white shadow in it, somehow present, but not really.

Only now and then, when I'm in very high spirits, roaring along with my pencil and motor scooter, I feel like a halfway decent cross between Rilke and Hemingway. Now and then, on cocky days . . .

Translated by Jerry Glenn and Jennifer Kelley

ERICH WOLFGANG SKWARA

I TAKE MY ILLUSIONS SERIOUSLY

"Austria is where I am," as Wallenstein once said—I cannot actually make that claim, so I would like to change the quotation a little. Austria is in my memory as well as in my goal as an author. I suffer from the fact that in my native country I am read even less than in the Federal Republic, which is essentially alien to me. (I avoid saying "Germany"— the word makes me uncomfortable.) Like almost all Austrian authors I am published in the Federal Republic, and it hurts me when a German publisher asks me why I don't sell better in my home land. I don't know why. Should I say it is because no one in Austria wants to get acquainted with me?

After all, one reaps what one sows. And what does my country mean to me, other than as a past? When I fly "home" (and it's a nice long trip and costs quite a bit of money from where I "live"), I am dropping in on memories. The present does not attract me to Austria—but then the present doesn't really attract me anywhere else either. If I am asked about my place in Austrian literature, I have to reply (almost) truthfully that I have none in Austria. If someone would like to know how I rank myself, I have to be careful so people won't think I am crazy. But I dare say that without certain Austrians who have lived and written before me, I would not enjoy living and working at all—that is the measure of how very much my predecessors are part of my world.

My encounter with Georg Trakl has proved decisive for me since I was sixteen years old, and my poetry developed on his model and yet became autonomous. In prose, Hermann Broch was my model, especially with his mature work, *The Death of Virgil*. From Broch's work I formed the standard as well as the loftiness of my ambition and of my ethical concern. How Broch converts knowledge into feeling; how science, philosophy, and literature become one—I would like to strive for such universal reconciliation. Then, there is also Franz Kafka: to become ever more specific and transparent, to be obliterated by a wide-awake here-and-now—I yearn to travel that road too. And finally, to go beyond those who are dead (if only biographically), I love and revere Peter Hanke. No one in contemporary world literature works with greater precision, patience, rigor and—above all—love.

Living and working in reverential agreement with these standards is a powerful counterweight—especially to a success that is far too slow in coming. With my writing I aim to fight against time and death. Where beauty and love are so transient, I want to leave a track that endures. I take my illusions seriously.

Translated by Richard H. Lawson

Wilfried Steiner

To anchor my own position among the diverse tendencies of contemporary Austrian literature seems to me to be an impossible undertaking, for in my view these tendencies are not clearly delineated or definable. The oft-cited antagonism between "experimental" and "realistic" literature is relaxing more and more; literary groups with joint declarations about content and form are practically non-existent.

As a reader I have gained the most enjoyment and enlightenment from texts which neither seek to prove the impossibility of narrative (theorems turned prose), nor simply tell stories, as if science, epistemology and the literary avant-gardism of the twentieth century had passed them by without a trace. In other words, I want to read (and for me that also means: write) prose that knows all the tricks of modernism and yet understands how to incorporate the element of "plot" or, if you will, suspense into the construction of the text. The naive excitement with which we were able to enter a strange storybook world as children as if it were just another room is as impossible for me to recreate as is the idea of a homogenous, mimetically describable reality. And yet: the ability to reflect, more or less with a wink of the eye, precisely this undeniable craving for a story, seems to me to be fundamental to many substantial texts. In this regard, my role models are authors who have gone farther in this direction than I have been able to; I have found this sort of inspiration with such diverse authors as Elfriede Czurda, Gert Jonke, Elfriede Jelinek and Anselm Glück.

But the most explosive and most exhilarating prose texts from my literary point of view are found outside of Austrian contemporary literature: the range extends from Thomas Pynchon to the great Latin

Americans such as Borges, Fuentes, Cortázar or Carpentier to Arno Schmidt and Hans Henny Jahnn.

Translated by Heidi L. Hutchinson

GERALD SZYSZKOWITZ

A BRIEF INTERVIEW

Q: You are working on your twelfth volume of prose. Do you write all your novels and short stories according to a predetermined plan?

A: The form of the novel as it developed in the nineteenth century, that is, the telling of a story with an overall plot made up of the many intersections of the individual characters' stories, requires a carefully constructed overall plan. An example from *Der Thaya*: young Rudi Thaya is supposed to get married. In the many possible plots I devised for the Thaya novel, I tried each of the female characters in the marriage role and ultimately picked the plot variation that seemed most interesting to me. This method of construction, with its endless possibilities, proved very stimulating to my imagination. Especially since in the course of writing, a completely different woman—to my surprise and for a while even against my will—embraced and married the young man. That's the most interesting part: to give your characters complete freedom to develop. Even in the most stringent construction.

Q: Are you describing your own world in your novels?

A: I have always found it fascinating that a writer like Kafka didn't set his first novel in his own backyard but on a continent that he had never set foot on. It was because he wanted to write independent of everyday trifles. He was interested only in the plot. And that plot was taken not from his backyard, not from America, but from England, from the novel *David Copperfield*. He himself has characterized the first chapter of *Amerika* as a Dickens imitation. His first novel is literature about literature. And my first novel *Der Thaya* is, among other things, the continuation of another novel, of Theodor Fontane's *Der Stechlin*. I was interested in how I could tell this story, which took place a hundred years ago near Berlin, if I transferred it to the farthest corners of the Austrian Waldviertel, an area about whose development and peculiarities few have ever written. And my latest novel, *Die Badenweiler oder Nichts wird bleiben von Österreich*, owes not only the idea for its title, but also several other provocative ideas to Joseph Roth's *Radetzkymarsch*. For example, at the defining moment of *Radetzkymarsch*, the Kaiser appears. How, I had to ask myself, am I going to handle the appearance of the Führer in my retelling of the story? Do I dare? Can I have the most guilty of all guilty men speak in a seemingly everyday tone?

Q: Lastly, where, or, let's say, on what page do you see yourself in the book of today's Austrian literature?

A: As a footnote, on the last page. But definitely on the page where the writing hasn't stopped. But seriously, I see myself as a realist who holds up a critical mirror to our society, and who entertains the reader with irony, a well-constructed plot, and surprising observations, out of whose stories—now or at some time in the future—people can learn something about our country and our times that might otherwise be missed.

Translated by Heidi L. Hutchinson

Sylvia Treudl

What does it mean when a person writes? The world, of course. Or nothing at all. Or something very different.
So much paper that gets printed.
So many books—one could almost say innumerable.
Books that because of their sheer quantity could drive the most avid reader, the best-disposed reader to despair. So much that must remain unread. And new stories are continually appearing. What for? For the chaos of life.
But the world is invented only in books, in texts. Is it not?
Or is it bent into shape, commented upon, falsified, screamed at, and exorcised?
To write world/image. To hold a plumbline for the shallowness, to

have a sharp knife to cut oneself free; laughter in the specimen case and always a great yearning.

Translated by Beth Bjorklund

Elisabeth Wäger

My mother, in a different life, could have been a writer. In a different life my mother could have been a pianist. Her letters and her handwriting remain the only indication.

I come from an enclosed countryside; the mountains are castle walls, and roads run through them as if they were gates.

My memories dwell on the talented women in my family. Those who dragged their then unwritten writings along behind, the feathery formulations in their sentences, and their childhoods like lace handkerchiefs. I got caught up in those childhoods. Just as they were, those childhoods, forever transitory and distanced, they captivated me. All dreams put aside, just as was youth itself. With that in mind, they made it comfortable for themselves. Coffee on the veranda every day at the same time. (Only in childhood, so they said, were summers so hot that the windows could be removed.)

The theatrical light in the house when the Venetian blinds were lowered. At the death of Grandmother, that angel, they said she had faded away. They had faded away too and they accommodated to it. With a glance at the garden, their ritualized glances outdoors, their commentaries on the seasons. Off and on they dragged out a future as contemplated for me. For me everything would be quite different. For me they summoned up hazy views of the future, which they marked with their expectations. Thus they injured me in the same way they had been injured. Because any planning was simply beyond them.

When I wrote, their glances were mingled with deep distrust. They looked out into the countryside. And they thought I was betraying them. Perhaps. But what's what? Who were they? Which one am I?

Translated by Richard H. Lawson

WOLFGANG WENGER

I do not think an author should categorize himself; the press is ready enough to provide him with labels. Mine range currently from "New New Objectivity" to "apocalyptic." Through the intellectual "shelf" on which an author is placed, he becomes intellectual merchandise to be marketed. I don't object to categorization for this reason, but I grant myself the privilege of changing constantly. As far as what the new labels do for me, the public's memory is short, and the reader doesn't buy the "shelf," but the merchandise. Creativity means change to me, acceptance of the unpredictability of life. To be sure, there are basic themes in my work which attract me again and again, for example, the effects of technology on the consciousness of the human being, or the utopia of a symbiosis between man and machine. I try, however, to treat specifically these themes with as great a variety of approaches as possible. At the present time I cannot ascertain any relationships I might have with other authors of Austrian literature. With regard to form, I have been influenced through reading the works of the French writer Marguerite Duras, the Brazilian Clarice Lispector, the Mexican José Emilio Pacheco, and the Americans William Carlos Williams, Robert Creeley, William Carpenter, and Thomas Pynchon. In addition, the sculptural energy of Picasso, the "resonant" colors and forms of Kandinsky, and the music of Johann Sebastian Bach, Steve Reich, and Arvo Pärt. This list could go on and on; this does not mean, however, any perceptible systematic similarities with these artists, but rather correspondences with my present development. The unconscious mind, I contend, is the master of my seeing, hearing, reading, and writing.

Translated by Margaret T. Peischl

ARIADNE PRESS
Translation Series

Bosch
By Graziella Hlawaty
Translated by Lutz Kümmling

Crime at Mayerling
By Gerhard Markus
Translated by Carvel de Bussy

Love in London
By Theodor Kramer
Translated by Fritz Brainin
and Jörg Thunecke

Born-Where
By Robert Schindel
Translated by Michael Roloff

In Foreign Cities
By Anna Mitgutsch
Translated by Lowell A. Bangerter

The Giant File on Zwetschkenbaum
By Albert Drach
Translated by Harvey I. Dunkle

The Red Thread
By Gitta Deutsch
Translated by the Author

The Register
By Norbert Gstrein
Translated by Lowell A. Bangerter

Seven Contemporary Austrian Plays
By Gabriel Barylli, Wolfgang Bauer, Helmut Peschina, Werner Schwab, Brigitte Schwaiger, Peter Turrini
Edited by Richard H. Lawson

The Wild Woman and Other Plays
By Felix Mitterer

Shooting Rats, Other Plays and Poems
By Peter Turrini
Translated by Richard Dixon

Paracelsus and Other Plays
By Arthur Schnitzler
Translated by G.J. Weinberger

"It's Up to Us!"
By Jura Soyfer
Selected and translated by
Horst Jarka

*Thennberg
or Seeking to Go Home Again*
By György Sébestyen
Translated by Lisa Fleisher

Walk about the Villages
By Peter Handke
Translated by Michael Roloff

ARIADNE PRESS
Translation Series

Lerida
By Alexander Giese
Translated by Lowell A. Bangerter

Three Flute Notes
By Jeannie Ebner
Translated by Lowell A. Bangerter

Siberia and Other Plays
By Felix Mitterer

The Sphere of Glass
By Marianne Gruber
Translation and Afterword
by Alexandra Strelka

The Convent School
By Barbara Frischmuth
Translated by
G. Chapple and J.B. Lawson

The Green Face
By Gustav Meyrink
Translated by Michael Mitchell

The Ariadne Book of Austrian Fantasy: The Meyrink Years 1890-1930
Ed. & trans. by Michael Mitchell

Walpurgisnacht
By Gustav Meyrink
Translated by Michael Mitchell

The Cassowary
By Matthias Mander
Translated by Michael Mitchell

Plague in Siena
By Erich Wolfgang Skwara
Foreword by Joseph P. Strelka
Translation by Michael Roloff

Memories with Trees
By Ilse Tielsch
Translated by David Scrase

Aphorisms
By Marie von Ebner-Eschenbach
Translated by David Scrase and Wolfgang Mieder

Conversations with Peter Rosei
By Wilhelm Schwarz
Translated by Christine and Thomas Tessier

Anthology of Contemporary Austrian Folk Plays
By V. Canetti, Preses/Becher, Mitterer, Szyszkowitz, Turrini
Translation and Afterword
by Richard Dixon

Try Your Luck!
By Peter Rosei
Translated by Kathleen Thorpe

ARIADNE PRESS
Translation Series

February Shadows
By Elisabeth Reichart
Translated by Donna L. Hoffmeister
Afterword by Christa Wolf

Night Over Vienna
By Lili Körber
Translated by Viktoria Hertling
and Kay M. Stone

The Cool Million
By Erich Wolfgang Skwara
Translated by Harvey I. Dunkle
Preface by Martin Walser
Afterword by Richard Exner

Farewell to Love and Other Misunderstandings
By Herbert Eisenreich
Translation and Afterword
by Renate Latimer

Professor Bernhardi and Other Plays
By Arthur Schnitzler
Translated by G.J. Weinberger

Negatives of My Father
By Peter Henisch
Translated by Anne C. Ulmer

On the Other Side
By Gerald Szyszkowitz
Translated by Todd C. Hanlin
Afterword by Jürgen Koppensteiner

*I Want to Speak
The Tragedy and Banality
of Survival in
Terezin and Auschwitz*
By Margareta Glas-Larsson
Edited and with a Commentary
by Gerhard Botz
Translated by Lowell A. Bangerter

The Works of Solitude
By György Sebestyén
Translated by Michael Mitchell

Remembering Gardens
By Kurt Klinger
Translated by Harvey I. Dunkle

Deserter
By Anton Fuchs
Translated by Todd C. Hanlin

From Here to There
By Peter Rosei
Translated and with an Afterword
by Kathleen Thorpe

The Angel of the West Window
By Gustav Meyrink
Translated by Michael Mitchell

*Relationships
An Anthology of Contemporary
Austrian Literature*
Selected by Adolf Opel